Counsel for the Defence
The Bernard Cohn Memorial Lectures in Criminal Law

EDITED BY Edward L. Greenspan, QC

Published in 2005 by
Irwin Law
347 Bay Street
Suite 501
Toronto, Ontario
M5H 2R7
www.irwinlaw.com

Editor: Rosemary Shipton
Design: Sonya V. Thursby, Opus House Incorporated

ISBN 1-55221-102-9

Library and Archives Canada Cataloguing in Publication

Counsel for the defence : the Bernard Cohn memorial lectures in criminal law / edited by Edward L. Greenspan.

Includes bibliographical references.

ISBN 1-55221-102-9

1. Criminal procedure—Canada. 2. Criminal law—Canada.
I. Greenspan, Edward L.

KE8809.5.C69 2005   345.71'05   C2005-900862-8
KF9220.ZA2C69 2005

Printed and bound in Canada.

1 2 3 4 5   09 08 07 06 05

The Publisher acknowledges the financial support of the Government of Canada through the Book Publishing Industry Development Program (BPIDP) for its publishing activities.

Contents

Foreword

MR. JUSTICE SAUL NOSANCHUK

Bernard Cohn was born in Windsor, Ontario, on January 8, 1908, and died there on February 1, 1982. He lived his entire life in Windsor. He was a brilliant criminal lawyer whose remarkable legal career spanned fifty-two years. As a young man he decided to pursue a career as a criminal lawyer, and he was called to the bar in 1930. He quickly established a law practice devoted exclusively to criminal defence work.

Throughout his life, Cohn had great compassion for the underdog, and he was fearless in opposing injustice and standing up against any abuses of power by those in authority. He successfully defended clients accused of every type of criminal charge, ranging from minor traffic violations to murder. His immense talent as a criminal lawyer resulted in many acquittals in murder trials and other serious crimes. But no matter how minor or how serious a charge, Cohn was always totally committed to vigorously advocating his client's cause.

Bernard Cohn was an affable and a gregarious person, and he was affectionately called "Barney" by everyone who knew him. He was a colourful, humorous, and quick-witted character who enjoyed fine cigars and especially loved to wager on the outcome of sporting events. On any given day, he could be observed sporting a natty grey fedora and a custom-tailored navy blue suit, puffing on an ever-present cigar as he walked at a leisurely pace to the criminal court. In one hand he carried a British barristers' attaché case containing case reports, legal briefs, and notes in preparation for hearings or trials, while rolled up under the sleeve of his suit jacket was the *Detroit Free Press*, open at the racing or sports section. There was no doubt that Barney handicapped each sporting event as skilfully as he prepared for trial.

Cohn had an intense interest in the law, and he read voraciously. He was a scholar of the law who mastered the intricacies of criminal law, criminal procedure, and criminal evidence. The bookshelves of his modest downtown Windsor office were lined with every volume of the *Canadian Criminal Cases*, the *Criminal Reports*, and the *English Criminal Appeal Reports*, as well as every available textbook and periodical relating to criminal law published in Canada and in England.

In his practice, Cohn thoroughly mastered the facts of any case against his clients. He probed exhaustively into the circumstances of the alleged offence and did whatever was ethically necessary to prepare his client's defence. When he arrived at court to defend any client, he was totally prepared. He had a clearly focused strategy and a theory of the case. He was a superb cross-examiner whose questions were honed to razor sharpness. He never asked an unnecessary question. He penetrated to the vulnerable core of the witnesses for the prosecution.

In 1954, in a case that gained international notoriety, he defended Donald Ritchie of Windsor in extradition proceedings brought against him by the United States government on a charge of attempting to murder the famous UAW International president Walter Reuther in Detroit, Michigan. Cohn's devastating cross-examination of two Detroit detectives demolished the case for the prosecution and resulted in the exclusion of statements made by Ritchie. The application for extradition was dismissed.

Bernard Cohn had an elegant and gracious courtroom presence, just as he had a reputation as a counsel of impeccable integrity. Judges and opposing counsel trusted him. He always conducted himself according to the highest ethical standards. He was the quintessential mentor, and he was exceedingly generous in sharing his knowledge and wisdom with both civil and criminal lawyers. His door and his phone lines were always open to any lawyer who sought his counsel.

In 1939, with his criminal trial practice thriving, Bernard Cohn retained as his appellate counsel a young gold-medallist graduate from Osgoode Hall

Law School who had decided to specialize in criminal law. That young counsel was G. Arthur Martin, who would later become a justice of the Ontario Court of Appeal and, at the time of his death, was acknowledged as one of the greatest criminal lawyers in Canadian history. Cohn and Martin had a warm and collegial relationship as lawyers which lasted for thirty-four years, until Martin's appointment to the Ontario Court of Appeal in 1973.

Retired Superior Court Justice Patrick Hart was associated with G. Arthur Martin for fourteen years and became his partner in the firm of Martin and Hart. Justice Hart witnessed the close relationship between Cohn and Martin. He recalled vividly how, on many occasions, the two master criminal lawyers loved to debate intricate points of law and discuss trial strategy. They shared an encyclopedic knowledge of the law. Each was able to quote from memory names of cases, volume numbers, and page numbers on which the passages were written. Justice Hart saw Cohn and Martin as mentors to each other. He recalled also that Martin shared Cohn's love of horse racing and sports. The two spent many hours discussing, analyzing, and attending these events.

Bernard Cohn was a devoted husband to Helen and was blessed with two children: a daughter, Faye, and a son, David. When David was born Cohn had an opportunity to show his respect and gratitude for Martin's friendship. Following the Judaic tradition, he named David after his deceased grandfather but bestowed on him the middle name of Martin. Cohn was a wonderful father and mentor to his son, who has developed into an outstanding criminal trial lawyer. He would have been proud to know that David was invited to deliver the fourteenth annual Bernard Cohn Memorial Lecture—and that he delivered it superbly. It appears here under the title "You Can't Judge a Crown Brief by Its Cover."

The essence of Bernard Cohn was captured in a tribute paid to him by Justice G. Arthur Martin when he delivered the sixth Bernard Cohn Memorial Lecture:

> Bernard Cohn was a wonderful companion. He had a profound knowledge of human nature. He combined worldliness with compassion and understanding. He also had a great sense of humour, was fond of anecdotes, and was a gifted raconteur. Furthermore, he was a very learned, careful, and wise defence counsel. He would

carefully study the most recent judgments of the courts in Canada and Great Britain and, of course, the *Journal of Criminal Law*, the *Criminal Law Review*, and the *Criminal Law Quarterly*. He was a professional in the best sense of the word. Bernard Cohn was a great lawyer, but, even more important, he was a great human being."

The Honourable Mr. Justice Saul Nosanchuk
January 2005

Introduction

EDWARD L. GREENSPAN, QC

Bernard Cohn was a legendary criminal lawyer who practised all his life in Windsor, Ontario. On his death, his friends and colleagues decided to honour his memory by means of the Bernard Cohn Memorial Lecture Series Trust. The Honourable Carl Zalev, recently retired from the Superior Court of Ontario; Mr. Justice Saul Nosanchuk, of the Ontario Court of Justice; Harvey T. Strosberg, QC, a Windsor lawyer; and I are all members of the trust.

We had no idea when we created the lecture series in Cohn's memory that it would ultimately emerge as one of the most significant annual lectures at any law school in Canada. The Windsor Law School, which has become one of the finest law schools in the country, has always hosted the event and will continue to do so.

The former Chief Justice of Ontario, Charles Dubin, delivered one of the lectures. He was such a close friend of Bernard Cohn that he spent his entire lecture telling us anecdotes about Mr. Cohn in the context of their long friendship.

No legal system is flawless—and that is true of the administration of justice in Canada—but most participants in our legal system believe, as I do, that the Anglo-Canadian justice system is the least flawed ever devised. However, its success in attaining justice requires the limitless dedication, unbounded efforts, and fine-tuned advocacy of those who have devoted their lives to the defence of the accused. This book is a collection of essays by defence counsel in tribute to one of the great champions for justice, Bernard Cohn. Originally presented as fifteen lectures from 1987 onward, these essays address the strengths and shortcomings of our criminal justice system. They raise basic issues of guilt and innocence and pose questions concerning the fairness of the judicial procedure itself. Collectively, they demonstrate the strong commitment in this country to the defence of the accused.

In Part One, Proof and Innocence, the essays concentrate on two fundamental principles of our criminal justice system: the presumption of innocence and proof beyond a reasonable doubt. In "Innocence and Proof: *R. v. John Alexander MacKenzie*," Joel Pink, QC, one of the leading criminal lawyers in the Maritimes, tells of the jury trial on behalf of his client charged in a triple murder. In the face of a confession by MacKenzie a day after the deaths, Mr. Pink focused throughout the trial on his client's continued innocence and the Crown's burden to prove beyond a reasonable doubt that MacKenzie's statement should be believed. MacKenzie testified at trial, contrary to his statement, that he did not recall the fateful evening, as he had been drinking excessively and did not know how the pistol that killed the three men ended up in his possession. MacKenzie's friend testified he was with the accused at the time of the shootings. Mr. Pink persuaded the jury to weigh all the evidence, and, in the end, that jury acquitted his client.

Austin Cooper, QC, one of the deans of Canadian criminal law, lectured on "Susan Nelles: The Defence of Innocence." His essay is a remarkable account of how thorough and devoted counsel can ensure that justice is done at the early stages of the criminal process. Ms. Nelles, a nurse at Toronto's Hospital for Sick Children, was charged with killing four infants under her care. Despite the media circus and the seriousness of the charges, Mr. Cooper successfully persuaded the judge at the preliminary hearing that there simply was no evidence against his client.

One standard by which a legal system may be assessed is whether it convicts only the truly guilty. However, this standard is virtually impossible to apply, so a preferable test might be one of fairness. Was the jury deprived of evidence that might have assisted it in reaching a just conclusion? What of the system itself? In the drive to convict, did the system sacrifice some of its own integrity? Hersh Wolch, QC, in "The Presumption of Guilt: Experiences from *Milgaard* and Other Cases," directly raises these issues in exposing the short-

comings of our justice system. His observation that the presumption of innocence is really a presumption of guilt in practice comes from his years of experience in western Canada as both a prosecutor and a defence counsel. He has
seen this presumption of guilt start with the media headlines and carry on
through the trial as a result of tunnel vision by the police, when they single out
a suspect and then ignore all evidence that would exonerate that person.
Prosecutors, judges, and juries are also susceptible to the same biases, despite
the requirement that they remain impartial. David Milgaard was a victim of
overzealous police and prosecutors who, convinced of his guilt, withheld evidence at trial that would have proved his innocence. The Canadian justice system is not perfect, but when participants in our system interfere with the
proper administration of justice, there will be no justice for anyone.

Greg Brodsky, QC, another leading practitioner in western Canada, provides an analysis of a wrongful conviction for his client Thomas Sophonow,
who endured a mistrial and two convictions before being acquitted for murder by the Manitoba Court of Appeal. This case demonstrates the flexibility
of our legal system and its ability to correct itself. The appeal procedures in
our criminal laws are a long way from being impediments to the resolution of
a case or havens for trivial technicalities–though the media may often view
them as such. In fact, it is the provincial courts of appeal and, ultimately, the
Supreme Court of Canada that offer us the careful, dispassionate scrutiny of
trials that our system needs to prevent miscarriages of justice at the lower-
court level. In the Sophonow case, after two new trial orders, the entire bench
of the Manitoba Court of Appeal took the unusual step of acquitting
Sophonow of murder. Each appeal corrected previous trial errors, but the
Court of Appeal finally realized that a guilty verdict for Sophonow was not
the correct verdict. This account is a tribute to the importance of research,
preparation, and extreme perseverance in achieving an effective defence.

In Part Two, A Variety of Defences, the authors describe a range of
unusual and difficult defences in their efforts to ensure justice for their
clients. It is a basic tenet of criminal law that, save in the most exceptional
cases, accused persons must have *mens rea*–criminal intent–before they can
be convicted of a criminal offence. To inflict punishment where there is no
guilty mind may amount to nothing more than societal revenge. The essence
of the offence of murder is that the accused intended to kill the victim.
"Revisiting the Insanity Defence: The Capital Murder Trial of Matthew

Charles Lamb" is an analysis by Mr. Justice Saul Nosanchuk of his use of the insanity defence when he practised criminal law in Windsor in the same bar as Barney Cohn. Charles Lamb, charged with the senseless and unprovoked killing of a couple strolling down the street one night, was found not criminally responsible for the murders because he suffered from an acute psychotic reaction and was incapable of appreciating the nature and quality of what he did. When there is no intent, whether as a result of a disease of the mind or some other reason, there is no justice in a conviction–even if the act was committed. Mr. Nosanchuk is now a much-loved part-time professor at the University of Windsor Law School and a well-respected and admired judge of the Ontario Court of Justice. Before his appointment to the bench, he was one of the finest criminal lawyers in the province.

"Sleepwalking as Non-Insane Automatism: *R v. Parks*" is another case of someone who committed a terrible offence with no intent. Marlys Edwardh, one of the leaders of the Ontario criminal bar, details her representation of a man who drove to his in-laws' home one night, murdered his mother-in-law and seriously wounded his father-in-law, and then, covered in blood, drove to the police station. Ms. Edwardh convinced the jury that her client was sleepwalking at the time and had absolutely no intent to kill his in-laws–and, in fact, had no conscious control of his actions. Ken Parks did not have a disease of the mind; rather, he had no mind at all when he killed, and the only just result was his acquittal. It's a fascinating story, persuasively presented and effectively argued.

In "Automatism–Legitimate Defence or Legalized Responsibility: *R v. Joudrie,*" Noel O'Brien, QC, an innovative senior criminal lawyer in Alberta, discusses one of the most controversial defences ever advanced in a Canadian courtroom. Dorothy Joudrie, a sixty-one-year-old socialite, after years as a victim of her husband's abuse and suffering the consequences of alcoholism, got a gun and, with no immediate provocation, shot at her estranged business-magnate husband six times, nearly killing him. Mr. O'Brien effectively argued that, at the time of the shooting, Mrs. Joudrie was in a "dissociative state" and could not be held criminally responsible for the attack because she had no control over her actions. The public has historically viewed such a defence with sceptism. It is seen as a way of avoiding the personal responsibility associated with a crime and as a defence that is available only to the rich, who can afford to buy their own form of justice. Mr. O'Brien defends the use of this defence and explains that the criticisms are a result of a misunderstanding of the intricacies of the defence, unfair reporting by the media, and lack of information about the specifics of the case.

In "The Mystique of Science: The Influence of Experts of the Administration of Criminal Justice," my brother, Brian Greenspan, one of Canada's finest criminal lawyers, adds another element to the importance of advocacy on behalf of clients. He had prepared an important and crucial defence on behalf of his client, Dr. Mohan, a pediatrician charged with sexually molesting four child patients. He had scientific evidence from a psychiatrist that strongly supported his client's claims of innocence. The trial court refused to admit the evidence because it found that this doctor's conclusions were not sufficiently supported by his evidence. Dr. Mohan was convicted, and he appealed. The Ontario Court of Appeal found that the psychiatrist's testimony should have been allowed and ordered a new trial. The Supreme Court of Canada heard the Crown's appeal. Although the Supreme Court reinstated the conviction, it developed a four-part test for the admission of expert evidence at trial that has permanently changed the way such evidence is admitted. Although *R. v. Mohan* was an immediate victory for the Crown, defence counsel have successfully relied on this landmark decision ever since to exclude previously admissible evidence advanced by Crown counsel in the realm of behavioral science.

The defence of necessity is based on the idea that human beings are sometimes placed in situations in which there is simply no alternative than to commit an illegal act. In such situations, the law, without condoning illegal behaviour, may excuse it. "Taking the Law into Your Own Hands: Child Abduction and the Defence of Necessity" is a case of a father who kidnapped his children from their mother's custody and left Canada. The father returned seventeen years later and was arrested and charged with abduction. Raphaël Schachter, QC, a leader of the Quebec criminal bar, describes his successful use of the defence of necessity in demonstrating to the court that his client had an honest belief that his children were in imminent danger and that, in his mind, there was no alternative in protecting them but to abduct them. Their mother, despite being granted full custody, was an unstable and unfit caregiver.

These unusual defences confirm how crucial it is that defence counsel leave no stone unturned, no argument neglected when preparing their clients' defence. Sometimes the most unbelievable, questionable, and far-fetched defences may, in fact, be the truth, and justice cannot be done unless these defences are thoroughly prepared and vigorously argued in Court.

The public's view of defence counsel has often been that we are hired guns—that we don't care about the truth and that we will do anything to win at all costs. This view couldn't be farther from reality. The true advocate cares about nothing but the truth—the legal truth. We are advocates and must do everything to advocate on behalf of our clients, using the power of cross-examination and oral argument, and conducting independent investigations from the police. We are not driven by the need to figure out the real truth. Rather, we must ask vital questions: Did the police commit an abuse of process in the manner in which they conducted an arrest? Did the accused suffer from any illness at the time of the offence? Did the Crown meet its burden of proof beyond a reasonable doubt? In Part Three, Defence Counsel and the Truth, the essays deal with effective advocacy and, with that, the search for truth.

It is generally accepted that G. Arthur Martin was probably Canada's greatest criminal lawyer—and he was also a great friend of Barney Cohn. In his essay, "Reflections on a Half-Century of Criminal Practice," Mr. Martin references a number of cross-examinations and trials he conducted in his long and remarkable criminal law practice. He recounts his cross-examination of Dr. Keith Simpson in the *Truscott Reference*. That cross-examination is a fine example of how best to demolish an expert witness. The *Truscott* case has been in the public eye for nearly fifty years. It is still in the press and is still making law. Mr. Martin provides a fascinating analysis of his first murder case and of a few famous cases, including the Gouzenko spy case. He talks about the role of defence counsel and comments on the changes in the style of advocacy at the criminal bar that he witnessed in his half-century there. His essay allows us a glimpse into this great criminal lawyer's mind.

Gerald Allbright, one of Saskatchewan's finest counsel and now a judge of the Saskatchewan Court of Queen's Bench, provides insight into the art of advocacy and explains how an advocate's behaviour in a courtroom can win or lose a case. An effective advocate, he says, must always be in control of what is going on in the courtroom. That may mean creating friendships and mutual respect with the judge, jury, and Crown; using humour; and displaying confidence at all times. However, the most effective tool is the power of cross-examination. Using some fine anecdotes from one of his own cases, Mr. Allbright illustrates that the effective use of cross-examination and the leading question are the most powerful tools that advocates possess.

Preliminary inquiries are an important part of the criminal process (as we have already seen in the case of Susan Nelles). They provide an opportunity for the defence to test the Crown's case before trial and, possibly, to avoid expensive and unnecessary trials. They are a perfect vehicle to obtain full disclosure, to discover and appreciate the case to be made against the accused, and to identify weaknesses in the prosecution's case through cross-examination. David Cohn, a well-respected Toronto criminal lawyer, outlines a case in which, through effective advocacy at the preliminary hearing phase, he uncovered tremendous weaknesses in what seemed an airtight prosecution against his client, leading the Crown to stay the charges before the completion of the preliminary hearing.

Bernard Cohn would be proud to know that his son, an accomplished advocate in his own right, made an important contribution to the Bernard Cohn Lecture Series. To our great benefit, David Cohn shares not only his legal insights but also his personal insights about his father. At seventeen years of age, Bernard Cohn became the head of the household and responsible for his younger brother, when their father died of diabetes just months before insulin became public. For him, family always came first—unless, of course, it was during a raid at an unlicensed gambling venue by the Detroit police. David Cohn tells a marvellous anecdote of how he spent quality time with his father arguing with a customs officer at the Windsor/Detroit border when they were late for placing an important bet at the Detroit racetrack. Bernard Cohn was a legendary gambler, and it is no wonder that, in his practice of criminal law in a border town, he represented, and then became great friends with, Ed Curd, one of the great bookies in America in the 1950s.

I was honoured to present "The Murder of Bruce Lorenz: The Role of Defence Counsel," the first Bernard Cohn Lecture, in 1987. I discussed the trial of my client charged with the murder of a Toronto lawyer, Bruce Lorenz. This case is a perfect example of why defence lawyers should never, ever make any moral judgment about their clients in preparing a defence. According to all the evidence, my client appeared to be guilty. But he said he did not commit the crime, and I was determined to make sure he was not convicted.

Michel Proulx, QC, a formidable Montreal criminal lawyer and a recently retired judge of the Quebec Court of Appeal, addresses the distinction between "legal truths" and "real truths." The purpose of a trial, through the adversarial system, is to determine the legal truth of a matter, and Mr. Proulx recognizes that many lawyers believe, as I do, that this truth is the only one that matters, and that any personal judgment by a lawyer about the moral guilt or real truth is unnecessary and potentially harmful. He argues that defence counsel can, and should, involve themselves in the pursuit of real truth, and he provides four examples to support his case. I still stand by my belief that legal truth is all that should matter in a court of law, but I urge you to read his commanding argument and decide for yourself.

Part Four, From Law to Politics, includes a stimulating essay by Frank McKenna, QC, who, at the time of his lecture, was premier of New Brunswick. Mr. McKenna, an experienced criminal lawyer before his entry into politics, outlines some of the lessons he learned while practising law that later proved invaluable in his political career. Illustrating with his own war stories, he explains that in both criminal law and politics you must come to expect the unexpected, as he did in his defence of boxer Yvon Durelle, whose unreliable memory led to unpredictable testimony. He realizes that his years as a criminal lawyer, involving unequalled pressures, were an extremely good preparation for high-pressure moments in politics, such as the Meech Lake meetings. As well, he says that the practice of criminal law taught him to be fearless and to experiment with new and innovative ideas, trying always to do the best for his client and to provide the most effective representation–precisely what he later did as premier for the people of New Brunswick.

All the topics presented in this book are significant in the evolution of our criminal law. The essays not only highlight key criminal cases in Canadian law but, most important, provide entertaining and splendid tales from the trenches. All the original lectures made for great listening, and now they have a new life as equally exciting reading.

Without Bernard Cohn, there would be no lecture series. Without the Bernard Cohn lecturers, there would be no legacy. And without the following people, there would be no book. I wish to express my gratitude to Suny Virk, who gathered the lectures together and reviewed a number of them. He is a graduate of the Windsor Law School and articled with my firm, and he now practises criminal law in Toronto. My daughter Julianna Greenspan, a lawyer with my firm, and Kenneth Pritchard, a bright undergraduate student who has worked for my firm for several summers, ably assisted me in organizing the lectures for publication. Their comments were invaluable.

Dean Bruce Elman of the University of Windsor Law School has provided a fine forum for the Bernard Cohn lectures since his appointment in July 2000 and has also been most supportive of both the lecture series and this book project. The members of the Bernard Cohn Memorial Lecture Series Trust are truly in his debt. Finally, the guidance and assistance of the professionals at Irwin Law made publication of this book a genuinely pleasant experience.

Edward L. Greenspan, QC
January 2005

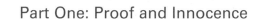

Part One: Proof and Innocence

Innocence and Proof:
R. v. John Alexander MacKenzie

JOEL E. PINK, QC

2002

Johnnie MacKenzie, as he was known to his friends, accumulated a host of criminal convictions during the years he lived in Ontario from the mid-1970s to the mid-1980s. These convictions included common assault, assault causing bodily harm, theft under $200, and wounding with the intent and discharging a firearm–for which he was sentenced to two years less a day.

In 1986 MacKenzie decided to return to his native Antigonish, Nova Scotia, to embark on a new beginning. He wanted to have a home on Beech Hill Road, an area where his parents and grandparents once lived. In August of that year, having accumulated a few dollars, Johnnie partially realized his dream by purchasing a piece of property at a tax sale in Beech Hill. The parcel of land, almost a hectare in extent, was used as a garbage dump by local residents. However, there was one clear patch of land on the property which Johnnie developed as the site for his mobile home. Once he settled in, his troubles began.

MacKenzie had three neighbours–John Boucher, Joey Deon, and Edmond Deon–who all lived within one or two kilometres of him. Over the next eighteen months, for reasons unknown to Johnnie, these men all relentlessly violated his peace and tranquility by continually harassing him, both as a group and individually. They dumped garbage on his property; tore up his front lawn and garden with an all-terrain vehicle; threatened to cause him death; chained and nailed his back door so he couldn't get out of his residence; committed a break and enter into his residence; knocked on his back door during the early morning hours to awaken him; dismantled his propane tank; bulldozed his driveway; tore down his front gate; captured his dog, put it on a rope, and dragged it down the dirt road behind an all-terrain vehicle, eventually killing it; placed stolen property on his property and then called the RCMP on him; killed his cat and left it on his back steps; shot holes in his mailbox; and fired gunshots in the vicinity of his trailer.

MacKenzie lived in constant fear of John Boucher, Edmond Deon, and Joey Deon. He pleaded with all three men to stay off his property, but they ignored him and laughed at him. They took advantage of him–a meek and mild man–at every opportunity. These men made life so miserable that it would have driven most people to move elsewhere. MacKenzie, however, never gave in to their cruel acts. He felt he had every right to live peacefully wherever he wished, and he wanted to live in Beech Hill. He refused to be forced out by these men. The harassment became so intolerable that MacKenzie began to sleep on his floor with prayer beads, hoping that the bullets fired in the vicinity of his trailer would not hit him. He turned to alcohol to calm his nerves. For the six weeks before June 23, 1989, MacKenzie never saw a sober day. On June 23, 1989, he drank most of the day with his friend William Cooger. According to a forensic toxicologist, Johnnie's blood/alcohol concentration at 4:30 a.m. on June 24 would have read between 281 and 330 milligrams of alcohol per 100 millilitres of blood.

Between 3:30 and 4:00 on the morning of June 24, Lorraine Boucher, the wife of John Boucher, testified that she heard gunshots. Not realizing the significance of what she heard, she drifted back into a sound sleep, without her husband by her side, until the morning. A neighbour, Daniel Girrior, heard three shots at 4:17 a.m. on June 24, then another two shots at 4:58 a.m., and, a few minutes later, he heard two more shots. He testified that, on each occasion, he looked at the clock in his bedroom. According to Girrior, it was not unusual to hear gunshots in Beech Hill at any hour of the day or night. William Cogger, who was staying with MacKenzie on June 24 in his trailer, woke up between 4:30 and 4:45 a.m., according to his watch, and saw Johnnie sitting at the kitchen table with a beer in his hand.

In the early morning hours of June 24, Lorraine Boucher discovered the body of her husband and called the RCMP. Officers responded to the scene immediately. They discovered John Boucher, deceased, on his front lawn. On further investigation in the area, the body of Edmond Deon was discovered in his bed with gunshot wounds. Finally, at the house diagonally across the road, the police found Joey Deon in his truck, fatally injured from a gunshot wound. He died from his injury a short time later.

The RCMP sent in a veteran investigator, Sergeant Robert Peebles, to assist Constable Kevin Cleary in the investigation. Sergeant Peebles arrived at the scene at 10:45 a.m. and was directed to the residences of John Boucher, Edmond Deon, and Joey Deon. Because of the numerous previous reports of harassment, John Alexander MacKenzie immediately became the prime suspect.

The police spent that entire day gathering evidence at the scene. When they drained MacKenzie's well, they located a pair of shoes and a .22-calibre gun, which later proved through forensic testing to be the murder weapon in the shooting of the three men. At approximately 7:30 p.m. the RCMP obtained a search warrant and went into MacKenzie's trailer residence. There they found a .22-calibre rifle, but they quickly determined that it had not been fired.

As a result of the information received, Corporal Kenneth W.L. Diamond and Sergeant Peebles went to the residence of George Levangie on the South River Road in Antigonish County, where they located Johnnie MacKenzie at 8:41 a.m. The RCMP described MacKenzie, when they first saw him, as a person "who was drinking heavily." They immediately placed him under arrest for the murders of John Boucher and Edmond Deon and for the wounding of Joey Deon. MacKenzie was given the standard police caution and read his rights under the *Charter of Rights and Freedoms*, before being escorted back to the detachment. A statement was not taken from him at that time because of his level of impairment, and he was remanded to the Antigonish County Correctional Centre.

On June 25 at 9:46 a.m., Sergeant Peebles and Constable Cleary summoned MacKenzie from his cell and took him to an interrogation room in the superintendent's office at the Antigonish Correctional Centre. Sergeant Peebles repeated the police warning: "You need not say anything. You have nothing to hope from any promise or favour, nothing to fear from any threat whether or not you say anything, but anything that you do say may be used as evidence." The officers also advised MacKenzie of his right to retain and instruct counsel. If he could not afford a lawyer, he was told, he could contact Nova Scotia Legal Aid, and counsel would be provided to him.

The interview began immediately and was completed at 10:37 a.m. At 10:05, Johnnie MacKenzie requested that he be allowed to phone his sister, to see if she could contact a lawyer for him. He made the phone call, and Sergeant Peebles was informed that a Legal Aid lawyer would be arriving shortly. Between 10:05 and 10:37, Sergeant Peebles remained in the interrogation room. The police knew Johnnie was a talkative person and would converse freely if the opportunity was presented. And he did.

The RCMP charged John Alexander MacKenzie with three counts of first-degree murder. In Nova Scotia, individuals charged with murder have the right to request counsel of their own choice. MacKenzie did not wish to accept the services of Nova Scotia Legal Aid. And so, after June 25, I received a call from Legal Aid requesting my services.

Shortly after I was contacted, I was informed that MacKenzie had made a statement to the police between the hours of 9:46 and 10:37 a.m. on June 25 and had also made a statement to his friend William Cogger. My challenge was clear: how was the defence ever going to manoeuvre around the admissions that MacKenzie had made in his statements to the police and to Cogger, along with the fact that the police had found the murder weapon and the shoes in MacKenzie's well? How was it possible to establish the legal defences of provocation and drunkenness?

The words of Viscount Sanky in the English murder case of *Woolmingtom v. The Director of Public Prosecution* rang loud and clear in my head:

> Throughout the Web of English Criminal Law, one golden thread is always to be seen, that is the duty of prosecution to prove the prisoner's guilty subject ... to the defence of insanity, and subject also to any statutory exception. If, at the end of and on the whole of the case, there is a reasonable doubt created by the evidence given by either the prosecution or the prisoner ... the prosecution has not made out the case and the prisoner is entitled to an acquittal.

The *Queen v. John Alexander MacKenzie* was an exemplary case to test the three basic principles of criminal law: the presumption of innocence, the burden of proof, and proof beyond a reasonable doubt. We would put these fundamental rights, guaranteed under the *Charter*, to a jury. And the jury members would make every effort, under the terms of their oath, to reach a verdict that was fair, just, and in accordance with the evidence and the law.

The presiding judge at trial, the Honourable Mr. Justice Alex MacIntosh, was a senior judge of the trial division of the Supreme Court of Nova Scotia. During the preliminary examination, or *voir dire*, to determine the admissibility of the statements, the police painted a picture of Johnnie MacKenzie as a sober individual who was fully aware of his surroundings, willing and eager to talk. Even after he requested a lawyer, he kept on talking, without any promises, inducements, or threats. As far as the Crown was concerned, any statements MacKenzie made were freely and voluntary given.

The defence, however, had to portray a different picture–one of an alcoholic who had not been sober for six weeks before the events at issue and was extremely hungover. My task was to try to develop a theory that any information elicited from Johnnie MacKenzie was not from a person with "an operating mind." I decided to throw in a possible *Charter* violation: the right to remain silent, once the police were informed that counsel was en route.

After hearing the defence evidence tendered at the *voir dire* from the forensic toxicologist, a psychiatrist, and MacKenzie himself, the trial judge made the following ruling:

> The two experts were given hypothetical questions consistent with the accused's evidence of his condition, and they were of the opinion that these conditions were consistent with symptoms of alcoholic withdrawal. Neither expert, of course, was present with the accused on June 25th. They both admit that, between individuals, there is a great difference between the effects of alcohol withdrawal–that is, not all individuals have the same withdrawal effects.

Justice MacIntosh continued in this vein. When Dr. Rosenberg, one of the expert witnesses, was asked what happens to a person who is going through the initial stages of withdrawal from alcohol, he replied, in the judge's words:

> "It's one of the most uncomfortable states I'm sure known to man. There's a progression of symptoms not necessarily the same in each individual over a period of time." Then at another point of his evidence, when asked if alcohol withdrawal varies greatly from individual to individual, he replied in the affirmative once again. In light of such a scenario, I am unable to accept the opinions of these experts

as to the lack of ability of the accused on June 25th to appreciate the consequences of making incriminating statements to the police and giving up the right to counsel. Having had the opportunity to assess the evidence given by the accused has buttressed my decision to reject the above noted opinions. Despite being an alcoholic, he is clearly not a man of low intelligence. During his testimony, he exhibited a very selective memory capacity when it suited his purposes. Consequently, I find his evidence suspect in many respects ...

I accept the evidence of the two experienced police officers, Sergeant Peebles and Constable Clearly that on June 25th the accused was sober, alert and aware of what was going on. Their handling of the accused was adjudicatively fair as well as meeting the test set forth by Justice MacIntyre in Clarkson v. The Queen, that is, with respect to those statements made by the accused to the police on June 25, 1999, between 9:46 a.m. and 10:05 a.m., the latter time of which the accused exercised his right to retain legal counsel. Although no questions were asked of the accused subsequent to 10:05 a.m., the continued presence of the police in the same room with the accused could be taken in the instance as urging the accused to continue talking. In my opinion, it could be considered adjudicatively unfair, and such statements are therefore inadmissible. So, to recap, those statements made between 9:46 a.m. and 10:05 a.m. are admissible; those subsequent to that time are not.

The Crown had thrown the first pitch, and it was a swing and a miss for the defence. However, there have to be three strikes before you are out. I, as defence counsel, never gave up hope. You never know when a new development may benefit your client as a case unfolds. Most important, MacKenzie had the advantage of his case being heard by a jury–twelve men and women who apply common sense to the issues–and I felt sure they would be sympathetic towards him.

The learned trial judge's ruling allowed the jury to hear the content of the earlier statement MacKenzie made to the police between 9:46 and 10:05 a.m. It was transcribed as follows:

MacKenzie: I think they're dead. They never leave me alone, the cocksuckers. I told them to stay away from my property, but that cocksucker, John Boucher, landed up the other night with Bill Cogger trying to let on he dropped a rock on his foot. He came looking for beer, then he left at around 3 a.m. Then that fucking Joey Deon came to the door. I told him to fuck off, that I was asleep. Then I guess it started bugging me and I snapped and I went down and shot them. First down was John Boucher's place and I couldn't see him. Then he came out and started shouting, "What are you doing around here?" I said, "I came to kill you, cocksucker," and I shot him.

Constable Cleary: How many times?

MacKenzie: I don't know, perhaps five. I figured I shot one, I might as well do them all. Then I went to Joey Deon's and rapped on the door. I heard a moan. He was in the truck, drunk, so I put two in the cocksucker. Then I went up to Eddie's. He wouldn't open the door, so I put three in him through the door. Then I went in and finished him off. I was going to shoot myself, but I wanted to get another drink, so I ran home.

Constable Cleary: What did you do with the bullets?

MacKenzie: Threw them in the woods. I put the gun in the well and the dress shoes in the well.

Some of the facts as related by MacKenzie in his statement could be proven to be inaccurate—for example, how many shots were fired.

The defence had also overcome the comments made to William Cogger at approximately 4:40 a.m. on the day in question, June 24. When the Crown attorney asked Cogger during the trial about his conversation with MacKenzie, the exchange took a different angle:

Q. And what can you say, any conversation with him?

A. Not too much then because I didn't stir too much. I just woke up. I got on my one elbow and I could see Johnnie sitting at the end of the table.

Q. And ... did you have any conversation with ... Johnnie MacKenzie?

A. Well, I got up, no. I don't know when ... at a quarter to five or something like that ... he came in and he told me that he got the three sons of whores last night.

Q. Okay, what did you say to that or was there any further conversation?

A. No, there wasn't much more conversation. I told him I didn't want to hear about it at all. But I figured it was just a dream or something that he was re-enacting. He's a pretty good storyteller and he acts the stories out.

Q. How many times did he tell you this?

A. Oh, maybe twice before I faced him. I went eye to eye with him and I said, "Johnnie, tell me this is not the truth or say something to the effect," and he said, "No, brother, it's not true."

On cross-examination I somehow had to minimize Cogger's evidence. I asked him the following questions:

Q. My learned friend asked you about the conversation that you had with Johnnie MacKenzie in the morning. As I understood it, after he made some initial comments, immediately thereafter, he, in fact, told you he didn't know whether or not it was a dream. Is that not true?

A. He did, yeah.

Q. And then when you pushed him a little further, he said, no, brother, it is not true.

A. That's correct.

Q. In fact, Johnnie MacKenzie when he's been drinking, has been known to talk a lot of nonsense. Would you agree with that, sir?

A. Story after story.

Q. In fact, you've told the jury about other problems that he may have been having, Then he said on some other occasions he was going to shoot them, and then he was going to take his own life. He was drinking at the time, wasn't he?

A. Oh, every time he told me that.

Q. But you didn't take him seriously?

A. I told him on one occasion, "Johnnie, that would be a very poor trade."

Q. And, in fact, you did not take him seriously?

A. I did not, no.

Q. Let's face facts, Mr. Cogger. When you are drinking the amount you were drinking on this particular day, your memory of events is clouded and you cannot honestly say for sure what Johnnie MacKenzie told you during the early morning hours of June 24, 1989.

A. No, not really. I could recollect some stuff, but it's possible that I can't remember a lot of stuff he said.

Q. Johnnie MacKenzie was, or is, a private person who likes to be alone and to basically be with nature. Would you agree with me there?

A. Yes, very much so.

Q. And, in fact, during the afternoon of the 23rd, you, together with Johnnie, took some peanuts and went down to feed the squirrels?

A. Yeah, he has a squirrel station down in the woods just a ways down and he feeds them.

Q. He not only has a squirrel station but also has a calf, a little baby calf?

A. Right.

I figured now that I had taken some of the bluster out of the direct examination. I would still, however, have to deal with my client's statement to William Cogger during my final address to the jury.

Another hurdle that the defence had to overcome was the evidence of Lorraine Boucher. She portrayed her husband as a well-liked man who was a good neighbour and who would never cause harm to anyone. She claimed he was a friend to Johnnie MacKenzie. I had to discredit her without making the jury feel sorry for her as the grieving widow. Throughout her evidence she was tearful. She would not succumb to my suggestion that Eddie and Joey Deon and her husband were best friends. She described them as casual acquaintances, but insisted that Joey and Eddie Deon were good friends of MacKenzie.

I began my cross-examination of Lorraine Boucher by stating:

Q. Would you agree that friends would not harass one another and then use their tractors to dig up each other's driveways?

A. That's right.

Q. Would you also agree with me that a friend would not tear down their friend's gate that was erected to keep persons off their property?

A. That's right.

Q. And would you agree that a friend would not take another's animal, such as a cat, and kill it?

A. Yes.

Q. And would you also agree with me that a friend would not take another friend's dog, drag it behind an all-terrain vehicle and kill it, then dump it on their lawn. Would you agree that that would not be a friend?

A. Right.

Q. If, in fact, Mrs. Boucher, either your late husband, John Boucher, Joey Deon or Edmond Deon, did any of these things, would you agree that they would not be acts of a friend?

A. No, I'd say they'd be the acts of an enemy.

I tested Johnnie MacKenzie during the *voir dire*, and he did not make a good impression on the trial judge. Although that was unfortunate, the real test would be whether the jury would believe him or be left in reasonable doubt after hearing his evidence at trial. MacKenzie did testify before the jury and he presented his evidence in a credible manner. In fact, the courtroom was so full that the Sheriff's Department brought in the fire marshall to enforce the fire regulations and escort the overflow of spectators from the courtroom. At one point MacKenzie testified:

Q. Now, Mr. MacKenzie, what was your condition when you went to sleep on the floor that night?

A. Well, I was passed out. From the moment I hit the floor until I was awakened at five after three with a lot of kicking and banging at my door. I looked at my clock, I have my electric battery clock on a mantelpiece, to see what time somebody was coming to bug me. I could tell by the time who it was, because none of my people ever came at that hour of the morning. It was five after three a.m. that morning, the morning of the 24th.

Q. Who was it?

A. It was Joey Deon and I told him to go way, we're sleeping, leave us alone. He slammed the door. There was talking and cursing going on, then I laid back on the floor. I didn't get up and I didn't look out the window, but I did hear people's voices. I also heard bottles rattling motors revving up, and I did hear tires spinning and gravel flying in my driveway. I don't know how long this took place, maybe ten minutes, but they eventually left.

Q. Now what effect, did this, of course, have upon you?

A. Well I, like I said, I never got up off the floor. I tried to get back to sleep because Billy Cogger and I had plans at 7 o'clock that morning. We were going to go down to St. Augustine's Monastery, to the Shrine, and we were going to meditate and pray and I had no intentions of staying drunk that day. I was going to sober up because I had to be able to work Monday morning. So while I was trying to get back to sleep on the floor, I was thinking about all the problems that I was having, all the persecution with these people, and I could not get back to sleep. So I got up, and thought, "I'll go to sleep now." I grabbed a mickey of rum I had, Captain Morgan Light, and I drunk four big mouthfuls. Then I opened up a bottle of McEwin's Ale and used that for a chaser. Then laid back down on the floor thinking I'd go to sleep now. I continued to stay awake and the harassment and torture kept running through my mind, so I said there's one alternative to this, I've got stronger alcohol than rum. I went into the washroom, and poured a good shot of Aqua Velva, which I know is 70 proof, and put some juice in it, in the kitchen. I drunk it down very fast so I couldn't smell it or taste it. Then I opened a beer for a chaser and I laid down on the floor again.

Q. What happened after you took the swig of Aqua Velva?

A. Well, after I took the Aqua Velva, I opened up a beer and I laid down on the floor. The next thing I can honestly remember is waking up on the floor. I don't know how much time had passed. I had a coat on, cap on my head, and shoes on my feet. I also had the idea that I had seen bodies on Beech Hill Road that night.

Q. And what bodies had you seen on the Beech Hill Road that night?

A. Well, to the best of my knowledge I, I thought it was a dream, and I thought I saw John Boucher, Joseph Deon and Edmond Deon. I thought, this is what I thought I had seen, Sir.

Q. What's the next thing you saw, Mr. MacKenzie?

A. The next thing I, well, this was disturbing to my mind. I got up off the floor and the first thing I saw was a .22 pistol laying on my counter. I couldn't remember if it had been given back to me or not, I wasn't sure. The last time I saw it, it was taken from me before I entered Lorraine Boucher's car. So, I went to the fridge and I sat down thinking, the gun is here and I think I've seen bodies. If I walked by the bodies and if the gun is here, it looks very much, whether I am guilty or innocent, that I am going to be blamed anyway because I am a number one suspect because of the feuds that we've been having on Beech Hill. So, I saw Billy Cogger kinda make a turn on the chesterfield and I went over and talked to him. I told him what I had dreamt. He said, "You're absolutely crazy. You never left the house." I said, "I pray to God I didn't, Bill, but the pistol is on the counter and I haven't seen the pistol for twelve days. I was fighting with Boucher to get the pistol back when Boucher, he said, he was talking to Corporal Seewald. Corporal Seewald said he knows I've got the pistol. Then Boucher told me he said, "I'm going up to Ray MacKenzie's place to get the pistol." Boucher said, "Lorraine is not giving you the pistol back until the police raid your place and until you sober up."

Therefore, I told Billy Cogger and I said, "There's the pistol and I think I saw bodies. I walked by the bodies. I'm definitely going to be the number one suspect." So I asked, "Bill, do you think it's wise if I get rid of the shoes and the pistol if I walked by the bodies?" He said, "I, it's up, I don't know, Johnny." He thought I was fooling. He said, It's up to you. I guess so." So, I was in no state of mind to reason. If I thought I saw bodies, the most reasonable thing to do would be to phone for help for these people, bur I didn't. I don't remember throwing the gun and the shoes in the well. I didn't know I put them there until the RCMP told me in the Antigonish lockup.

Q. Tell me, Sir, in the early morning of June 23rd, today, do you have any recollection of shooting John Boucher, Edmund Deon, and Joey Deon?

A. No, I do not, Sir. And I do not have the nature to kill people under any circumstances, animals or humans.

It is not the role of defence counsel to judge a client's story. That is the role of the jury. It was my goal to present to the jury members a case that would leave them in reasonable doubt as to John Alexander MacKenzie's guilt. If the jury was convinced beyond a reasonable doubt that it was MacKenzie who fired the gunshots, then the jury would still have to deal with the issues of provocation, drunkenness, and the offence of manslaughter.

The Crown did not call any rebuttal evidence to refute MacKenzie's evidence about the gun. It was then left up to me to try to convince the jury that there was a reasonable doubt about who in fact fired the shots. I decided to approach the issues before the jury as follows:

There are some real questions in this case which I must leave with you to consider. First, has the Crown proved beyond a reasonable doubt that it was Johnnie MacKenzie who actually did the shooting? If you should so conclude this, then you may proceed on to answer these questions.

I then listed the other questions for the jury members to consider and continued my address:

Going back to the first question of Who did it? It's not a matter of looking at the evidence and saying to yourselves: In light of all the evidence, who else could have done it? That is not the issue. The issue is: Has the Crown proved beyond a reasonable doubt that, in fact, it was Johnnie MacKenzie who, in fact, shot John Boucher, Edmond Deon and Joey Deon?

In light of the evidence that you heard in this courtroom, can it be said that the Crown has met that burden?

The Crown has called two witnesses, and they will try to tell you that from their evidence you can conclude it was in fact Johnnie MacKenzie. Well, do you remember the two witnesses called?

Daniel Girrior was the neighbour who stated that he placed the time of the first shot at 4:17 a.m, the second set of shots at 4:58 a.m., and the third set of shots a few minutes later. He also stated that he heard gunshots in the early morning on several other occasions and that it was not an unusual occurrence in the Beech Hill area to hear gunshots. He said there were differences in what he, in fact, heard. The Crown wants you, I informed the jury, to infer that these times were, in fact, the precise times of the shootings. But, I continued, you cannot be unmindful of the evidence of the Crown's other witness, William Cogger, who said that when he woke up at 4:45 a.m. and looked at his clock, Johnnie MacKenzie was in the trailer. Who, I asked, fired the other shots at 4:58 and a few minutes later? To be precise, Cogger looked at his watch again at 5:03, and Johnnie was sitting at the table drinking a beer. Accepting what both of these Crown witnesses have said, can it be said beyond a reasonable doubt that Johnnie MacKenzie shot these three men?

There was no evidence to refute MacKenzie's evidence that Lorraine Boucher was the last person to be in possession of the gun, I reminded the jury. In fact, the unrebutted evidence was that, a week earlier, MacKenzie could not find his gun. Turning to face the jury, I said, "I'm sure the Crown's going to say to you, Mr. Foreman and Ladies and Gentlemen, 'Well, how did the gun get into the trailer?'" Well, that is not for us to answer, I replied, that is for the prosecutors to prove. Sure, they could prove it was the gun that killed those three people, but they still have to put Johnnie MacKenzie behind the gun with his finger on the trigger before the jury could say that he committed any type of homicide.

In light of the evidence of Danny Girrior, who said he heard the second shots at 4:58 a.m., the Crown wanted the jury to infer that MacKenzie shot Joey Deon at that time. But, I reminded the jury, William Cogger, another Crown witness, testified that MacKenzie was at home then. And, a few minutes later, Girrior heard a third series of shots, which the Crown wanted the jury to believe was when Johnnie shot Eddie Deon. Yet Cogger said that he looked at his clock at 5:03 a.m., and MacKenzie was at home drinking.

There was one initial question to be addressed, I advised the jury: "Has the Crown proven beyond a reasonable doubt that John Alexander MacKenzie fired the gunshots that claimed the lives of John Boucher, Joey Deon, and Edmond Deon?" When dealing with MacKenzie's statement, I reminded the jury members that once a confession has been ruled admissible, it is in the same position as any other evidence, and they might accept it or reject it in whole or in part. The same could be said about any statement made by Johnnie MacKenzie to William Cogger. It was the jury's prerogative, after examining all the evidence, to decide whether to accept it in whole, or in part, or not at all. The opinions of the judge, the Crown, or the defence are not pertinent.

At the end of my address, I declared, "As I commenced my address, so will I end it by stating that the mere fact that Johnnie sits before you does not mean that he must be guilty. There is no burden upon Johnnie to prove that he is innocent. The burden is solely upon the Crown and that burden never shifts." I completed my address with these words:

Ladies and Gentlemen of the jury, when you listen to his Lordship's instructions concerning reasonable doubt and you hear his instructions regarding the Crown's burden of proof, these are not empty slogans. They are the foundation of the criminal justice system of Canada. They are what our system offers my client as a way to answer such a serious allegation, a way to make a defence. Not only because of the great impact a conviction would have in these circumstances on my client and those close to him, but also because it is necessary for the law to recognize the errors, inaccuracies and misconceptions that sometimes result. When we try to judge the truth of what a person says, or when we try to infer, where there are gaps in the evidence as there clearly are here, then the words reasonable doubt will have a significant meaning. Listen carefully to his Lordship's instructions.

I sat down–and hoped for a favourable jury charge by the trial judge.

In his jury address, Justice A.L. MacIntosh made some pertinent remarks that a jury could grasp in deciding whether the Crown had proven its case beyond a reasonable doubt. The judge's charge was fair and well balanced:

> A reasonable doubt is an honest doubt, a fair doubt based on reason and common sense. It is not imaginary or frivolous doubt that you might use to avoid your responsibilities as jurors. The accused is entitled to the benefit of a reasonable doubt on the whole of the case with respect to each count and on each and every issue in the case.

> In this case the accused himself gave evidence. He is in the same position as any other witness as far as credibility is concerned. Shortly I will instruct you how to weigh testimony, but for the present let me tell you that if you believe the accused that he did not commit the offence or what he did lacks some essential element of the offence, which I will describe later, or if the evidence of the accused, either standing alone or taken together with all the other evidence, leaves you in a state of reasonable doubt, then you must acquit him.

Statements of the accused:

> You've heard the evidence of Sgt. Peebles and Cst. Cleary regarding the statements made by the accused to them on June 25th. The fact that these statements were given does not mean that they were made or that they were true. That's up for you to decide. It's for you to decide whether the statements were made and if you have a reasonable doubt about whether or not a particular statement was made in whole or in part, you must reject it entirely or reject those parts for which you have a reasonable doubt as to the making. If you find statements were made, you may believe all of the statement, part of it, or you can reject it entirely. Here we recall that the accused

is saying he doesn't remember anything of what happened, that these statements he gave is what he heard from other people. If you decide to accept part or all of it, it will be considered by you with the other evidence you decide to accept. You, of course, must reach a verdict on the whole of the evidence that you decide is worthy to believe. For the accused, as a witness, you can accept earlier testimony as the statement that the police, the Crown alleges he made to the police. You can accept that as the truth of what happened as opposed to what he said in court ... If you find that his evidence at trial represents the true facts, or if you have any reasonable doubt about it, you will reject entirely the earlier statement.

4. The evidence of William Cogger:

It's obvious that certainly at 4:45 a.m. there's no doubt that the accused was at the trailer.

Keep in mind the times that the other people said about hearing shots and so on. It's up to you to decide just what significance you put to those times. You can consider how well you rely on people when they tell you times, and so on. Use your common sense in judging the weight you give to the evidence.

The judge's charge to the jury lasted four and a half hours. The jury returned at 4:30 p.m. on the first day of deliberation to rehear the evidence of William Cogger, Lorraine Boucher, and Daniel Girrior. The jury deliberated for two and a half days and, at 2:23 p.m. of the third day, it reached a verdict.

The townspeople crowded the courtroom. There were even people outside waiting for the verdict:

Clerk: Members of the jury, have you agreed upon your verdict?

Mr. Foreman: We have.

Clerk: What's your verdict on the first count?

Mr. Foreman: The verdict on the first count is not guilty.

Clerk: What's your verdict on the second count?

Mr. Foreman: The verdict on the second count is not guilty.

Clerk: What's your verdict on the third count?

Mr. Foreman: The verdict on the third count is not guilty.

Clerk: Members of the jury, you have found the accused not guilty.
Are you in agreement?

Jurors: Yes.

The Crown attorney then requested that the jury be polled and that the clerk ask each juror individually the verdict on all three counts. Each one responded, "Not guilty."

Those in attendance applauded. The judge, without thanking the jury or discharging the accused, said, "Well, the court stands adjourned."

John Alexander MacKenzie was free to return home. As he exited the court, several townspeople clapped and cheered him. I gave him a ride home to his sister's residence. In the car he thanked me for my assistance but said it wasn't my work that had him acquitted him—it was God's wishes. He had become a very religious person. I accepted his words without comment. We shook hands, and I returned to Halifax to see if the Crown would appeal.

* * *

The date of the acquittal was April 20, 1990, and, on May 17, just three days before the thirty-day limit would have expired, the Crown appealed the verdict on eleven grounds. The appeal was heard on February 13, 1991, before a panel of three justices of the Nova Scotia Court of Appeal: the Honourable Justice D. Chipman, the Honourable Justice G. Hart, and the Honourable Justice G. Freeman.

On April 11, 1991, the Court of Appeal handed down its 108-page decision. The majority, which included Justice Chipman and Justice Hart, found an error in law, allowed the Crown appeal, and sent the matter back for a new trial. Justice Freeman dissented.

When I reported the decision to my client, I informed him that I had done my best. It must have been God's wish that he have a new trial.

MacKenzie decided to appeal this decision to the Supreme Court of Canada. On April 22, 1991, I filed a Notice of Appeal based on the following questions of law from the dissenting judgment of Justice Gerald Freeman of the Nova Scotia Court of Appeal:

1. That the learned Trial Judge erred in law in instructing the jury that the appellant's out-of-court culpatory statement must be rejected entirely if the appellant's testimony at trial raised any reasonable doubt, thereby misdirecting the jury on the doctrine of reasonable doubt and the proper method of deliberating on the evidence as a whole.

2. That the Learned Trial Judge erred in law in excluding from the evidence certain statements made by the accused to police officers on the basis that the appellant had exercised his right to retain legal counsel and the taking or admission of these statements would be considered " adjudicatively unfair."

3. That the majority erred in law in holding that the verdict might have been different, therefore usurping the function of the jury, which amounted to an error in law.

After presentation of the arguments, the Supreme Court of Canada reserved its decision. The court narrowed in on the issues dealing with MacKenzie's statement and the trial judge's instructions pertaining to it. The court closely examined the trial judge's instructions to the jury, in particular where he stated that "they must reject the accused statements if they had a reasonable doubt as to whether the statement was made." Further, when the trial judge invited the jury members to reject the statement if they had a reasonable doubt as to its veracity, as stated by Justice La Forest:

> In my view, it is acceptable for a trial judge to focus the jury's atten-
> tion on the vital issues of its inquiry. Perhaps the jury should not be
> directed to compartmentalize their deliberations, but at the same
> time it is unrealistic to view a jury's decision as some epiphanic pro-
> nouncement of guilt or innocence. Rather, the jurors engage in a
> deliberate process of evaluating the evidence presented to them. In
> this case, the jury deliberated for two days on the evidence from a
> trial that lasted more than three weeks. To restrain jurors from reject-

ing evidence during this process is to impose an artificial constraint on their mandate. Having said this, a trial judge should proceed with the utmost caution in advising the jury that certain evidence may be rejected. If the trial judge ventures into this realm, then the advice must be complete. He or she must go on to stress to the jury that this rejection must not be done in isolation. The evidence is not to be evaluated in a piecemeal fashion.

In this case, the decision continued, where a statement by the accused at a trial is entirely at odds with one of his previous out-of-court statements, and the jury believes the statement at trial or is left in reasonable doubt that it is true, the jury must reject the out-of-court statement. The accused must be given the benefit of the doubt. In arriving at that conclusion, the jury should, of course, give consideration to the evidence as a whole.

The contradictory statements of the accused were a key element of this trial, and the judge was entitled to give the jury some guidance on how to handle this discrepancy in the evidence. As a matter of logic, the two stories could not be reconciled, and the evidence to reject one of them is an acceptable way to deal with the dilemma. When a judge ventures into this kind of instruction, a reviewing court will have two concerns: first, the jury must know that its job is not to choose the most believable of the versions, but the version most favourable to the accused is entitled to the benefit of the doubt; second, the two versions cannot simply be pitted against each other in isolation, but all the other evidence must also be considered.

The Supreme Court of Canada relied on its decision in *R. v. Morin*, where the court states:

Morin demonstrates that it is both acceptable and desirable for a trial judge to focus the jury's attention on vital issues, and to direct their minds to the proper burden of proof on those discrete questions. In my view, this is exactly what the trial judge has done in the present case. As Freeman J.A. commented in the court below, at p. 389: the words of Mr. Justice MacIntosh referred to above, to say nothing of his instructions as a whole, would have left the jury in a state of mind no different than if he had charged them in the words of Mr. Justice Lamer in Nadeau.

Chief Justice Lamer in his judgment in Nadeau states:

> However, the jury can and must decide whether the whole of the
> evidence establishes, beyond a reasonable doubt, the individual
> facts necessary to support a conviction. This must, of necessity, be
> done in a sequential manner, and I agree with La Forest J. that it is
> unrealistic to expect the jury to have an "epiphanic" experience in
> rejecting its verdict. In Morin, Wilson J. stated that the process of the
> jury's deliberation with respect to the Crown's evidence "requires a
> fact elicited through the mouth of a witness to be assessed by the
> jury in the context of all the evidence and to be rejected if it has not
> been proved beyond a reasonable doubt." Therefore, while the jury
> never rejects evidence, it can and must decide whether to accept or
> reject. The factual assertions made by that evidence before it uses
> those factual assertions to support or infer other factual assertions
> towards reaching its verdict. Such factual assertions can only be
> accepted and used by the jury to convict the accused if they are
> established by the evidence beyond a reasonable doubt. Facts which
> are not established cannot corroborate or be allowed to "bootstrap"
> other doubtful facts. Any lower standard would present the possibil-
> ity than an accused could be convicted on the basis of facts which
> are established as matters of conjecture only.

An analogy I often used in charging juries, especially in cases where the
Crown's case was circumstantial, was that of a fisherman's net. The evidence
presented at trial by the Crown seeks to establish factual propositions. Once
established, facts may be used to imply other facts. In this way, factual propositions intertwine to construct a net of such propositions. If a factual proposition is established as a mere probability or likelihood, and not beyond a reasonable doubt, it cannot be used to imply any further facts. The interweaving
of facts breaks down and there is a hole in the net. A net with a hole, however small, is not a useful net because a critical factual proposition remains that
is not consistent with the accused's guilt. Thus, a fact that is not established
beyond a reasonable doubt can play no part in the jury's decision to convict,
either as a fact on which they rely to find an essential element of the offence
or as a fact used to imply such facts. Although it is a misdirection to instruct

juries to reject evidence, it is correct in law to tell juries to reject factual propositions that the Crown's evidence does not establish beyond a reasonable doubt.

In the Supreme Court decision, Justice Lamer goes on to state:

> It is also important to understand the relationship between the jury's assessment of credibility and the criminal standard of proof when the jury is faced with conflicting accounts from the Crown and the defence witnesses. It is a clear error for a trial judge to instruct the jury to choose the most believable, persuasive or creditable of the two accounts in such circumstances. As with all facts on which a conviction is to be supported, the factual propositions in the Crown witnesses' evidence must be established by that or otherwise evidence beyond a reasonable doubt. If the jury does not believe the Crown witnesses' version, or any part of it, beyond a reasonable doubt, it cannot be used to convict the accused, even if they do not believe the contrary version of the defence. It may very well be that both versions are wrong, and the accused is entitled to the benefit of this doubt with respect to the credibility of any witness.

In the circumstances of this case, however, the trial judge was not in error in inviting the jury members to reject the factual proposition in one of the two statements, depending on which they believed, because both statements emanated from the accused and, as La Forest states, could not logically co-exist. There was only a single determination of credibility to be made. If they believed the accused's exculpatory evidence at trial, they must of necessity disbelieve his inculpatory statements to the police. It must be remembered, though, that the accused need never establish his or her version of events beyond a reasonable doubt. That standard only and always applies to the Crown. The accused, in giving evidence, must raise only a reasonable doubt, even where he or she bears an evidentiary burden.

The judgement of the court was handed down on January 5, 1993. The court upheld the instructions of Justice MacIntosh and stated that he did not err when he said:

> It's for you to decide whether the statements were made, and if you have a reasonable doubt about whether or not a particular statement

was made, in whole or in part, you must reject it entirely or reject those parts of which you have an reasonable doubt as to the making. If you find the statements were made, you may believe all of the statement, part of it, or you can reject them entirely. You are the sole judges of whether an unsworn statement alleged to have been made by the accused, in whole or in part, is an acknowledgement by the accused of the truth of the matter contained in it.

The Supreme Court of Canada allowed John Alexander MacKenzie's appeal and reinstated the acquittal of the jury.

I chose this case not because I was successful before the Supreme Court of Canada but because the case encompasses every basic principle of law that we learn in a first-year criminal law course. Regardless of the charge, never forget that these three basic principles of law always apply: presumption of innocence, burden of proof, and proof beyond a reasonable doubt. If at any time there is doubt, it must be found in favour of the accused. This case also highlights the importance of the jury as triers of fact. The question of credibility and the weight to be given to any evidence is for the jury to decide, and the opinions of the trial judge, the Crown attorney, and even the defence counsel are irrelevant.

As for Johnnie MacKenzie, he left Beech Hill Road and moved to live with his sister, Josephine Levangie, in Antigonish. Approximately two months after his acquittal, a nephew of one of the victims decided to take the law into his own hands and went looking for MacKenzie. He fired a .303 rifle shot into the side of Levangie's trailer. Fortunately MacKenzie, who was home at the time, was spared from any injury. The nephew was arrested and charged with dangerous use of a firearm. He pleaded guilty and received a sentence. In this particular incident, because of the unusual circumstances, justice was tempered with mercy, and the nephew was placed on probation, with the direction to stay away from Johnnie MacKenzie.

Since the day of his acquittal, Johnnie MacKenzie has suffered continuously from post-traumatic stress illness.

Susan Nelles:
The Defence of Innocence

AUSTIN COOPER, QC

1990

Between January 11 and March 22, 1981, four infants who were patients in the cardiac ward at the Hospital for Sick Children in Toronto died as a result of the deliberate administration of overdoses of a heart drug called Digoxin. Although, at the outset, there was some speculation that "mercy killing" was the reason for the deaths, it soon became clear that there was no motive for the killings. In fact, some of the babies could have recovered from their illnesses and led reasonably normal lives.

The usual reasons for one person killing another, such as matrimonial discord, jealousy, revenge, self-defence, drunkenness, or provocation, were all irrelevant. There was no apparent motive. Accordingly, these crimes were strange indeed, and, as the lawyer retained to defend the person charged, it appeared plain that the killer who snuffed out the lives of the babies had to be a strange person. Any normal, right-thinking, healthy person would not extinguish the lives of four helpless infants in their cribs for no apparent reason. It was therefore with some curiosity that I anticipated the first meeting with my client, Susan Nelles, at the Metro West Detention Centre in March 1981.

What sort of creature would I see? The first thing that struck me on that cold Sunday afternoon in the little room assigned for lawyers to meet their clients was how small she was. She appeared barely five feet tall. Apart from that, she certainly was not typical of the young women I had seen within the confines of prisons. There was a freshness about her appearance and a polish about her manner that set her apart from other inmates I had met.

As we sat at the table provided for us and discussed her pending application for bail, I noticed that she was clear eyed, reserved, polite, considerate, and, above all, apparently quite sane—at least to my non-medical eye.

Later, while interviewing the witnesses to be called at her application for bail before Mr. Justice Steele, I was impressed by the quality of her friends. Her best friend and confidante with whom she shared an apartment was Alison Woodbury, a law student and a person whose wholesome manner and integrity were immediately apparent. She is now a lawyer with a large firm. The evidence she gave at the bail hearing was impressive and it reinforced my initial reaction to this case: it was highly unlikely that the strange person I expected to have committed such senseless and bizarre crimes would have friendships with people of Alison Woodbury's quality.

If one assumed that the person who had committed these unusual crimes had to be an aberrant personality—a twisted, warped individual—the staff in our office quickly concluded that Susan Nelles did not appear to fit the role. For that reason alone (and, later, there were others), we began to speculate that perhaps the police had arrested the wrong person.

To test our thesis, we decided to have her examined by a psychiatrist of some eminence and by a senior psychologist on the staff of a major hospital. We wanted professionals whose qualifications, expertise, and impartiality would be unquestioned, so we turned to a psychiatrist and a psychologist who, although perhaps not well known around the courts, were the chiefs of their departments at teaching hospitals in Toronto. The chosen psychologist was Dr. Leonard Goldsmith at the Toronto General Hospital. He administered a battery of psychological tests to Ms. Nelles and gave us a written report that concluded she was the most well-adjusted person it had ever been his privilege to examine. We felt good about that.

We also arranged to have her examined by Dr. Stanley Greben, who was chief of the medical staff and head of the Department of Psychiatry at Mount Sinai Hospital, in Toronto, a former president of the Canadian Psychiatric Association, and a professor of psychiatry at the University of Toronto. He had an impressive background of scholarship and experience and had written extensively in his specialty. In his written report, Dr. Greben concluded that Susan Nelles was sane, socially well adjusted, and a person to whom the killing of other humans, particularly infants, was an abhorrent concept. She was a nurse, and her instincts and outlook were focused on comforting and healing, not killing. These reports further confirmed our first impression that Miss Nelles did not fit the role cast for her by the prosecution. She simply was not the type of person who could be expected to murder helpless infants for no apparent reason.

What did the evidence show? Did it bear out our thesis that the wrong person was accused of four murders of the first degree? What contact, if any, could the prosecution prove Susan Nelles had with Janice Estrella, who died on January 11, 1981; Kevin Pacsai, whose death occurred on March 11; Alana Miller, who died on March 21; and Justin Cook, who died a day later on March 22?

Before the preliminary hearing, we conducted a detailed analysis of the hospital records. It demonstrated that Miss Nelles was one of the five-member nursing team on ward 4A, the team on duty when all four children died. Further, she had been assigned to care for babies Pacsai, Miller, and Cook during the long night shifts when each of them died—she had access to each of those three children during the seven to eight hours before their deaths. However, the records also showed that at various times during those shifts other nurses had relieved her and, therefore, had access to those three infants.

Our analysis of the nursing notes and hospital records relative to the fourth child, Janice Estrella, showed that Susan Nelles was not on duty during the night shift for the seven or eight hours before her death. We searched the records for the preceding twelve-hour day shift and found that although Miss Nelles was on duty as part of the nursing team, two other nurses had been assigned to care for the baby under circumstances of "constant nursing care," meaning one of those two nurses always had to be present and tending to the child. Whenever one nurse took a break for coffee or lunch or to use the washroom, the other had to be there. In other words, the records indicated that Susan Nelles had no contact with Janice Estrella during the twenty-hour period preceding her death. Accordingly, our preliminary analysis of hospital and nursing records tended to confirm our impression that perhaps the police had the wrong person. We began to think that the prosecution was in trouble, and we had a reasonable chance of having the charges tossed out at the preliminary hearing. We hoped the oral evidence at the hearing would bear that out.

The preliminary hearing commenced on January 4, 1982, before Judge Vanek of the Provincial Court. As the evidence unfolded relative to Janice Estrella, it was established that the child, who had been prescribed Digoxin, had fatal levels of the drug in her blood at the time of her death. It was confirmed that Susan Nelles was off duty during the night shift when the baby died, that the two nurses assigned to the baby on the preceding twelve-hour day shift had watched her continuously, and that Susan Nelles had not been near her. We felt that the prosecution was truly in deep water. We also began to wonder who had killed baby Estrella. It was never determined who administered the fatal dose of Digoxin to Janice Estrella, but it became clear that it could not have been Susan Nelles. She simply had no access to the child in the twenty hours during which the fatal dose of Digoxin had been administered.

From the outset and throughout the proceedings we contended that the same person had to be responsible for all four killings. The crimes all followed the same pattern:

- all involved infants on the cardiology ward;
- all were killed by Digoxin overdose;
- there was no motive for any of the murders;
- all died early in the morning and while members of the same nursing team were on duty;
- all had to have been killed by an unusual assailant;
- one could not expect, in the light of common human experience, that two people operating independently of each other could have had the strange need to snuff out infants in this way; and
- there was absolutely no evidence of a conspiracy among two or more persons to murder in this manner.

Ultimately, the court accepted this thesis, as did the Crown in its argument. We felt that the facts proved in relation to baby Estrella should put an end to the case against Susan Nelles. However, the prosecution turned that argument around and submitted that, because the crimes could have been committed by only one person, if there was some inference that Susan Nelles had access to and perhaps killed Miller, Pacsai, and Cook, the Court could infer that somehow she had obtained access to Estrella and murdered that baby too.

Fortunately, a month or so into the preliminary hearing the defence received further support when we learned that, following an order of the attorney general, the body of a fifth infant, named Stephanie Lombardo, had been exhumed. Baby Lombardo had been a patient on the cardiac ward for five days during the latter part of December 1980. She died suddenly on the ward while recovering from an apparently successful heart operation. Lombardo had not been prescribed Digoxin, yet, when her body was exhumed in December 1981, a year after her death, an analysis demonstrated that her tissues were laced with Digoxin. The expert evidence confirmed that baby Lombardo very likely died as a result of a Digoxin overdose. The hospital employment records and the nursing records for December 1980 showed that Susan Nelles was on holiday during the whole period in which Lombardo was in the hospital. This fact was confirmed at the preliminary hearing by the oral evidence of the staff who attended the baby. With the introduction of that evidence, we felt that the case against Susan Nelles had all but disintegrated and that we had an innocent client. Ultimately, Judge Vanek agreed in his ruling on May 21, 1982, when he gave his reason for discharging Susan Nelles: "Since admittedly the same person must have killed all four children, the evidence relating to Estrella is positive disproof that [Nelles] is the person who poisoned Cook, Pacsai and Miller. Moreover, the Crown's theory that Susan Nelles is the person who killed all four babies is inconsistent with the circumstances surrounding the death of Stephanie Lombardo."

During this enormously complicated but immensely interesting case, we faced several tactical and evidentiary problems. Here is how we tried to deal with them. We realized from the outset that the legal test by which the judge presiding at the preliminary hearing had to guide himself in determining whether to send the case to trial was a narrow one. He did not have to be convinced beyond a reasonable doubt before he could commit for trial. The test that Judge Vanek was required to apply was enunciated by the Supreme Court of Canada in *U.S.A. v. Sheppard*: was there evidence on which a reasonable jury, properly instructed, could convict the accused? During the three-and-a-half-month preliminary hearing, we had to be sensitive as to whether some evidence might be led against Susan Nelles on which a reasonable jury could convict. We realized, on the authority of *Sheppard*, it did not have to be very much evidence for Judge Vanek to conclude that the case ought to be sent to trial.

Some areas of the evidence caused us concern in this regard, such as the evidence of Dr. Rodney Fowler. He was the staff cardiologist and chief of the cardiac ward during March 1981, and he testified that he saw Miss Nelles in the early morning of March 22, 1981, shortly after Justin Cook had died. Cook was the last of the four children to expire. As Dr. Fowler was leaving the hospital, he saw Miss Nelles sitting at one of the desks in the nursing station, apparently writing up the final report in Justin Cook's medical chart. (She was the nurse assigned to that child during the evening shift on which he died.) Dr. Fowler gave evidence that he knew she had been previously involved with baby Pacsai and had given the prescribed Digoxin to that child before his death. By that time, it had been confirmed that Pacsai had died of a Digoxin overdose because an inquest had been made into the death. Dr. Fowler was anxious to see what Miss Nelles looked like in the early morning after Cook's death. He said he glanced in her direction and saw a very strange expression on her face, one showing no sign of grief. He thought it was unusual for her to have this appearance after such a terrible thing had happened. We appreciated that this evidence was tenuous but felt it could prove troublesome and might be the straw that would convince the judge to let a jury decide the case in a trial. As a result, we prepared Dr. Fowler's cross-examination very carefully. The cross-examination proceeded this way:

Q. Now, as to Susan Nelles, was she a close friend of yours?

A. No.

Q. Did you ever visit her house?

A. Never.

Q. Or her apartment?

A. Never.

Q. Has she ever visited your house?

A. Never.

Q. I think you said you knew her for one year?

A. Just because she was on the ward.

Q. On the ward?

A. Her brother is a resident on the ward and I knew her father.

Q. Have you ever had lunch with her?

A. Never.

Q. Or coffee?

A. Never.

Q. Or dinner?

A. Never.

Q. Ever had a sort of meaningful conversation with her about any-thing other than whether a baby has or hasn't had its medication or has turned blue?

A. Never.

Q. Okay, so you never worked a twelve-hour shift in her company?

A. Never.

Q. Did you ever see her since her arrest on March 25 other than around the Court or whatever?

A. No, I've never seen her since then.

Q. Did you ever see her grieving after a relative had died?

A. I have never seen her grieving because I don't know her. I've never seen.

Q. Did you ever see her upset, ever?

A. Never.

Q. Ever see her cry?

A. No.

Q. Did you ever see her angry?

A. No.

Q. Did you ever see her depressed or elated?

A. No.

Q. Did you ever see her sad or shocked?

A. No.

Q. Well, I'm going to suggest that you really don't know much about the lady's emotional range. You'll agree with that?

A. I've seen many nurses who are looking after sick patients, and her reaction, again, was very unusual.

Q. Well, I didn't ask you that. I asked you – I suggested that you don't know much about her emotional range?

A. No.

Q. You just don't know much about it?

A. No, except that it's unusual, under the circumstances, for a person to have that reaction.

Q. Okay. Well, a number of witnesses here have described Susan Nelles as being a cheerful person. Do you know her well enough to even know about that?

A. No.

Q. She's easy to get along with. Do you know her well enough to even know that?

A. No. I don't work with her.

Q. You don't work with her. She's conscientious and eager. You don't know that, I guess?

A. No, I don't know that. I presume that she does her job well or she wouldn't have been working on the ward.

Q. Do you think those people, whether nurses or doctors, who have worked on shift with her, would be in a better position than you to describe her emotional states. Someone who knew her well and worked with her on shift. Do you think?

A. I'm not talking about her emotional state, I'm talking about her appearance under a situation, and I explained what she looked like. I don't know anything about her reactions, her emotional reactions.

Q. Well, my question was, do you think those who have worked on shift with her over a period of weeks or a year, twelve hours a day, would be in a better position than you to describe Susan Nelles' emotional state?

A. Well, I'm not sure about that.

Q. You're not sure about that.

A. Because they haven't seen her in exactly the same situation that I saw.

Q. Oh, I see. Well, we've had some witnesses here who spoke about that. There was a Mrs. Ober who gave evidence in this courtroom, and I've got it as exactly as I can that, "After Justin Cook's death, Susan Nelles looked tired and strained and pretty upset." Is that the type of reaction you would have expected from a nurse after a death?

A. Yes.

Q. We have Mr. Cook himself, Justin Cook's father, who gave evidence here just a couple of weeks ago. He said, "There were tears in Susan Nelles' eyes and she said she was sorry." Is that the type of reaction you would have expected from a nurse after a death of an infant that she was looking after.

A. Yes, that's what I would have expected.

Q. You would have expected that. Another nurse, Susan Reaper, said in this courtroom under oath, after the death of Justin Cook "Susan Nelles was upset. She was smoking a cigarette." Is that the type of reaction you would have expected?

A. I'm not sure. I don't know.

Q. Mrs. Lyons, Evonne Lyons, one of the nurses on 4B, gave evidence in this courtroom that "Susan Nelles, after the death of Justin Cook, seemed to be in shock." Is that the type of reaction you might expect to see after the death of a child who you were looking after?

A. I don't know what that term means, I'm not sure.

Q. Well, you said she looked strange. Do you know what that term means?

A. Yes.

Q. Phyllis Trayner, who is the same lady Mr. McGee asked you about and whom you said you knew by sight anyway, the head nurse?

A. I just know her by sight, just the way I know Miss Nelles.

Q. She swore in this courtroom, just a couple of weeks ago, that, "After Justin Cook's death, Susan Nelles was very upset. There were tears in her eyes." That's the type of reaction you would have expected?

A. That's what I would have expected, but there was no evidence of that at all when I witnessed her.

Q. When you witnessed her. Bertha Bell, a nurse on 4B swore in this courtroom some short time ago that "After the death of Justin Cook, Susan Nelles was upset. She was very quiet. I know Susan Nelles, well, I know when she was upset." That's the sort of thing you'd expect after the death of a child you were looking after?

A. Yes.

Q. Janet Brownless, a nursing assistant, a registered nursing assistant, on 4A, said that "Susan Nelles helped Brownless bathe Justin Cook after the death of Cook, and that Susan Nelles was upset." Again, that's the type of reaction that would be normal?

A. Yes.

Q. And Mrs. Whittingham, who was also on duty, I believe on 4B, said, "Everybody was upset and feeling badly after Justin Cook's death, including Susan Nelles." Again, that's how you'd expect the nurses to react?

A. Yes.

Q. Right. Now you swore that you didn't see Susan Nelles, according to my notes, until you were leaving the ward?

SUSAN NELLES: THE DEFENCE OF INNOCENCE **37**

A. That's correct.

Q. After the death of Justin Cook?

A. Yes.

Q. So you didn't see her during the arrest or right afterwards, did you?

A. No.

Q. You might not have had the same opportunity as these other people whose evidence I've outlined for you?

A. Yes.

Q. Right. You took a glance at her, I think you said?

A. Yes.

Q. She was seated at a desk, writing out a description of what happened?

A. Well, I don't know what she was writing, but she was writing something.

Q. I thought you said she was writing a report?

A. No, I don't know what she was doing. I presume it was a description of the final events, but she was writing something at the desk.

Q. Well, it would be her duty to write out such a description, wouldn't it?

A. Yes.

Q. Yes. She was looking down at a piece of paper while she wrote?

A. Yes.

Q. Apparently concentrating?

A. Yes.

Q. And you felt from your glance at her as you left the ward that her expression was strange?

A. Yes, it was not in keeping with a person who had just had a patient die under her care.

Q. So it was strange in that there was no appearance of grief?

A. Of grief, right.

Q. That's why it was strange, is that correct?

A. Correct.

Q. Are you really in any position to tell this Court how she was really feeling at that time. Are you?

A. All I can do is tell the Court what I saw.

Q. What you saw. You have no idea what she was feeling, do you?

A. That's an inference that you'll have to make yourself.

Q. Well, you just don't know, do you, how she was feeling?

A. No, I just know what she looked like, and I've seen many, many people who were in that situation who don't appear like she did. In other words, she had no signs of grief.

Q. She had no signs of grief and that was strange to you?

A. Yes.

Q. Right. But you don't know how she was feeling. I mean, are you prepared to agree with that or not?

A. Yes, I can't say that.

Q. You can't say. And you certainly don't know how she was feeling during the arrest or when the baby was pronounced dead or immediately afterwards when talking to her nurses on the floor, do you?

A. No. I didn't speak to her at all during that period.

Judge Vanek concluded his reasons for discharging Ms. Nelles with these words: "I am unable to find any evidence of guilt from what a doctor thought from a passing glance was a "strange expression."

It was also an area of concern for us that, apparently after the arrest of Ms. Nelles on March 25, 1981, there were no deaths of infants that could be attributed to a Digoxin overdose. We were concerned that Judge Vanek might conclude that this fact led to an inference of complicity by Miss Nelles, enough to compel him to send the case on for trial. However, we were able to elicit some facts in cross-examination that we felt were able to neutralize any such inference. First, after the death of Justin Cook, all Digoxin was locked up in a narcotics cabinet. Before that, it had been readily available to anyone who sought it. As well, after Cook's death, all Digoxin had to be signed for by two nurses on an inventory sheet, and the inventory control was tightened considerably. Since Digoxin was a prescription drug, it became very difficult for any person to obtain access to it, certainly without considerable risk of exposure.

Second, we argued that, with the arrest of Miss Nelles, any further killings by Digoxin would attract attention to the real offender still at large. That person might be expected to keep a low profile.

Third, the evidence revealed some bizarre happenings at the hospital after the arrest of Susan Nelles. They tended to support our contention that someone with a twisted personality, the type of person who might have caused the senseless killings charged to Susan Nelles, might still be on the loose in the ward. We were able to adduce through cross-examination of members of the nursing staff that a series of ominous and threatening telephone calls had been made to nurses and members of the hospital staff and their families after the arrest of my client. Someone, a female, who was familiar with the deaths of the babies and with the nurses on duty, was calling people at the hospital for no apparent reason and was making death threats to two particular nurses on the ward. In addition, we were able to show that a series of strange marks in lipstick was made on the locker doors of the same two nurses on the cardiac ward, on the door of the apartment of one of them, and on the rear window of a car.

We established through alibi evidence that Susan Nelles was unable to have made some of those telephone calls–for example, she was on an airplane to Vancouver when one of them was made. She was out of Toronto when some of the lipstick markings were placed–a bridesmaid at a wedding in Ottawa, for instance, when one of the marks had to have been drawn.

Another bizarre incident occurred at the hospital after the arrest of Miss Nelles when two nurses found Propanolol, another heart drug, in the food they had brought to the hospital from their homes. During a 2:00 morning lunch break, one nurse found the drug in her soup, which was in a Tupperware container, while the other nurse found the drug sprinkled in her salad in a similar plastic container.

We were able to establish through cross-examination of most of the witnesses called for the Crown that Susan Nelles had not been in or near the hospital since the day of her arrest. We were therefore able to argue that some human being with an aberrant personality was loose both in the hospital and outside. A disturbed person was still operating, undeterred by Nelles's arrest. We argued that this evidence was consistent with the fact that the real killer had not been apprehended. Judge Vanek concluded on this point:

> Any inference of Nelles' guilt from the fact that there was a decrease in the number of deaths on Wards 4A and 4B after her arrest is off-set by equally valid inferences of innocence for the reasons previously stated [i.e., the locking up of all Digoxin and the realization by the killer that he/she might attract attention by further killings] and the long list of unusual incidents and mysterious happenings at the hospital.

After we learned that the exhumation of baby Lombardo had confirmed that her body was loaded with Digoxin, although not prescribed, and we confirmed that Susan Nelles was on holiday for the five days that Lombardo was in hospital, we could see that the prosecution was demoralized. Their case was disintegrating. We met with the prosecution and police at the El Toro Steak House in Toronto for dinner. We gave them copies of our psychiatric and psychological reports that indicated Susan Nelles was sane and well adjusted. We suggested that the prosecution be stopped. We told the prosecution that we intended to file those reports or call the doctors who wrote them at the preliminary hearing to show that Nelles was not an aberrant personality. We felt they would be potent evidence at the hearing.

The Crown responded by requesting an examination of our client by a psychiatrist. We said we would allow it, but we wanted the examination to be by doctors who were not usually consultants to the Crown at that time. We asked for doctors who were staff at teaching hospitals in Toronto and professors or associate professors of psychiatry at the University of Toronto. We gave them a list of seven or eight names of suggested doctors who had those qualifications. However, the Crown would not accept any of the doctors on the list, so we were never able to agree on a doctor to conduct the examination. In any event, the Crown was not prepared to stop the prosecution, even if a psychiatric report obtained by them confirmed that Susan was sane and well adjusted.

In the end, we decided not to file our psychiatric and psychological reports. We were concerned that an adverse inference might be drawn against us because we were unwilling to permit a doctor selected by the Crown to see her. We had in mind the case of *R v. Sweeney*, a murder case in which the defence was insanity. The defence had psychiatric reports, and the Crown had asked for a psychiatric examination of the accused. The defence agreed on the condition that the Crown psychiatrists confer with the defence psychiatrists before examining the accused. This offer was declined by the Crown, so no examination was done. At the trial, however, the defence proceeded to call its psychiatric evidence in support of the defence of insanity. The Crown then led evidence of the refusal of the defence to permit their doctors to examine the accused. The accused was convicted and subsequently appealed to the Ontario Court of Appeal. That court held that the evidence of the refusal of the defence to permit the psychiatric examination was relevant and admissible: it implied that the defence of insanity was either contrived or weak. Mr. Justice Zuber said in the decision:

> It is, after all, the accused who has raised the defence and made his sanity an issue. Can it be said that he has the exclusive right to call psychiatric evidence and also to deny the prosecution even the ability to explain why the Crown has called no evidence to meet this issue? ... In my view, the rational conclusion in this case is that the impugned evidence was properly admitted as a fact to be weighed in assessing the merit of the defence.

In light of this decision, we decided to keep our psychiatric reports in our file. We knew our case was very good, and we did not want to provide the Crown with an iota of an inference that the judge might consider evidence within the rule in *U.S.A. v. Sheppard*.

At about the same time, the prosecution requested a lie detector examination of Susan Nelles. We were still hoping they would withdraw the charges. We wanted to convince them to do so, but we had doubts about the accuracy of the lie detector. Eventually we agreed to permit her to undergo a lie detector examination on two conditions. First, if the results were negative, those results could be filed on consent before Judge Vanek. They would provide the final nail in the coffin that the Crown's case had become. Second, if the results were positive (i.e., the machine was in error), no reference could be made to that fact at the preliminary hearing. The prosecution refused to accept our conditions, and no lie detector test was administered.

In a long judgement on May 21, 1982, Judge Vanek found that the circumstantial evidence tendered against Susan Nelles was not sufficient to meet the test laid down in *U.S.A. v. Sheppard* and that she should be discharged on all counts. In his reasons, the judge went further and, in effect, exonerated her from all complicity in the murders by stating, "There's evidence that points in a different direction." Subsequently, Mr. Justice Grange, after a lengthy and intensive public inquiry, confirmed that Susan Nelles was indeed innocent and suggested that the province of Ontario pay her compensation.

Overall, I found the case a fascinating one because of the unusual and sometimes bizarre facts we had to deal with, the sensitive tactical decisions we had to make, and the daily courtroom drama in which I was involved.

The Presumption of Guilt:
Experiences from *Milgaard* and Other Cases

HERSH WOLCH, QC

1993

In late January 1970 a jury was deliberating on the fate of David Milgaard. At that time, I was a young Crown attorney beginning my career and, like many Crown attorneys, I was self-righteous and pompous. I don't like those types of Crown attorneys very much, yet I was definitely one of them.

It was great being a Crown attorney in those days for several reasons. I won almost all my cases. I had no *Charter of Rights and Freedoms* to worry about. I had no pressure groups telling me to proceed in cases I did not believe in. I had control over what I did. All I really had to do was get over the "presumption of innocence" and "proof beyond a reasonable doubt" hurdles, and that wasn't difficult. In those days, when we had a jury trial in my juris-diction, the accused sat in the prisoner's box with two guards standing beside him. When the jury came in to be selected, the clerk would say, "Prisoner, look at the juror; juror, look at the prisoner," and they'd be challenged to stand aside. What a start to the presumption of innocence! Getting beyond the rea-sonable doubt hurdle was easy as well. I would always tell the jury in my address that the defence was going to talk about "beyond a reasonable doubt" and explain that it doesn't mean "beyond a shadow of a doubt." I also scrapped the word "presumption" by saying it's a legal kind of term, but we now know better. I also enjoyed explaining the word "until." The legal term is not "unless" you're proven guilty but "until" you're proven guilty. In other words, if I say to you, "I'm going to speak today until I become sick," my sentence conveys a meaning that it's going to happen. However, if I substitute the phrase "unless I become sick," it conveys a different matter entirely. I would say these words in every case to make sure the jury didn't feel any particular sympathy for the accused.

For me, a trial became a forum where an accused is guilty but can be proven innocent. I knew back then, and I still believe today, that we have a presumption of guilt, particularly in high-profile crimes. Consider the headlines for these crimes, such as this one from the *Windsor Star*. It read, "Relief, Rage, Reap Arrest in Slane." Does it say a person presumed innocent was arrested? Of course not, that wouldn't get many headlines. The first paragraph read, "Two years of fear are over for the residents of two Southern Ontario cities." I would have thought that relief and rage come after a conviction, not for the presumed innocent. All of us presume these arrested persons to be guilty, and they will eventually have to satisfy a jury they are not guilty.

While the reporting in these high-profile cases is understandable, I am always disturbed by the police press conferences. In drug busts, for example, there are usually three police officers with silly smiles on their faces holding up the dope. It's always been the largest bust this month, last month, or forever, and it's always $27 billion worth of dope. Their announcement that they have the guilty people once again undermines the presumption of innocence. I remember a case a few years ago in Manitoba. During the press conference, the attorney general and the chief of police announced the arrest of two judges and seven or eight lawyers. It was judicial corruption of the highest level, and everybody believed that Manitoba had the most corrupt judicial system. That press conference was even carried in Czechoslovakia. However, at the end of the investigation the most they proved was that one magistrate had accepted two tickets to a Winnipeg Jets hockey game. Unfortunately, the damage from the press conference was enormous.

What happens is that the publicity settles and people get locked into position. The exercise appears to be, "Can we secure a conviction for the person who we all know did it?" I'm reminded of a jury trial I defended in which, before the start of trial, the prospective jurors were milling about and I overheard one say to another, "Where's the guy who did it?" The other prospective juror pointed to the accused in the prisoner's box. This is the attitude we take into the courtroom. Just as an aside, I worked that into my jury address and got into trouble. I tried challenging the jury with their own prejudices by referring to the anecdote I had overhead, but, for the only time ever, I was admonished by the trial judge and the jury for giving evidence in my closing address.

Once the trial process begins, people get locked into positions. The police aren't bad guys, but by the time the trial arrives, they are 100 percent convinced they have the right person. Furthermore, they've been promoted, they've been in the newspapers, and they've gotten applause from everybody around them. They are psychologically locked in and they get tunnel vision. Most of the time they are right–but not always.

I'll use an example to illustrate tunnel vision and how dangerous it can be. A few years ago a taxi driver named Daliwal went missing in Winnipeg. Police later found his cab and, a few miles away, his body. About ten months later, two men named Bunn and Ross were charged with his murder. Evidence was given by Ross's ex-common law wife and by Bunn's mother. The ex-common law wife said that she had been there and had seen it all. The mother said that her son told her he was there, but that the other guy killed the driver. There was tremendous public pressure. During the preliminary hearing, cab drivers lined up for miles with their vehicles to come into the court. I was virtually satisfied that the main witness was lying, but I held back because her evidence was ridiculous. We knew the last call for the cab was from the heart of town, which these two accused would never frequent. Both were very distinctive men with criminal records, one for manslaughter, but nobody saw them there. The men were accused of driving the cab for miles, without anybody seeing them. The case made no sense. Furthermore, when this ex-common law wife was asked where the party was that she claimed to have called the cab from, she couldn't describe it. She didn't know where she was or who she was with. In addition, before trial, the police found fingerprints on the meter of the cab, a place passengers never touch. They belonged to a young man whose sister lived at the last call of the cab driver. This young man had no connection with Bunn and Ross, who were much older men. The blond-haired young man had only a minor criminal record, and he offered an explanation. He said that six months earlier he had broken into the cab. That was how his prints got on to the meter.

I salivated at this trial. First I was going to break down the main Crown witness. Then the Crown would call the fellow with the fingerprints, and I would get him to confess. It was going to be my day in the sun. The main witness took the stand, and suddenly it happened. She admitted "Yes, I'm lying, I'm lying. I made it all up." I was waiting for my chance, and the Crown attorney broke her down instead. The judge directed the jury to acquit right then and there. I had the real killer waiting for me to break down, but the jury had to go and acquit. I told the judge, "No, I want to hear more," but, after two or three tries, he still forced the jury to acquit.

It wasn't long until the police issued statements saying, "We have the right guys. Somebody must have gotten to the witness." The fellow whose fingerprints were on the meter got concerned, wondering why the police weren't questioning him. He went to his friends and said, "I killed a cabby. Why aren't they questioning me?" The friends told other people, but the police still didn't come to him. The poor fellow became exacerbated and started writing to the media. He wrote letters saying, "Look, I'm the guy who killed the cabby. Why aren't the police talking to me?" He even sent the media his picture. The media went to the police, but they said he didn't do it. Eventually, the police went to him and he confessed. Interestingly, out of the blue came a witness who was always available and who had seen the cabby fighting with a blond young man in the area. He never spoke to us at all but had always been available. Unfortunately, the police had a tunnel vision theory as to who committed the crime.

Later on in my career, I was counsel to the Aboriginal people in the Aboriginal Justice Inquiry in Winnipeg. The same investigator who handled the Bunn and Ross case was handling this one as well, and he was scheduled to testify at 10:00 one morning. However, fifteen minutes before he was due to take the stand, he took his own life with his service revolver and left two notes. One note talked about the inquiry itself: it was a reasoned police view of what the inquiry had become. The second note was addressed to me and contained only a few words. It said, "Bunn and Ross are guilty." By now, the man who had confessed to the crime had been tried and convicted by a jury. After being convicted, he stood up and begged for forgiveness, giving more details of how he killed the cab driver, and then he went back to the cell and took his own life. Despite these events, the police officer who investigated Bunn and Ross still thought they were guilty. Granted this may be an extreme example of tunnel vision, but it shows that police officers, when they get their mind focused in one direction, can sometimes find it very hard to look another way.

Police aren't the only ones to get tunnel vision, however. Crown attorneys are influenced by the police, for example, and are basically counsel to the police. I can always recall addressing the jury as a Crown attorney and saying, "We never win or lose." If you believe that, however, why are there parties after the accused is convicted?

The judge, too, sometimes enters the picture. In many cases where judges believe that the accused is guilty, they will steer the case in that direction. I once had a sexual assault case that resulted in an acquittal. I was speaking to the judge in her chambers after the trial when a more senior judge came in and said to her, "I hear you lost your first case." Although this comment was meant as a joke, it goes to show that judges are not immune to the same biases.

Once the trial process is under way, another element becomes significant: the credibility of witnesses. Crown witnesses are generally presumed to be telling the truth, while witnesses for the defence are presumed to be lying. All presumptions are rebuttable, but Crown experts always have an advantage over the defence experts because they are more readily believed, no matter what their credentials. I remember one trial in which I asked the Crown expert what he was getting paid for his services, and I was admonished by the judge not to ask that kind of question. The judge said that the expert was a man of high repute, and my suggestion that he would offer his evidence for money was not proper. I was stunned. In the very same trial, the Crown asked my expert the same question several weeks later and, when I objected, the judge said, "No, it goes to credibility."

Another interesting aspect of trial work is jailhouse confessions. People who would never be believed in their own trial are suddenly credible. It struck me as interesting in David Milgaard's case, when we called two such individuals to say they had heard "confessions" from Larry Fisher. Both of these men approached us, not the Crown, and sought a favour, but we couldn't give them any. One of them is now a prison guard, which certainly speaks to his credibility. However, at the time, they were "virtually ignored." Another man came forward to the RCMP and gave graphic details of how Fisher had confessed to the murder of Gayle Miller while he was raping him. Imagine the headlines! We refused to call him, and we told the Crown in Saskatchewan that we didn't want to hear from a witness who we didn't believe. A further difficulty in trial work is that, when witnesses recant, they are almost never believed. Take spousal abuse: once a spouse says the attack did not take place, everybody believes the opposite.

Some types of witnesses are more credible depending on the case itself or whether they are called by the prosecution or the defence. If an accused calls a prostitute, for example, as an alibi, the judge may physically move away to avoid being tainted by this witness. But suppose the Crown calls the same witness in a charge of living off the avails: that witness suddenly becomes very credible.

Despite all these difficulties in trials, when we advance to the appeal level, the courts are reluctant to interfere. I find it interesting when I appeal a decision. I might be told by the court, "Your client didn't testify and answer all these allegations, so why should we overturn this verdict?" Alternatively, I might be told: "Your client did testify and wasn't believed. The jury didn't believe your client, so why should we interfere?" Yet there are only two choices—either you testify or you don't—and either one can help lose an appeal. Fortunately, most people convicted are guilty, but there's a lot to learn in the appeal process.

David Milgaard walked into that judicial system. It was a high-profile case in which the police had an initial theory—the right theory—that there was a rapist in the area named Larry Fisher who killed a nurse, Gayle Miller. Unfortunately, Fisher's victims were no help in identifying him. Months were passing, and there was a lot of public pressure. Then a young, mentally disturbed young man named Albert Cegrain, who had been grilled by the police for days, finally mentioned that he thought his drug-using hippie friend, David Milgaard, may have had blood on him the morning he came into town. This allegation would have gone nowhere, except that a trail of articles from the scene of Miller's death led to Cegrain's house. That evidence proved to be compelling. What the police didn't know was that Fisher lived in the basement of Cegrain's house. After that, the police grilled two young kids, Nicole John and Ron Wilson, and eventually persuaded them to incriminate Milgaard. Yet, previously, all three—John, Wilson, and Milgaard—had been interviewed by the police separately, with no chance of collusion, and they all gave identical stories that nothing happened that morning in the forty-below-zero weather in Saskatoon. It was only months later, when the police brought in a professional interrogator from Calgary who showed the impressionable teenagers bloodstained clothing and scared the devil out of them, that they made statements implicating David Milgaard. After those statements, Milgaard was arrested, and the press picked up on the story. He was portrayed as a young hippie with reefer madness. The police had their man, or boy (he was only sixteen), and everything proceeded from there.

How did this miscarriage of justice happen? First, the presumption of guilt continued, and, second, two major developments emerged in the courtroom. Nicole John, the young woman who incriminated Milgaard, could not remember anything under questioning about the murder she had told the professional interrogator she saw. Most criminal lawyers are familiar with the rule from the Milgaard case about the use of statements. That rule comes from Nicole John and her having no memory of what she once said she saw. Had Nicole John stuck to her statement, I believe David Milgaard would have been acquitted because her actual statement made no sense. It was factually impossible. In essence, she said that, after a news bulletin, Milgaard confessed, or gave words to that effect. The fact that everyone stayed and partied after the confession didn't seem to matter. In addition, the jury didn't find out that four other people in the room all heard the remark and understood it as a joke.

The police had tunnel vision—and that was the main cause for Milgaard's arrest and conviction. The police would not disclose anything that would take away from their theory or cause others to question that theory. Our first application to the minister of justice had been turned down and our second, almost identical application was already submitted when I learned for the first time that another young woman had been attacked seven hundred yards from Gayle Miller, five or so minutes after she was murdered. This young woman, who now has a senior position in Toronto and is wholly reputable, was going to school when a man she later identified as Larry Fisher attacked her. She reported it to the police that same day, and they told her her attacker killed a nurse. However, none of this evidence was ever disclosed. The fact that Gayle Miller would never have been on the street where Wilson and John said she was attacked was not exposed either. Two roommates knew that Miller never walked down that street, but that information was never revealed.

Most telling of all, in October 1970, before David Milgaard's appeal, Larry Fisher was arrested in Winnipeg and confessed to a number of crimes in Saskatoon. These crimes occurred before and after Gayle Miller's attack, and all of them closely resembled the attack on Miller. You would think the police would parade this man, who has attacked at least four women in Saskatoon, and the story would be written up in all the newspapers, but that did not happen. Instead, the chief investigator for the Milgaard case was sent to Winnipeg, where he took the statements from Fisher. He sent the statements to the prosecutor for David Milgaard's trial, who in turn sent them to the man who was currently handling the Milgaard appeal. Then Larry Fisher, who was being tried following a direct indictment, went into the High Court at 2:00 p.m. and pleaded guilty in Regina to the crimes in Saskatoon. However, the victims in Saskatoon were never told. The police still felt that Milgaard was the right guy, and they didn't want to muddy the waters by releasing Fisher's confessions.

Towards the end of the Supreme Court hearing, I learned that another nurse had been attacked at 8:00 a.m., two weeks before Miller's murder, and two blocks away, by a man who matched Fisher's description. That is how miscarriages of justice occur. They start with the presumption of guilt and tunnel vision by the police. That leads to non-disclosure of important evidence. Add in young, malleable witnesses, and you have the makings of a wrongful conviction.

What is most disturbing is that, once questions come up about a conviction, some people prefer to protect the system rather than expose the mistake. I was shocked to hear the man who handled the Milgaard appeal say publicly that the preservation and integrity of the system are more important than the innocence of one individual. In 1969 a lawyer addressing the special lecture series at the Law Society of Upper Canada said: "Notwithstanding so many years spent defending criminal cases, I happen to believe that there are more innocent people charged with crimes that is commonly supposed. I have heard many unlikely stories in my time, and some of them, surprisingly, turned out to be true." This man has gone on to lead a distinguished career. He went on to prosecute a number of people in a very confident manner and to become a member of parliament in Saskatchewan. The lawyer who made this comment is Justice Arthur Martin.

David Milgaard was sixteen years old in 1969. He went to a jail where your worst nightmares come true, especially when you're a good-looking sixteen-year-old boy. He tried to escape, only to be shot in the back. He went on to have a mental breakdown and today wanders the streets, pan handling. He is not convicted. There is no semblance of a case against him, and there is ample evidence leading to Larry Fisher–who I have no doubt killed Gayle Miller. No one has ever even apologized to David. Where is the presumption of innocence?

Thomas Sophonow:
A Long Road to Innocence

G. GREG BRODSKY, QC

1989

On December 23, 1981, Barbara Stoppel, a pretty sixteen-year-old girl working alone in a donut shop in Winnipeg, was strangled to death. One year later, on December 12, 1982, Thomas Sophonow was arrested for her murder. Sophonow, a door attendant from the Laugheed Hotel in Vancouver, was placed in a line-up and positively identified by eight eyewitnesses. He made two incriminating statements to police, saying he was the only one who had the opportunity to be the killer. He also made some remarks to an undercover police officer about the inside of the donut shop, points that could be known only to the killer. In the course of his third trial, he made a number of positively incriminating statements to some fellow jailhouse residents. In addition, Sophonow had a unique kind of twine, a twine made by only one company in the world, in his car. The same twine was found around Barbara Stoppel's neck. Sophonow had the motive to commit the crime, according to the police, because he had just had a dispute with his wife, was angry, and wanted to dispense this passion in some strange way. Finally, he had the opportunity. He came to Winnipeg en route to a holiday in Mexico. Right after the killing he went back to Vancouver.

Given all this incriminating evidence, the case was difficult. It would challenge the ingenuity, the perspicacity, and the stamina of any defence counsel. Before it was over, it would leave a history of a mistrial at first trial, a conviction at second trial, and a conviction at third trial. Finally, the Court of Appeal ordered an acquittal. Along the way it went to the Supreme Court a number of times. On the last occasion, the Supreme Court agreed with the Manitoba Court of Appeal that there should be no more trials of Thomas Sophonow, no matter how many times he has been convicted. This bizarre case demonstrates that lawyers can take nothing for granted, cases cannot be prepared only in the office, preparation cannot be left to the police or hired investigators, and counsel must be robust in the presentation of their case.

The defence at the first trial proceeded on the basis that Sophonow couldn't be the killer because he couldn't be in two places at one time. At the first trial, it was thought that the killing of Barbara Stoppel took place at a minute or two after 8:00 p.m. Sophonow, between 7:52 and 7:58, was eleven miles away on the other side of Winnipeg, where phone records at the Canadian Tire store at that location showed he made a call to his mother. Despite all the eyewitness identification, the evidence of the twine, and the confessions, the defence argued that Sophonow couldn't be the killer because he wasn't at the donut shop at the time of the murder. The jury went out and deliberated. And there was a mistrial.

I was retained three days before the second trial was set to proceed. The first thing I was told was that the case for the defence had improved. The witness who had put the time at a minute or two after was wrong. When she said she drove by the intersection where she saw the big clock, which gave the time as 8:00, she was correct. However, that clock was right only twice a day: it hadn't worked in five years! New evidence now put the time of the killing at 8:15, which gave Sophonow just enough time to get there. The case for the defence had, in fact, gotten worse. We now had a difficult case to present.

Sophonow's defence was as bizarre and unusual as the facts of the case proved to be. His defence, which was not presented at the first trial and was not told to the police at the preliminary inquiry, was that at the time of the killing he was handing out Christmas stockings to little kids in the hospital who didn't have parents to take them home for the holiday. It was a difficult story to try to prove.

The full story went this way: Sophonow worked as a door attendant for the Laugheed Hotel in Vancouver. He came to Winnipeg en route to a holiday in Mexico to drop off some presents for his child, because he and his wife were not living together. He left the presents at his wife's sister's house shortly before 3:00 in the afternoon. Unfortunately, his car wasn't working properly, so he went to Canadian Tire to have it fixed. The mechanic told him the brakes were in bad shape and certainly couldn't last in hot weather. It was December 23, and the parts for the car would not be ready until December 27. He decided to go back to Vancouver, to go home for Christmas. He phoned his mother at 7:52 and told her his plan, then went across the parking lot to the Safeway store, where he bought a big bag of candy stockings. He returned to the Canadian Tire, where they were still working on his car, shared some chicken and chips with a little girl whose mother was also waiting for her car to be fixed, and returned to the Safeway store once his car was ready. He bought another bag of stockings, and the clerk asked what he was doing with so many of them. He said he was going to deliver them to the kids who couldn't go home for Christmas, and he asked if there was a hospital nearby. The clerk told him there was one across the street, so he walked there. Sophonow went to St. Boniface Hospital, then to Misericordia Hospital, and finally to Grace General Hospital, dropping off the Christmas stockings. That was his defence. The Crown attack was that none of the nurses could identify Sophonow as being the fellow who dropped off the stockings, the Safeway clerk couldn't identify Sophonow as the one who bought the stockings, and the woman at the Canadian Tire couldn't identify him as a customer.

The battle lines were drawn, the fight was on. The mood when the second trial began was electric. Minimally contentious matters took on great significance. For example, during the jury selection, Mr. Justice Skullen opined that at the rate it was going, "Only people who are absolutely illiterate, deaf, or blind, or a combination, are in fact going to escape the net." Again, after a few more jurors were successfully challenged, he said, "I can see I'd better explain in a bit more detail, perhaps with a bit more lucidity, what we are trying to do here. It's not the selection of a hockey team. It's not a question whether the chap is a good skater or a bad skater or if any of you are a fast forward." The *Globe and Mail* reported these comments together with my question to the next potential juror: "You're not afraid of the judge, are you?" He said, "Yeah, I'm nervous. I'm very nervous." So that was the start of the case. Eventually we got the jury together.

The evidence from the bystanders in the donut shop, as called by the Crown, was that a tall, scruffy-looking stranger wearing a cowboy hat walked from the front of the shop to the back and into the ladies' washroom, closely followed by Barbara Stoppel, the waiter. The man exited the washroom alone, walked to the front of the store, turned the sign from "Open" to "Closed," and walked out carrying a small cardboard box that he picked up near the cash register. Outside the donut shop, watching these proceedings, stood John Doerksen, who had been selling Christmas trees in the adjacent parking lot. He testified that he followed this man to the bridge, caught up with him half way over, and grabbed on to him. The man whirled around and pulled out a knife, so Doerksen let go of him. He returned to the parking lot, stopping to say hello to a fellow named Marcel, who had told him to go after the cowboy in the first place. Doerksen then went home, had a few beers, and phoned the hospital to ask about Barbara Stoppel's condition. He gave a statement to the media explaining his encounter with the cowboy, and he made a statement to the police the next day. Despite Doerksen's description, Marcel was never found, nor was a man resembling Doerksen's description of Marcel ever seen by any of the other people gathered around the parking lot outside the donut shop.

Nearly three months after the murder, on March 12, 1982, John Doerksen was called into the police station in Winnipeg for a line-up identification that included Sophonow. Doerksen failed to make the identification in that line-up. Later, however, news that the suspect in the Stoppel murder had been arrested peaked Doerksen's curiosity. While he was waiting for a ride to see the proceedings in court two days later, he was arrested for unpaid parking tickets. While in the cells, he was taken to see Sophonow. Following this encounter, Doerksen made positive identifications of Sophonow in a second line-up and in court. I addressed the validity of his eyewitness identification in my cross-examination:

> Q: And on that day you were on your way to court, in any event, to see the fellow that had been arrested?
>
> A: That's correct.
>
> Q: You still had the paper in your pocket when you saw him in the hallway, the newspaper, remember the article?
>
> A: Yes.
>
> Q: But you couldn't identify him in the line-up?
>
> A: Yes. I told the guard, yes, I did.

Q: You asked the guard if you can go see that fellow again?

A: Yes.

Q: You showed the paper to the guard and told him that you tried to identify the killer earlier?

A: Yes.

Q: And you asked him if that was the fellow that had been arrested for the killing?

A: No. I had asked him if I could see him. I didn't make any mention of anything.

Q: Didn't you ask him if you could see the fellow charged with the killing.

A: No, I didn't say that, in my own words, but the association of the news article and me saying that was me, that I'm sure he got the impression that is who I wanted to go see.

Q: There's no doubt in your mind that he was taking you to see the killer.

A: That's correct, yes.

Q: I am suggesting to you, Mr. Doerksen, in order to be as fair as I can to you, the reason you picked him out as the killer is because the guard took you to him and presented to you the fellow charged with the killing and that reinforced in your mind the familiarity that you talked about when you saw him in the hallway.

A: Well, the first time that I'd seen him passing in a hallway got my suspicions right there. And like I said, I didn't sleep the night before so I wanted to be reassured for the final time and to look at him, and the guard took me down and I looked at him and I'm sure he's the person.

Needless to say, his identification of Sophonow in the line-up following that suspicious encounter should have been brought to the jury's attention by the trial judge, but it wasn't. The reinforcement that he was correct from both the police and the media should have been pointed out by the trial judge, but it wasn't. The repeated appearance of Sophonow's picture in the media should have been remarked on by the trial judge, but it wasn't. Doerksen testified that the difference between the first line-up, when he failed to make an identification, and the second line-up was that Sophonow had shaved off his beard. However, that testimony was demonstrably false, as the photographs of the line-up showed Sophonow to be clean-shaven in both.

Further issues concerning eyewitness identification by other witnesses were presented at cross-examination. Seven eyewitnesses picked Sophonow out of a photo pack line-up. You have to be very careful with photo packs, and this case demonstrates as well as any what is wrong with them and with positive identification. The witnesses were given the photographs, and each one picked out Sophonow. That might seem to be a solid identification, but you also have to consider the details: nine photos were plastic, one was cardboard; nine had a white border, one had no border; nine were the same size, one was larger than the rest; nine subjects were hatless, one had a hat; nine were in a room, one was outside. Needless to say, the nine were fakes, and the one was of Thomas Sophonow. That was the identification we had to contend with. As well, Mr. and Mrs. Janower, two witnesses who had nothing to gain from lying or exaggerating, testified that the last time they saw the photograph they picked out, it was in the hands of the Crown attorney at the preliminary inquiry, and that the photograph presented to them at the trial was not the one they had picked out. Clearly, there were problems with the photo pack line-up.

In terms of identification, we didn't rest with what the police presented by way of evidence. We thoroughly investigated the background of what happened before and after the line-ups. We had someone from the law office watch the line-up and knew, when a witness identified Sophonow as the killer, that it was not a simple matter. For example, before one woman picked him out, she hesitated for fifteen minutes while she asked, "Could you have the last five come back again?" Then she commented: "The second one from the end, that could be him. Looks like him." When I asked her in cross-examination why she thought it looked like him, she said, "By the way he walked." I called the police officer, who said that no one had seen him walking because he wasn't one of the five who came back. In any event, no one could see how the five walked because the viewing room was arranged so they could see only the top portions of their bodies.

We also looked to other things to try to destroy the identification evidence. For example, the composition sketch that was presented in court had a picture of Sophonow and a description under it. This sketch was put out by the police and presented at the preliminary inquiry, the first trial, and the second trial. Between the second trial and third trial I went to the exhibit box to look at all the exhibits that hadn't been accepted at the preliminary hearing or weren't tendered. There I found what turned out to be the original of that composite sketch. What everyone thought was the original sketch in fact was not the original. As well, at the bottom of the composite sketch were the signatures of the people who made up the sketch. Only one of them had been there at 8:00 in the evening when the killer was in the donut shop with Barbara Stoppel. One of the people who participated in making the composite sketch was a man with a psychiatric history who testified that he saw Sophonow on the bridge around 9:15, an hour after the killing took place. The other person, Marina Labustier, who testified that she was involved in making the composite sketch, said that the man she was helping to describe had been in her shoe store at about 3:30 in the afternoon. Yet at that time Sophonow had been at his sister-in-law's house, dropping off the presents for his daughter. Overall, these examples demonstrate that you can't rely on what comes out in court. You have to prepare your case and you can't take anything for granted.

One of the points of appeal held that insufficient care had been given to the law with regard to identification evidence. Mr. Justice Skullen, in his charge to the jury, said: "When you consider the evidence of the witnesses, consider their evidence as people. That's the bottom line." In fact, one witness had thirty-three charges dropped in return for his evidence. He wasn't just a man–he was a fellow who had much to gain from the story he gave in court. The Court of Appeal thought, on that ground alone, there should be a new trial. Another ground of appeal involved the gloves that the cowboy threw off the bridge. The gloves had twine on them that matched Barbara Stoppel's sweater. They were the gloves of the killer. I had Sophonow try the gloves on in court and he looked like a duck with webbed feet: the gloves were too small. The Crown attorney tried them on and they fit, but we didn't tender the Crown's hand!

One of the new issues we faced at the third trial were Sophonow's purported jailhouse confessions. Everybody who wanted early parole, bail, charges dropped, transfer to a less secure institution, or bonus points of some kind had overheard Sophonow confessing to the killing. All these witnesses had different details, some of which were impossible, some of which weren't. Although there were twelve or fifteen confessions, the Crown called witnesses to testify to only three. We investigated the background of these criminals. One fellow, Douglas Gordon Martin, had a multitude of convictions for false pretence. Martin's cross-examination commenced with the fact that he wasn't a stranger to testifying against co-prisoners:

Q: So the jury won't be misled, Mr. Martin, giving evidence against other prisoners is not a stranger to you, is it?

A: This is my third time.

Q: The third time you have testified against other prisoners?

A: Yes.

Q: Mr. Martin, you've lied and cheated your way through most of your life time?

A: Certainly I have lied, yes.

Q: And cheated?

A: Yes.

Through a little digging and obtaining the transcripts of his previous cases, I had the following ammunition to use in this case:

Q: You made deals in connection with other occasions?

A: No. One time I gave evidence. It was mentioned in court, but I don't believe I was given any deal.

Q: When was that?

A: 1982.

Q: Where?

A: In Brandon.

Q: You don't think you were given a deal?

A: No, I don't.

Q: Then you say you didn't give evidence in order to get yourself a lighter sentence?

Armed with the transcript, I bulled ahead. He had testified that the authorities didn't know who he really was because he was sworn under a different name. He also had thirty-six charges and an application for parole. As well, he wanted a one-year sentence as opposed to the two-year sentence, which the Crown was asking for. It took him a lot of work, but after he testified in the other case, he got the one year.

Another witness named Adrian Charles McQuaid was a bootlegger. He said Sophonow confessed to him in jail that he was the killer. I called him a bought witness, which I think was fair in light of his testimony:

Q: You told Mr. Walsh [McQuaid's lawyer in an earlier case] to get you $10,000, is that the amount?

A: No.

Q: How much was the amount Mr. Walsh asked for?

A: He asked for five. $5,000.

A: Yes.

Q: You were going to tell this story providing police paid you $5,000?

A: Not now.

Q: But that's the deal you tried to make?

A: Yes. Before, yes, I did.

He further testified that he was facing a number of break and enter charges.

Q: And you knew that in the past when you were facing criminal code charges, you always went to jail for a length of time?

A: Right.

Q: You were able to have Mr. Walsh have the charge of break and enter and theft dropped?

A: Yes.

Q: I am suggesting that the plea bargain was based on your agreeing to testify, you saying that you had something to sell, that is an incriminating statement from a fellow the police are anxious to convict?

A: Yeah, I know that.

Q: But that's what you were selling?

A: For money. I wasn't worried about possession of stolen goods, I just wanted the money.

Q: You told us you were a bootlegger?

A: Yes.

Q: Are you a bootlegger today?

A: Yes.

Q: Are you afraid of going to jail for it?

A: No.

Q: Weren't you arrested with respect to being a witness on this case [he was arrested as being a material witness]?

A: Yes, I was. That was last week.

Q: Isn't that what you were talking about to the police. And the police told you you're going to sit in jail if you don't testify?

A: Yes, that's right. I don't like the public safety buildings. They were going to hold me two weeks there, until I called the Crown to testify. So I decided to testify, you know, give them a statement, say I'd testify instead of spending two weeks in a public safety building.

Q: When?

A: A little bit before they let me out. They said they'd let me out if I gave a statement, so I did.

I got that transcript of his bail hearing too. His cross-examination proceeded with the following eye-opening and peculiar demonstration of our judicial system. This evidence came during Sophonow's third trial, with the chief justice of Manitoba sitting as the judge. The chief justice had also sat on the bail application for McQuaid. In my cross-examination at the trial, I said to McQuaid:

Q: Did you tell the judge that the reporting conditions were no good for you?

A: That's right.

Q: Tell the jury what you told the judge.

A: So they gave me hours to report at ten and three o'clock, and I told them the hours were no good because I bootleg all night, so I can't sleep during the morning.

Q: So you can't what?

A: Sleep in.

Q: You can't sleep in?

A: Right, I wouldn't get no sleep.

The confrontation with McQuaid finished on a note that Thomas Sophonow took to heart:

Q: I am suggesting to you, Mr. McQuaid, that he never admitted to the killing. He never admitted that he was responsible, that you made all this up in order to sell something to the police. Wasn't that true?

A: Well, if you'd like, I'd like to take a lie detector. I'll take one with Mr. Sophonow if you like, I don't mind that.

Sophonow took the lie-detector test and passed, but not with my concurrence. I didn't encourage it and I didn't participate in it, but sometimes you can't control some of your clients. I was happy he passed, though.

The last of the jailhouse confession witnesses was a fellow who came forward at the second trial and said he was also part of the prison system. He came from Hong Kong and had thirty-three charges against him, all of which were related to honesty. He made a statement to the police after he tried and failed to get bail five times. The day after he made the statement, the police dropped all but three of the charges. However, this witness didn't appear for the third trial. I argued before the court that Sophonow should be allowed to confront his accuser because he was a crucial witness. He had said Sophonow confessed to him that he did the killing and described how he did it. I argued that the witness made it up after reading newspaper reports. I wanted to confront him because I had even more information than I had with McQuaid to put to him. However, because we weren't able to find him, Mr. Justice Hewatte ordered that the transcript of the previous proceedings be put in evidence. The saw-off for me was that I was allowed to put the fact that this witness had got into trouble three more times since the last trial, that the charges had been dropped in connection with those as well, and that he had been allowed to emigrate from Canada. The Manitoba Court of Appeal said that Justice Hewatte's decision was not right and ordered a new trial.

The third trial did not end uneventfully either. On the fifth day of deliberations, at 7:38 Saturday night, March 16, 1985, the trial judge received a note. It was read into the record of the trial by the foreman of the jury: "Your Lordship, with all respect, we have a juror who speaks of psychic powers and special gifts. We have tried with all diligence, sincerity and reason to reach a unanimous decision in this case. We are unable to do so because we feel this juror is mentally unable to deal with arguments or discussion over the evidence as it is before us, or to communicate their thoughts clearly to us. We cannot deal with this." The whole case was bizarre: after so much tension and the apprehension of the trial, five days of deliberations, not to mention all the years presenting this case in previous trials, it all came down to one psychic juror.

The Crown moved that the juror be discharged. The defence asked that the juror not be discharged without some evidence of mental incapacity. The Crown argued that the note, together with the length of time that this jury had already taken, called for the discharge of a juror for reasonable cause and incompetence. I argued that any infirmity disqualifying a juror must be demonstrated by proof subject to challenge. A doctor should determine the competence of the juror to continue, and the issue should not be left for the majority. After five days of deliberations, if it's eleven to one, it's clear that some anger will be directed towards the one individual who will not agree. I wanted some evidence, not merely the opinion of the majority minus one. The trial judge nevertheless at 8:18 had the jury parade out. The foreman was asked to stand and read the note. The foreman said, not under oath, that the juror claimed she was psychic and had special gifts. The psychic juror, who also was not sworn, was asked to stand and to respond to the note and the challenge. She began by denying that she had said she was a psychic. She denied that she said those things attributed to her in the note and denied that she had any special powers. Still, the judge discharged her 8:35. At 8:47, twelve minutes later, the jury returned a guilty verdict.

The Court of Appeal dealt with this case by pointing out that counsel for the defence had argued that no one could inquire into the deliberations in the jury room to see whether they were rational and reasonable and according to anyone's liking. Counsel for the defence submitted that the judge was not entitled to ask for the reasons for a verdict, and the jury was not entitled to give the reasons for a verdict. The Court of Appeal agreed. The defence counsel argued, alternatively, that if one juror was alleged to be suffering from a disqualifying infirmity, it must be demonstrated by proof, which was subject to challenge. The jurors' note was not subject to challenge and could not be acted on. The Court of Appeal agreed with that point too. Counsel for the defence further argued that if the judge thought illness might be established, he could send for a doctor to make an examination and report to the court. The Court of Appeal found that the claim by counsel on the right to cross-examine the juror was valid: "The unsworn statement of the foreman of the jury was an insufficient basis upon which to act. The denial by the juror that she claimed psychic gifts or special powers could not be rejected out of hand without an inquiry. The accused had a vital interest in any inquiry that would be held and had a right to participate in it by cross-examination and making representations. In the case before us, the discharge of the psychic juror deprived the accused of a verdict of twelve of his peers, and for that reason the verdict cannot stand and must be set aside."

The Court of Appeal did not order a new trial, and the court entered an acquittal by a unanimous decision. The Supreme Court of Canada affirmed. That decision marked the end of the Sophonow case.

Part Two: A Variety of Defences

Revisiting the Insanity Defence:
The Capital Murder Trial of Matthew Charles Lamb

MR. JUSTICE SAUL NOSANCHUK

1999

The capital murder trial of Matthew Charles Lamb is a tragic one. It begins with a shocking and senseless event that occurred at 10:30 on the warm summer night of June 25, 1966, on a residential street on the east side of Windsor. Six young adults in their early twenties were strolling down Ford Boulevard, walking in the direction of a bus stop on Tecumseh Road. Suddenly they were ambushed by Matthew Lamb, age eighteen, who stepped out in front of them from behind a tree. He pointed a shotgun in their direction and said, "Stop or I'll shoot." When Edith Chaykoski put up her hands, he shot her in the abdomen. When Andrew Woloch stepped forward, Lamb fired, striking him in the abdomen as well. Ms. Chaykoski died of those gunshot wounds within two hours. Mr. Woloch died nineteen days later. Lamb then shot and injured a woman whose silhouette he observed in the doorway of a nearby house. He walked to a house several blocks away, knocked on the door, and threatened to kill the elderly woman who answered. When she called to her husband to phone the police, Lamb ran out of the house and threw the shotgun in a nearby field. Finally, he went to his uncle's home, where he had been residing, and went to sleep.

The police soon identified the weapon used in the killings as coming from the home of Lamb's uncle. There was no doubt that Matthew Lamb had removed the weapon from that home on the evening of June 25. The next day he was arrested and charged with the capital murder of Edith Chaykoski. He faced a mandatory death penalty if convicted of that crime.

On Lamb's first court appearance, he sat in the prisoner's dock at the magistrate's court without counsel. He was remanded by the presiding magistrate for a psychiatric examination to determine whether there was reason to believe he was mentally ill.

Dr. Walter Yaworsky, a Windsor psychiatrist in private practice, conducted the examination. When he appeared in court, Dr. Yaworsky testified that, in his opinion, there was reason to believe that Matthew Lamb was mentally ill and unfit to stand trial.

The presiding magistrate remanded the accused into custody of the Ontario Hospital at Penetanguishene for a period of thirty days, as set out in the *Criminal Code*. At the end of this period, Lamb was certified as mentally ill and unfit to stand trial. He was confined to the Ontario Hospital until the psychiatric staff there concluded he could be returned to Windsor as fit to stand trial.

At the end of August 1966 Lamb was sent back to Windsor with the requisite report from the hospital. The report indicated that he was capable of understanding the nature of the proceedings against him and of instructing and communicating with counsel. At this point I undertook to represent him as defence counsel, assigned under the Legal Aid Plan then in existence in Essex Country. In 1966 many lawyers in Ontario represented indigent clients on a pro bono basis. A number of civil and criminal lawyers volunteered to serve on the panel, and cases were generally assigned in rotation. I willingly accepted the assignment to represent Lamb on this very serious charge. First, however, I needed to determine whether Lamb was satisfied to have me act as his assigned counsel under the Ontario Legal Aid Plan. He had no hesitation in signing a written retainer authorizing me to represent him.

I tried to find out as much as I could about the circumstances of the case and Lamb's background. After my initial talk with Lamb, I intended to continue my investigation by interviewing witnesses, reviewing the prosecution evidence, examining relevant police records, and considering all available psychiatric evidence, including the results of any psychological tests administered to Lamb. In addition, I would fully explore the legal issues in the case.

At our first interview, Matthew Lamb presented himself as a slightly built, quiet, and detached eighteen-year-old. He was boyish in appearance, with an agreeable and polite demeanour. He was most appreciative and grateful that I had undertaken his defence. When I asked him about the events on the evening of the killing, he became tentative and confused. He seemed to view these events as though he was not really involved in them and had not wanted to participate in them. He claimed he could not clearly recall intentionally taking the gun and loading it or killing people. He seemed to have only a dim recollection that such an occurrence might have happened. He had watched a movie on TV earlier that evening that involved a person who had shot and killed several people, and he did not know whether he had acted out what had happened in the movie. He appeared to be little concerned with the repercussions of the charge against him, even though he faced the death penalty if convicted of capital murder. He seemed quite prepared to let justice take its course.

Matthew Lamb discussed his background reluctantly. He seemed detached and emotionally uninvolved with people in his life. He hardly knew his mother, whom he had seen rarely over the years since she abandoned him as an infant. He did not know his father at all, and he had been raised primarily by his grandparents, as well as by uncles and aunts. As a result of later interviews I conducted with relatives, friends, and neighbours, I learned that Matthew's mother was only fifteen years old at the time of his birth on January 5, 1948. His grandparents brought him up in an atmosphere of emotional and physical abuse. His grandfather in particular resented his presence and rejected him, frequently calling him a "little bastard."

As a small boy, Matthew witnessed acts of violence between his grandparents. Moreover, he started exhibiting violent traits in his early years. He was known to have lured young cousins into his bedroom, where he locked them in a closet and frightened them with threats of bodily harm. On one occasion Lamb beat one of his cousins so badly that the child needed medical attention.

As he grew up, Mathew had very few friends. To other people he seemed detached, adrift, and lacking of any sense of purpose. At an early age he developed an interest in rifle cartridges and a fascination with weapons. He began to carry a knife with him and got into fights at school. He did not hesitate to exhibit the knife, though there was no evidence that he stabbed anyone. His fascination with violence continued, and he started to fashion bombs made with gunpowder. At one point, he almost blew himself up.

At the age of fourteen, Matthew Lamb repeatedly struck a burly police sergeant in the face in the presence of a crowd of people in front of the Riverside Arena. He was charged with assault under the *Juvenile Delinquents Act*. He received a custodial sentence of six months to be served at the House of Concord, a Salvation Army facility for young people guilty of delinquent behaviour. On his release, he returned to Windsor to reside at his uncle's home. He attended high school briefly before he quit and looked for work. Unfortunately, Lamb never succeeded in holding jobs.

In 1965, Lamb committed his first offence as an adult offender. At that time, persons who had attained the age of sixteen were prosecuted as adult offenders. Lamb had broken into a local sporting goods store, where he stole a number of rifles. After the break-in, he was involved in a shoot-out with the Riverside Police. No one was injured, but he was tried and convicted for breaking and entering, committing theft, and being in possession of an offence weapon for a purpose dangerous to the public peace. The presiding magistrate, J. Arthur Hanrahan, an experienced jurist, requested and received a pre-sentence report on Lamb. It painted a picture of a youth who was exceedingly dangerous and prone to violence. Hanrahan sentenced Lamb to a two-year term in a federal penitentiary for the offences on which he was convicted. It was rare for a sixteen-year-old first-time adult offender to be sentenced to a federal penitentiary, especially when no victim had suffered any physical harm. Magistrate Hanrahan apparently concluded that the prospects for rehabilitating this violent and dangerous offender in the community were slim. He must have thought, for public safety, that Lamb needed to be separated from society for a long period.

Following Lamb's admission to Kingston Penitentiary in 1965, psychiatric examinations and psychological tests showed him to be an extremely immature sixteen-year-old who was fascinated with weapons. Tests further indicated marked aggressiveness, little control over behaviour, and a lack of discipline. Not long after Lamb arrived, a guard observed him kneeling on his bed, with a broom handle stuck up his rectum. He was seen immediately by Dr. George Scott, the director of psychiatry at the penitentiary, who examined and sedated him. In his report Dr. Scott stated, "I think this young man is developing a mental illness of hypomanic nature," and, he continued, Lamb required "much therapeutic work." He asked for a further psychological assessment. This assessment showed that Lamb harboured elaborate fantasies involving robberies, fights, and shootings, all of which demonstrated enormous hostility.

In March 1996, only three months before Lamb was released from Kingston Penitentiary, his behaviour bordered on the psychotic. He threw food at one officer, and another officer found him with a broomstick shoved up his rectum, dragging it on the floor while laughing peculiarly. Lamb told Dr. Scott that he was just trying to bother the officer. Dr. Scott again noted a mental illness of a hypomanic nature developing in Lamb and admitted him to Kingston Psychiatric Hospital on March 18, 1966. At that time, Dr. Scott wrote that he did not know whether Lamb was putting on an act or was really breaking down.

On April 18, 1966, Matthew Lamb was released from hospital. The prognosis was poor. The psychiatric assessment determined that he would probably return as a recidivist. That same day Dr. Scott stated that Lamb was in "a marginal state of mental pathology" and that a schizoid element in his behaviour had developed.

Dr. Scott had to consider whether Lamb should be hospitalized instead of being released from the penitentiary when his sentence expired. Although Dr. Scott was not optimistic about releasing Lamb into the community, he did not believe that he could certify Lamb as requiring hospitalization because his clinical symptoms were not florid. Even though Dr. Scott had misgivings about whether Lamb was well enough to be discharged, he did not bar his release from the penitentiary on June 9, 1966. Seventeen days later, Lamb gunned down and fatally wounded two innocent people during their Saturday night stroll.

The picture of Matthew Lamb emerging from interviews with his family and friends and from the review of the penitentiary reports was of a deeply troubled individual who was capable of bizarre and violent behaviour. He was facing a charge of capital murder, and, if convicted, he would be executed. There was no doubt that he performed the killings. He did not act in self-defence, and there was no evidence of provocation capable of reducing the offence of murder to manslaughter. Nor was there evidence of drunkenness, which could also affect his capacity to form the intent to commit the act of murder and thereby reduce murder to manslaughter.

In light of Lamb's background of psychiatric difficulties and emotional problems, I was obliged as his counsel to explore the defence of insanity.

Section 16 of the *Criminal Code* provides that "No person shall be convicted of an offence in respect of an act or omission on his part while he was insane." Section 16(2) provides that "For the purpose of this section, a person is insane when he has a disease of the mind to an extent that renders him incapable of appreciating the nature and quality and acts or omission or of knowing that an act or omission was wrong." Section 16(4) provides that "Everyone shall until the contrary is proved be presumed to be and to have been sane." The burden of proof would clearly fall on the defence to prove insanity. The question remained whether the defence could discharge that burden of proof.

The report from the Ontario Hospital at Penetanguishene concerning Lamb's fitness to stand trial did not speak to the insanity issue. To establish the defence of insanity, it would be necessary to mount psychiatric and other evidence that would satisfy the burden of proof set out in section 16(2).

I began my psychiatric investigation with Dr. Walter Yaworsky, the first psychiatrist who examined Lamb following the killings. Dr. Yaworsky had conducted a sixty-five-minute examination of Lamb, which led him to the conclusion that Lamb showed signs of mental illness justifying his remand to the Ontario Hospital for observation. This examination took place on June 27, 1966, at 12:30 p.m., less than two days after the shooting.

Dr. Yaworsky found Lamb to be hyperactive and agitated. Lamb was unable to sit still. He stood up and paced around, then sat quietly for a few moments until he again became exceedingly agitated. He was euphoric and laughing elatedly. The psychiatric term for this conduct is "hypomania"–the same term used by Dr. Scott to describe Lamb's behaviour while he was at Kingston Penitentiary. Lamb's responses to Dr. Yaworsky's questions were shallow, and he did not appear very concerned about the interview. Rather, he seemed to treat the charge lightly and laughed when he was asked why he was in jail. Lamb giggled and said it was all unimportant and that he needed a lawyer. He said he never worried about things. He moved around the room, continuing his hypomanic behaviour. When the doctor asked Lamb what he did when he got angry, he responded that he did not get angry. When asked how he was feeling in December 1965, when he violently struck a peace officer in front of the Riverside Arena, Lamb said he did not feel anger and that he did not get mad.

During the interview, Lamb spoke in a confused manner, leaping from topic to topic. He stated that he had the kind of friends that most people avoid. When asked what happened on the Saturday night, he said he just wanted to be happy like any other teenager, buying a car and saving money. He spoke in an off-hand casual manner, not at all in keeping with the degree of concern expected. When asked if he felt bad about the incident, Lamb said he never felt bad about anything he did. A few seconds later, he casually said in an off-hand manner that if he had actually committed the crimes he was charged with, he would kill himself. Then he giggled, said "Poor broad," shook his head, and smiled.

When Lamb was asked about his mother and father, he responded in a very different manner, saying he didn't remember. In fact, Lamb avoided talking about people. His descriptions were vague, as if he had little concern about other people. When asked where his mother was, he said "Somewhere"–and laughed again. When asked what he was laughing about, he said he did not know.

Lamb told Dr. Yaworksy that he heard all kinds of voices, such as the flushing of toilets in the cell. Lamb huddled close to the doctor as if he did not want the guard to hear. When asked about the night of the shootings, he related that he could not remember the act of shooting. All he could remember was coming home in a cab, which he thought was strange. Then he remembered his uncle shaking him. Dr. Yaworsky believed that Lamb's lack of memory at the time was credible. What was also quite remarkable to Dr. Yaworsky was that Lamb had sustained this hypomanic mood for over one hour. In his opinion, it was not likely that Lamb was putting on an act.

Dr. Yaworsky's original diagnostic impression was that, at the time of the shooting, Lamb was a psychopathic personality who had suffered an acute psychotic reaction. He explained that a psychotic reaction involves a severe disorganization of personality in which the patient fails to evaluate reality effectively. Referring back to the definition of insanity in section 16, Dr. Yaworsky was of the opinion that Lamb was suffering from a disease of the mind at the time of the killing. Lamb's disease of the mind was his psychopathy, which involved a lack of integration of affective components in his personality. He suffered from a marked defect in his capacity to feel or appreciate emotional behaviour. Not only was there an impairment of feeling but there was also an absence of remorse, guilt, or shame–all characteristics of a psychopathic personality. The acute psychotic reaction occurred because of a fragile and flimsy personality structure, resulting, in Lamb's case, in his having no appreciation of the nature and quality of the acts he was committing. Lamb was out of touch with reality at the time of the shootings because of his mental illness. Dr. Yaworsky would, later, be a critical witness in support of the defence of insanity.

Next I interviewed Dr. James Dolan, the clinical director of psychiatry at the Ontario Hospital at St. Thomas. He had examined Lamb at the request of the Crown two days after he was seen by Dr. Yaworsky. Lamb told Dolan that he had worked in a woodworking job until 3:00 in the afternoon of the day of the shootings. He said he drank six beers between 3:00 and 9:00 p.m., then went to sleep. He awakened shortly thereafter and loaded his uncle's shotgun, intending to kill himself. The next thing he knew, he was on the street.

Lamb told Dr. Dolan that he saw people as though they were on television. He heard a sound of gunfire as if it were fired from a distance. Lamb said he heard a voice say "Put up your hands." Then he remembered the sound of a shot and seeing a woman fall to the ground. Then he had a vision of a terrified man before him. There was another shot, and he remembered crossing the street and seeing the figure of a girl in the doorway. Lamb believed that he somehow shot at her. He said that he had fired the gun at a passing car and that everything seemed unreal. The next thing Lamb recalled was confronting an old lady in a nearby house. The entire time he was wondering what he was doing there. He then recalled taking a cab from Pillette and Tecumseh Road back to his uncle's house, which was a block away from the shooting.

Dr. Dolan agreed with Dr. Yaworsky that, at the time of the shootings, Lamb had suffered an acute psychotic episode. Lamb was divorced from reality when he gunned down the two victims. Dr. Dolan was of the opinion that, at the critical time of the shooting, Lamb was suffering from a disease of the mind that rendered him incapable of appreciating the nature and quality of his actions.

The defence team now had two very important psychiatric witnesses who supported the defence of insanity. It turned out to be very significant that both Dr. Yaworsky and Dr. Dolan had examined Lamb shortly after the killings occurred. Next I reviewed the evidence from the Ontario Hospital at Penetanguishene, where Lamb had received a full battery of psychological tests and had been under close scrutiny for sixty days.

In early October 1966 I received a report from the Ontario Hospital. That report confirmed that Matthew Lamb had a lengthy history of impulsive, dangerous, and psychopathic behaviour. On examination at

Penetanguishene, Lamb showed no evidence of any psychotic thought disorder or thought content. He was glib, plausible, and seemed cheerful in mood. At first, he claimed amnesia for the events for which he was charged, but later changed his story: he related all the events in detail and admitted freely to his part in them. Lamb showed a most unusual lack of concern for what he had done. He knew the consequences, but did not seem to appreciate the situation in any genuine feeling or affective way and showed no emotion about it. Nevertheless, Lamb could state quite clearly to the psychiatrists that what he had done was wrong and that he wished he had not done it. He was remorseful, but clearly did not have any real underlying feeling of remorse. While his insight into the situation was quite good and he recognized precisely what he had done, he did not seem to appreciate that he might be ill in any way. His judgment was seriously impaired as a result of his affective disorder.

The psychological testing showed Matthew Lamb to be extremely aggressive, with little or no internal controls. While he had an appreciation of social laws, they had no personal meaning for him. He suffered from a disease of the mind as a pathological, anti-social, or psychopathic personality. This recognized psychiatric disorder was listed in the International Classification of Medical Causes of Diseases.

Dr. George Darby, Dr. Barry Boyd, and Dr. Elliot Barker, three psychiatrists from the Ontario Hospital at Penetanguishene, concluded that Lamb understood what he was doing when he did the killings. He knew he had a gun, he knew he had loaded the gun, and he knew that he was firing the gun. However, each of the psychiatrists was of the opinion that because of Lamb's marked emotional immaturity and his affective insufficiency, he could not appreciate the full force and significance of what he was doing. He did not have the capacity to appreciate what was involved in killing another human being and, therefore, could not appreciate the nature and quality of the act of killing another human being. The opinions of each of those psychiatrists supported the defence of insanity as defined in section 16 (2) of the *Criminal Code.*

Dr. Basil Orchard, another psychiatrist on staff at Penetanguishene, differed from his three colleagues. In his opinion, Lamb knew what he was doing when he shot Edith Chaykoski and Andrew Woloch, and he knew that it was wrong. To find him insane would open the floodgates for other psychopaths to try the same defence.

Despite the fact that the weight of the psychiatric opinion favoured the insanity defence, the prosecution maintained that Lamb was criminally responsible for the killings. To bolster its case, the Crown also secured the evidence of Dr. Wilfred Boothroyd, a senior psychiatrist at Sunnybrook Hospital in Toronto, who had reviewed all the psychiatric and psychological reports in the case. Dr. Boothroyd came to the conclusion that Lamb knew he was shooting at human beings, knew right from wrong, and could appreciate the nature and quality of the act of killing another person. In the opinion of Dr. Boothroyd, Lamb was criminally responsible for his conduct.

The stage was now set for the trial. The prosecution sought a conviction for capital murder and the death penalty. The prosecutor would vigorously contest any defence that Lamb was insane and not criminally responsible at the time of the killings. As defence counsel in this case, I had to make a number of important decisions.

In 1967 an accused person found not guilty by reason of insanity was placed in strict custody at the pleasure of the lieutenant governor. That meant that the accused could be released only by an order of the Ontario Cabinet acting on the recommendation of an advisory review board, which consisted of a Supreme Court judge, a psychiatrist, other mental health and legal professionals, and lay persons.

Dr. Yaworsky believed that Lamb would probably spend the rest of his life in an institution for the criminally insane if he was found not guilty by reason of insanity.

Even though Lamb faced the death penalty on the charge of capital murder, it was open to defence counsel to approach the prosecution and offer a plea of guilty to non-capital murder. A conviction for non-capital murder would result in a mandatory term of life imprisonment, but with parole eligibility after serving ten years in the penitentiary.

I was obliged to get unequivocal instructions from Lamb if I was to advance the defence of insanity. I gave him time to reflect on what instructions he wanted to give me. On my next visit to prison one week later, he told me in writing to advance the defence of insanity. He understood that, if he was found not guilty by reason of insanity, he could be detained in custody at the Ontario Hospital for the criminally insane for the rest of his life.

Another critical decision that had to be made was whether Lamb would testify on his own behalf at the trial. Sometimes this decision is deferred until defence counsel determines how the prosecution's case unfolds. In this case, the decision was made before the trial commenced.

The defence case stood or fell primarily on psychiatric evidence. The psychiatric evidence of Dr. Yaworsky and Dr. Dolan and the three psychiatrists from Penetanguishene supported the defence of insanity. Another important development was that Dr. Scott, from Kingston Penitentiary, was now prepared to testify that, in his opinion, seventeen days after release from the penitentiary, Lamb was so emotionally fragile that he probably suffered an acute psychotic episode at the time of the killings. According to Dr. Scott, Lamb was in a fantasy world and was out of touch with reality at the time he did the shootings. There would be no point in calling Lamb as a witness. He presented himself on the surface as a calm, rational person. The jury might have difficulty believing that Lamb did not really appreciate the nature and quality of the act of shooting and killing two human beings. Moreover, a rigorous cross-examination of him could be devastating. I received written instructions from Lamb that he did not wish to testify at his trial on the charge of capital murder of Edith Chaykoski.

Before the trial and in the course of preparing the defence, I sought an independent opinion from Dr. Emmanuel Tanay from Detroit, one of the leading forensic psychiatrists in the United States at the time. He had testified in support of the defence of insanity at the trial of Jack Ruby, charged with the murder of Lee Harvey Oswald, the assassin of President John F. Kennedy. When I called Dr. Tanay, I told him I was defence counsel for an accused charged with capital murder in Windsor and I had taken the case on a pro bono basis. I asked him whether he would be prepared to provide a psychiatric consultation without payment. Dr. Tanay graciously agreed to meet with me and with junior counsel Brian Clements at his office at Ford Hospital in Detroit. The meeting lasted one hour. Dr. Tanay reviewed and discussed the circumstances of the case, the antecedents of the accused, and the available psychiatric evidence. He concluded that Lamb, at the time of the killing, was probably in a dissociative state. Dr. Tanay stated that he would support the opinion that Lamb was mentally ill at the time of the killing and had suffered an acute psychotic episode. That opinion bolstered my confidence in the strength of the evidence of Dr. Yaworsky, Dr. Dolan, and Dr. Scott.

I decided it was not necessary to have Dr. Tanay interview Matthew Lamb or testify at the trial. I also had some trepidation about calling Dr. Tanay as an expert witness for the defence in this case: I thought it could backfire before a jury. I also reflected on the fact that Ruby's insanity defence had failed and that he had been convicted of the murder of Lee Harvey Oswald.

The stage was now set for the trial, which commenced on January 21,

1967. This was the first murder trial heard in the new Essex County Courthouse, completed in the previous year. Because the charge was murder, exclusive jurisdiction to hear the case was vested in a court composed of a judge and jury, presided over by a justice of the Supreme Court of Ontario. Appointed to preside at the trial was the Honorable Mr. Justice Alexander Stark, who had recently been appointed to the High Court of Justice of the Supreme Court of Ontario. Justice Stark had little or no experience in criminal law. In private practice he had served as general counsel for the *Toronto Star* for many years, before his appointment to the bench. This case was the first criminal jury trial over which he presided. Despite his lack of experience in criminal law, Justice Stark was an excellent jurist and conducted the trial in a patient, attentive, and even-handed manner.

After the jury was selected, the indictment was read to Matthew Charles Lamb, charging him with the capital murder of Edith Chaykoski. He pleaded not guilty. Immediately, I advised the court that an admission was being made under section 562 of the *Criminal Code* that Lamb was the person who shot Chaykoski to death. I indicated that the defence would be that, at the time of the commission of the act, Lamb was insane because he was suffering from a disease of the mind that rendered him incapable of appreciating the nature of the act of killing Chaykoski.

Justice Stark made an order allowing all the psychiatrists and psychologists who were to testify on this case to remain in court. He also asked the jury to weigh all the evidence that it would hear as calmly and as dispassionately as possible. He reminded the jurors that they were the supreme judges of the facts. He told them that all persons in the community had to be satisfied that Matthew Charles Lamb received a fair trial. The jurors were admonished by Justice Stark not to discuss the case until they began their deliberations. They were sequestered and confined to their quarters at the Norton Palmer Hotel in Windsor for the duration of the trial.

The Crown began its case by calling an uncle of the accused. He testified that only three hours after the killing, Lamb told him he must have done it. Lamb had been babysitting for his uncle and aunt. The uncle had left a double-barrelled shotgun in the closet. When he returned home an hour after midnight, he learned that a disturbance had occurred in the neighbourhood at about 10:00. When he entered the house, he saw a half box of sixteen-gauge shotgun shells used in his gun on the kitchen table. The remainder of the shells and the double-barrelled shotgun were both missing. At about 6:00 in the morning, he went to police headquarters and told the police the story of the gun. That missing shotgun was later identified as the gun used in the killings.

Lamb's uncle said that Matthew had come to live with him after being released from Kingston Penitentiary. When he spoke to Matthew in the early morning hours after the shooting, he never got any clear-cut answers to the questions he asked. It was the first time since his release from prison that Matthew was not responsive or cooperative. Previously, he had always asked for permission to have cigarettes or baths or anything else he needed to do in the house. He had been exceedingly cooperative with his uncle and family.

The prosecution then called as witnesses the remaining people who were walking with Edith Chaykoski to a bus stop on Tecumseh Road and Ford Boulevard. They testified that a small, thin-faced young man wearing dark clothing emerged from behind a tree, confronted them, spoke coldly and harshly, and said, "Stop, don't move." When Chaykoski, age twenty-one, moved forward, she was shot in the abdomen from a range of six feet. She died two hours later from abscess wounds in the abdomen. The assailant repeatedly ordered the other people to stop. When Andrew Woloch, age twenty, put up his hands, he was shot and fatally wounded, dying nineteen days later from internal wounds involving complications from a liver abscess. Edith Chaykoski's brother, Kenneth Chaykoski, was also shot and injured, but his wounds were not serious. After the shootings, the assailant fled across the street and shot and injured Grace Dunlop, who was standing in the side door of her residence. She suffered internal injuries but recovered soon after. Fifteen minutes later Ann Heaton, who lived two blocks west of the shooting, said she heard a knock on the door. After turning on the entrance light, she found the accused a few feet away, pointing a double-barrelled shotgun at her. He threatened to shoot her. When she called for her husband, Lamb walked away.

Each of the witnesses who testified described Lamb as calm, cool, and collected. On cross-examination, the defence focused on eliciting evidence of Lamb's unusual calmness. Witnesses conceded that Lamb appeared exceedingly detached and lacking in emotion. He paid no attention to a loud party that was going on nearby. When he was in the Heaton residence, he looked scared, his conduct was strange, and he suddenly ran from the house.

The defence was endeavouring to establish that the killings were not only senseless and pointless but that Lamb was moving around in a disconnected manner. Each officer who testified agreed that, when the police arrested him, he was unusually calm and quiet. When his uncle came home not long after the shootings, Matthew Lamb was fast asleep.

In his opening statement, the prosecutor sought to create a picture of a killer who had the presence of mind to take out a shotgun, load it, walk out in the street, and hide behind a tree. He knew he was stopping the group of walkers, he issued warnings, and he hid the gun. Although he did not readily admit what he had done, there was every indication that he knew what he was doing and intended the natural consequences of the act of shooting human beings with a loaded shotgun.

In my opening statement to the jury, I gave an overview of our case. I conceded that the defence had to establish insanity on a preponderance of credible evidence. I told the jury that I would be calling psychiatric evidence to demonstrate that Lamb had a disease of the mind at the time of the killings and did not appreciate the nature and quality of the act of killing another human being. I pointed out that each expert witness for the defence was initially engaged by the state to examine Lamb. The evidence for the defence would illustrate that Lamb was a young man with a very fragile personality who, at the time of the killings, was insane. The judicial interpretation of what constituted a disease of the mind that rendered a person incapable of appreciating the nature and quality of an act was set out in *R. v. O.* by Chief Justice McRuer of the High Court, where he stated that the defence would have to establish the following fact: "An accused was laboring under a disease of the mind to such an extent as to render him or her incapable of foreseeing and measuring the consequences of his act or estimating a right or perceiving the full force of his act."

Dr. Walter Yaworsky provided the first psychiatric evidence called by the defence. He testified that he saw Lamb only two days after the shooting at the request of the Crown. Dr. Yaworsky recounted the detailed evidence he had disclosed to me in earlier interviews. He observed that Lamb, in describing the events of the evening, was giggling and exclaimed "Poor broad." In fact, for the only time during the trial, Lamb giggled when Dr. Yaworsky was giving his testimony. It was the first time he showed any reaction after three days of trial. Dr. Yaworsky testified that Lamb also said to him, "If I did this, I will kill myself." Lamb said that he went for the gun with the thought of killing himself and then dashed out into the street.

Dr. Yaworsky testified that he examined Lamb further in December 1967 and in January 1968 on a total of four occasions. By then, Lamb remembered confronting the people on the street, but said that everything felt fuzzy when he pulled the trigger. Lamb told Dr. Yaworsky that it was as if he were invisible. The next clear memory he had was standing in the Heaton living room minutes later with a gun in his hand. He immediately ran out and, according to Dr. Yaworsky, at that point reality returned to Lamb. Dr. Yaworsky told the jury that Lamb was divorced from reality at the time of the shootings. He had suffered an acute psychotic reaction in a psychopathic personality. He was unable to appreciate the nature and quality of the act of killing another human being.

The next witness for the defence was Dr. James Dolan from the Ontario Hospital at St. Thomas. Dr. Dolan testified about the details he disclosed to me during my interview of him before the trial. He told the jury that when the shooting occurred, Lamb suffered a psychotic break and was divorced from reality. He said that at the critical time, Lamb was suffering from a disease of the mind that rendered him incapable of appreciating the nature and quality of the act of killing another human being.

Both Dr. Yaworsky and Dr. Dolan were cross-examined vigorously by the prosecutor, Eugene Duchesne, QC. Duchesne knew the contents of the psychological reports that were done while Lamb resided at the Ontario Hospital in Penetanguishene. Those reports determined that Lamb had an IQ of 127, which meant he was highly intelligent and placed in the ninety-third percentile of the population for persons his age. Duchesne suggested to each psychiatrist that it would be a simple matter for Lamb, with his psychopathic personality and his intelligence, to contrive a story that he had lost touch with reality to avoid responsibility for consciously shooting at a group of people to gratify his hostile impulses to kill. Both Dr. Yaworsky and Dr. Dolan had testified before the jury that they could not rule out the possibility that Lamb, given his intelligence, made up a story. Nevertheless, each psychiatrist steadfastly held to the conclusion, based on his clinical observations, that Lamb was insane at the time of the killing. To each of them, Lamb was in the throes of a psychotic break at the critical time. The acute psychotic reaction did not have to be triggered by an external set of events. It emerged from within Lamb's tortured personality, and he was unable to control it before it exploded.

To further demonstrate the mental fragility of the accused, the defence called John Robinson, the governor of the Essex County Jail. Governor Robinson testified that on December 10, 1966, five weeks before the trial commenced, Lamb, for no reason, went on a rampage. He set fire to blankets, broke scores of windows, flooded a cell, and smashed plumbing. The episode lasted three hours. Robinson observed that Lamb's pupils were dilated and his eyes were bulging out like that of a crazy man at the time. While it was arguable that Lamb's behaviour involved an explosion of hostility consistent with the extreme acting out of a psychopathic personality, it was such bizarre behaviour that the defence argued that it confirmed the extent of Lamb's mental illness.

To support the theory that Lamb was divorced from reality at the time of the shootings, the defence called Dr. George Scott from the Kingston Penitentiary. Dr. Scott was in an awkward and delicate position. Lamb's psychiatric history at the penitentiary indicated that in March 1966, slightly more than three months before the events of June 25, Lamb had been hospitalized at the penitentiary hospital because of bizarre behaviour, such as the time he shoved a broom up his rectum. It had been obvious to Dr. Scott at the time that Lamb was mentally ill. However, by the time of the expiry of his sentence, Lamb's symptoms had subsided. Scott considered, therefore, that he was not in a position to have Lamb committed to Ontario Hospital instead of releasing him into the community.

Dr. Scott testified before the jury that Lamb lived in an unreal fantasy world that had existed for him from the time he was a little boy. His bizarre behaviour stemmed from the fact that he fantasized himself to be an actor playing the part that his emotions decreed. Scott confirmed that when Lamb left the hospital, the prison officials were concerned about his welfare. In his opinion, when the killings took place, on June 25, 1966, Lamb's pre-psychotic state developed into a schizoid episode–he was split from reality. At that time, Lamb was psychotic, and he was divorced from reality. He suffered a disease of the mind that rendered him incapable of appreciating the nature and quality of the act of killing another human being. In cross-examination, Dr. Scott was pressed as to why Lamb would be released by responsible prison officials if he was in a pre-psychotic state. Scott responded by conceding that even though Lamb was in a marginal state of mental pathology, he was not certifiably insane at the time of his release from prison.

To further support the defence of insanity, I called three psychiatrists and one psychologist from the Ontario Hospital at Penetanguishene. Dr. George Darby, the clinical director, testified that Matthew Lamb changed his story three times, that he was not a reliable witness, and that no one could believe what he said. He confirmed, however, that Lamb was an anti-social and hostile person with a psychopathic personality. He said that Lamb did know about the events of June 26 in an intellectual way but was incapable of appreciating the events emotionally. He lacked the ability to foresee and measure the consequences of his acts, to estimate rights, or to perceive their full force. In some ways, Darby's evidence confirmed the Crown's theory that Lamb was an untrustworthy, intelligent psychopath, capable of lying and distortion.

Dr. Elliot Barker, another psychiatrist from the Ontario Hospital, testified that Lamb told him in an interview that he treated everyone like bugs, except for his uncle and his grandmother. When asked by Justice Stark whether Lamb could comprehend the horror of his crime, Barker said that it would mean nothing more to Lamb emotionally than for most people to swat a fly. In his opinion, Lamb was not capable of appreciating the full force and significance of the act of perpetrating the killing of two human beings.

Dr. Barry Boyd, superintendent of the Ontario Hospital, agreed with his colleagues that Matthew Lamb was incapable of appreciating the full force and significance of killing another human being. Lamb told Boyd: "I hate everybody on the street; I will probably kill someone else before I die. It doesn't bother me. It's like killing a bug." Boyd observed a series of tattoos on Lamb's arm, including a heart, knife, snake, dragon, and skull and crossbones.

While the psychiatrists at the Ontario Hospital differed from Dr. Dolan, Dr. Yaworsky, and Dr. Scott as to whether Lamb was psychotic at the time of the shootings, they unanimously agreed that he was incapable of appreciating the nature and quality of the act of killing another human being, in the sense of foreseeing or measuring the consequences of what he did or appreciating what those consequences would be. Each one conceded on cross-examination that Lamb was cognitively aware of his acts but lacked the emotional capacity to appreciate the real significance of the consequences of his actions.

To round out the evidence from Penetanguishene, the defence called Elizabeth Willett, a psychologist who had tested Lamb at the hospital. According to Ms. Willett, the tests showed that Lamb was between three and a half and six years old emotionally. The IQ test placed him at the university level in the ninety-third percentile, or in the top 7 percent of his age group.

He had a psychopathic personality capable of an acute psychotic episode. The picture of Lamb emerging from the test results was that of an extremely aggressive individual with little frustration tolerance and, consequently, little or no control of his behaviour. Though he was intellectually aware of society's sanctions, these curbs did not have any emotional impact on him. Lamb possessed the negative attitudes associated with a sadistic, destructive orientation in which he had little or no compunction about the means used to achieve his goals. He used few defence mechanisms and acted out almost all his impulses. His major defence mechanism was denial–a defence mechanism used frequently by psychotics or small children. Lamb told Ms. Willett: "Subconsciously I must feel something, but when I pull the trigger, I feel nothing. It's just like a cap gun." That statement verged on fantasy, but Lamb, in commenting on the June 26 shootings, indicated clearly that he was not living in a fantasy at the time. His lack of emotion in discussing the shooting demonstrated that he had only a cognitive and not the usual affective understanding of the results of his actions. Deficits in his personality control and conscience were illustrated by comments in this vein: "I shot a guy before and never lost any sleep over it. I would do it again if I had the chance." Ms. Willett's evidence was supportive of the testimony of the three psychiatrists from Penetanguishene and provided the psychological information they relied on for their opinions.

To rebut the psychiatric evidence of the defence, the Crown called two psychiatrists. Dr. Basil Orchard, one of the psychiatrists who had examined Lamb at the Ontario Hospital, testified that Lamb dropped all pretence of amnesia during an August interview. Once the second shooting victim died, he saw no point in maintaining the story of not remembering what had occurred. Orchard saw no evidence that Lamb suffered from a disease of the mind: he was simply a youth with strong impulses who controlled those impulses at some times and not at others. He was most certainly capable of appreciating the nature and quality of what he did and of knowing it was wrong.

The prosecution also presented the testimony of Dr. Wilfred Boothroyd from Sunnybrook Hospital. In his opinion, Lamb acted out of strong emotions of hatred and bitterness. What he wanted to do was hurt somebody. Boothroyd testified that Lamb was aware of the consequences of his actions and fully intended those consequences. Dr. Boothroyd believed that Lamb was mentally ill in March and mentally ill two days after the shooting, but he was essentially a person with a psychopathic disorder or disability who did not suffer from a disease of the mind at the time of the shootings. In his view, Lamb was capable of a wide range of feeling except for feelings of guilt and conscience.

Over the course of Dr. Boothroyd's testimony, Justice Stark intervened and commented that Boothroyd's opinion differed from that of every other doctor who had testified. Justice Stark also queried how Dr. Boothroyd could give a reliable opinion without having clinically examined Lamb. I reminded the jury of those remarks in my final address.

The stage was now set for the final addresses to the jury by the defence and the prosecution–a critical stage of the trial. Even though the witnesses for the defence outnumbered those for the Crown, it was impossible to predict how the jury, as the supreme judges of the facts, would ultimately deal with the disturbing facts of the case.

In addressing the jury for the defence, I knew it was important at the outset to concede that Lamb had committed a senseless act of violence and to express the utmost compassion and sympathy to the family, friends, and survivors of the deceased. I stressed that the defence of not guilty by reason of insanity, if successful, would not result in Lamb being released as a free man. Rather, the verdict would mean that Lamb was suffering from a mental illness at the time of the killing to the extent he could not be found criminally responsible. According to the terms of the *Criminal Code*, he would be held in strict custody in a secure hospital for the criminally insane "at the pleasure of" the lieutenant governor of Ontario. That meant Lamb could be confined in a hospital for the criminally insane for the rest of his life.

I reminded the jurors that each one of them now sat as a judge of the Supreme Court of Ontario, independent of the prosecution and the defence. Each one of them was a representative of the community standing between the state and the accused, and each of them was charged with the important task of doing justice in this case. The question that the jury would have to answer was whether the defence had established on a preponderance of credible evidence or a balance of probabilities that Matthew Lamb was suffering from a disease of the mind that rendered him incapable of appreciating the nature and quality of the act of shooting and killing another human being. I suggested to the jury that, even without any expert opinion to assist, they should scrutinize Lamb's actions on the evening of June 25 carefully.

Lamb had certainly acted in a bizarre and senseless manner. The victims were total strangers; he used no disguise; there were no accomplices; and he had nothing to gain from the act. He exhibited inexplicable behaviour by shooting at a silhouette in a doorway just after he shot at the group of people. Then he knocked on the door of a nearby home, made an idle threat to kill, and left, without anything happening. Was he conducting himself like a psychopathic killer or was this the behaviour of a severely disturbed, mentally ill young man who truly didn't appreciate the full force and significance of what he was doing? I also asked the jury to examine what Lamb did after the offence. He dropped the gun in a nearby field, where it certainly would be found. Shortly after that, he went home to bed and slept. Lamb made no real effort to avoid the consequences of what had occurred or to hide or cover up what had happened. What had to be obvious to every juror using common sense was that this young teenager had a glaring defect in his capacity to feel or appreciate what he was doing. He lived in a fantasy or dream world, disconnected from reality. Clearly, Lamb was insane at the time of the shootings.

I pointed out to the jury that there was overwhelming support for this conclusion, based on the evidence of six psychiatrists and one psychologist. Ultimately, three psychiatrists believed that Lamb suffered from an acute psychotic reaction and was entirely divorced from reality at the time of the killing. The other three psychiatrists and one psychologist were of the opinion that Lamb could not appreciate the full force and significance of what he was doing and that he did not really perceive the people he killed as human beings.

What was remarkable about this case, I informed the jury, was that not one of the experts called to testify by the defence was an expert solicited by the defence to give evidence in support of a theory. Each expert defence witness first saw Matthew Lamb in his or her capacity as a public servant. Dr. Yaworsky was the only defence expert witness in private practice, yet he saw Lamb at the request of the court. Dr. Dolan was a public servant who saw Lamb to give a second opinion at the request of the Crown. Dr. Scott was in the employ of the state when he dealt with Lamb over a lengthy period of time. It took courage and integrity for Dr. Scott to say, "When I released Lamb, he was in a marginal state of mental pathology." When he was asked, "Why did you not have him committed to a mental hospital instead of allowing him to be released into the community when he was mentally ill and capable of killing?" Dr. Scott stood his ground and gave compelling evidence of how sick and disturbed Lamb was only seventeen days after his release. I reminded the jury of Dr. Scott's forceful evidence that, at the time of the killings, Lamb was in a dream world. I suggested that if anyone could assess the difference between a psychopathic killer and a mentally ill or emotionally disturbed young man, it was Dr. Scott, who had vast experience with psychopathic and emotionally disturbed prisoners. Each psychiatrist who testified on behalf of the defence from the Ontario Hospital at Penetanguishene had the opportunity, on behalf of the state, to examine Lamb intensively for a period of about sixty days. None of them had an axe to grind, yet each concluded that Lamb suffered from a disease of the mind that rendered him incapable of appreciating the nature and quality of the act of killing he had committed.

I conceded that the burden was indeed on the defence to establish insanity on a preponderance of credible evidence. Jury members had to ask themselves whether the six psychiatrists and one psychologist called by the defence, each of whom was employed in a public service capacity at the time of assessment, were credible.

I suggested to the jury that the psychiatrists and the psychologist who were called for the defence were each able to probe beneath the surface to assess the emotional fragility of the patient. Even a person who was conscious of his acts could still be so deeply damaged emotionally as to be considered legally insane when those acts were committed. Even apart from the psychiatric evidence, the course of Lamb's life showed a deeply disturbed young man. He had been abandoned as an infant and experienced a troubled childhood. He was a victim of both psychological and emotional abuse and had few friends. Over the years, he had exhibited very strange conduct, marked by detachment. At the time of the shooting, he had an unusual fascination with guns and violence. He was a person whose behaviour tipped over the edge of sanity, and there was a touch of the bizarre in everything he did. Tragically, his acts were pointless, mindless acts of insanity. I urged the jury, as judges of the facts, to come to the only conclusion warranted by the evidence—the defence had mounted an exceedingly powerful case that established the insanity of Matthew Lamb at the time he perpetrated the killings. That finding, I argued, was supported by both science and common sense.

For the prosecution, Eugene Duchesne, QC, argued to the jury that this case was a cold-blooded shooting. The victims were a defenceless group of innocent young people shot while strolling in a residential area to a bus stop.

The assailant ambushed them. He was an ex-convict, released from Kingston Penitentiary only three weeks before the shooting. He had been labelled an anti-social psychopath. He gave conflicting versions to different psychiatrists of what occurred. He was very intelligent and capable of giving a false impression to suit his impulses. It would be a simple matter for the jury to regard him as a menace to the community who must be held criminally responsible for the tragedy he had perpetrated.

The prosecutor pointed out that five of the eight psychiatrists testified that Lamb must have known what he was doing. He invited the jury to examine the circumstances and not leap to the conclusion that Lamb could not appreciate that he was killing a human being, and so be absolved of criminal responsibility. Mr. Duchesne contended that the shootings were the acts of a violent young man who could not control his impulses. Lamb had to have his lust for violence gratified without delay. Why should this type of killer be exempted from criminal responsibility? Most psychopaths or sociopaths should be held legally accountable for criminal behaviour. A verdict of not guilty by reason of insanity might open the floodgates to sociopaths and psychopaths rushing to psychiatrists to get support for an insanity defence to avoid conventional imprisonment. Slick con artists might have a field day striving to be classified as insane and not criminally responsible. Moreover, the shrewd psychopathic criminal might have a much easier time in the hospital for the mentally ill than in a federal penitentiary. The jury appeared to be paying close attention to the well-reasoned arguments of the prosecutor.

In his charge to the jury, Justice Stark reviewed the evidence and advised the jury of the law of insanity as set out in the case of *R. v. O.* He pointed out that the weight of the psychiatric evidence favoured the defence, but reminded the jury that it had the last word because jurors are the final judges of the facts.

The jury members were poker-faced when they left for their deliberations. After retiring to consider a verdict, jurors often return and ask the judge questions to clarify any confusion in their minds. Those questions can be revealing. In this case, however, the participants and the spectators were not kept in suspense for long. The jury retired at 4:30 p.m. and returned before 7:00 p.m. The foreman read the verdict: not guilty by reason of insanity. Matthew Lamb showed no reaction.

Soon after, he was driven in police custody to the Ontario Hospital for the Criminally Insane at Penetanguishene, to be detained for an indefinite period until the Ontario Cabinet on the recommendation of an advisory review board made an order for his release.

What ultimately happened to Matthew Lamb? Treatment at the Oakridge Unit at the Ontario Hospital was amazingly successful. Lamb arrived at a time when a form of therapy called the Therapeutic Community was practised at the Oakridge Unit, directed by Dr. Elliot Barker, who had testified at the trial. Thirty-eight patients participated in an intense program in which the patients were involved in honest dialogue and communication among themselves and with therapists sixteen hours a day. Dr. Barker and other staff members monitored the behaviour and activities of each one. Patients were not allowed psychologically to manipulate each other, the doctors, or the staff. They actively participated in different group activities throughout the day and were encouraged to feel a sense of empowerment. Lamb thrived in this setting and became a model patient. At one point he was given the role of patient therapist. He performed that role successfully during his tenure at the hospital.

Matthew Lamb was respected very much in the hospital by both staff and the other patients. He even started a patients' newspaper. He wrote articles in that paper and encouraged other patients to write. The psychiatrists were so impressed with his recovery that they brought him with them to lecture sessions at the Ontario Police College at Aylmer as an example of the potential for this rehabilitative process. About five years after his remand to the Ontario Hospital, Lamb came before an advisory review board. The members of the board were Ontario Supreme Court justice Edson Haines, two independent psychiatrists not connected with the Ontario Hospital, one prominent lawyer and one respected lay person. That board recommended Lamb's release into the community.

The conditions of Matthew Lamb's release were that he reside with Dr. Barker and his family on a 200-acre farm, where he would be employed as a farm labourer. Dr. Barker and his wife described Lamb as an exceedingly industrious worker. He helped fence the farm and did every possible kind of chore for the Barkers, always looking for more work to do. He was trusted to babysit the Barkers' three-year-old daughter, who loved to have him around. He was described as treating her with healthy kindness and affection.

After working on the farm for about a year, Lamb told the Barkers that he wished to travel outside Canada and do something purposeful with his life.

He had read widely on the subject of psychiatry. Having read the classic book by Cleckley on the psychopathic personality, *The Mask of Sanity*, he believed he was a psychopath who would never be able to relate empathetically to others in mainstream society.

Lamb thought that involvement in military service in a highly structured environment could give him a sense of camaraderie and belonging. He admired the state of Israel. He purchased Israeli bonds from the savings he had accumulated through his work at the farm and from gifts from his grandmother. He wanted to fight for Israel in the Yom Kippur War, so he hitchhiked to the front in 1973 in order to join the Israeli Army. This war was difficult for Israel, and the morale of the soldiers was low. Lamb came into contact with many soldiers who did not want to fight in the war and who desperately wanted to leave the front. Disillusioned, Lamb left the front and the state of Israel.

Lamb's next destination was Australia. On his way to Australia he stopped in South Africa and Rhodesia and decided to join the Rhodesian National Army. In letters to the Barker family, he confided that he had found a new sense of self-worth and respect in the Rhodesian Army. He liked the discipline, the honour, and the esprit de corps. He felt strongly about duty and responsibility. While on leave, he came back to Midland to visit the Barker family. It was obvious to the Barkers that he had found a place for himself in Rhodesia with the military service.

Matthew Lamb's military career was short-lived. He was killed in action in November 1976, ten years and four months after the killings that had led to his trial. Lamb had escaped the death penalty in 1967 but was killed by gunfire at the age of twenty-nine. After his death, a friend sent a Rhodesian newspaper to Dr. Barker containing about a dozen obituary notices written by fellow soldiers who praised Matthew Lamb as an outstanding comrade. He was loved and respected as a soldier.

Lamb had confided in Dr. Barker that his concern about being killed or captured was that his past life would be revealed and that such revelation would embarrass the hospital, the army, and the Canadian government. Dr. Barker believed that Matthew Lamb was exceedingly aware that the hospital and the Canadian justice system had treated him in a humane way. Lamb was appreciative and deeply grateful that the Canadian justice system enabled him to receive treatment and ultimately allowed him to be free, despite the horrible acts he had committed. Ultimately, Lamb was satisfied that he had been treated justly–as indeed he was. He had received a fair trial.

There was ample evidence to justify the verdict of not guilty by reason of insanity, based on the law as it was in 1967. However, if Matthew Lamb had been tried in 1999, the year this lecture was delivered, would a jury have reached the same verdict?

Section 16 of the *Criminal Code* remains intact, except that the term "mental disorder" has been substituted for "disease of the mind." In addition, the interpretation of what is involved in the appreciation of the nature and quality of the act has been reconsidered since 1967 by the Supreme Court of Canada in *R. v. Kjelsden.* That case dealt with a dangerous psychopath who was charged with raping and killing his victim. The psychiatrists called by the defence in dealing with the definition of appreciation were of the opinion that it involved an ability not only to foresee the physical reaction but also to foresee and understand the emotional reaction of those affected.

Justice McIntrye, speaking for the court, adopted the statement from the judgement of Justice Martin in *R. v. Simpson*, where he stated:

> I do not think that the exemption provided by the Section extends to one who has the necessary understanding of the nature, character and consequences of the act but merely lacks appropriate feelings for the victim or lacks remorse or guilt for what he has done, even though such lack of feeling stems from a "disease of the mind." Appreciation of the nature and quality of the act does not import a requirement that the act be accompanied by appropriate feelings of the consequences of the act on other people. No doubt, the absence of such feelings is a common characteristic of many people who engage in repeated and serious criminal conduct.

How would this statement of law have affected the expert opinions of the psychiatrists and the psychologist from Penetanguishene who testified for Lamb's defence? I must concede that their opinions about Lamb's capacity to appreciate the nature and quality of his act would probably have been different. However, I submit that even if psychiatrists at Penetanguishene had come to different conclusions in 1999 about Lamb's ability to appreciate the nature and quality of his act of killing, the cornerstone of the defence evidence would have remained the powerful and graphic evidence of Dr. Yaworsky and Dr. Dolan–who made their clinical assessments of Lamb very close to the time of the killings–as well as the compelling evidence of Dr. Scott, who had observed Lamb's gradual breakdown over a period of more than one year.

I suggest that a jury properly instructed in 1999 would have been satisfied that the defence had established insanity pursuant to section 16(2) of the *Criminal Code*. A verdict of not criminally responsible on account of mental disorder would be the just and humane verdict delivered by that jury.

Sleepwalking as Non-Insane Automatism:
R. v. Parks

MARLYS EDWARDH

2004

In the late evening of May 23, 1987, Ken Parks lay down on the couch in his living room to watch television. His wife had just gone to bed. He was dressed in track pants and a T-shirt, his normal sleeping attire. He fell asleep between 1:00 and 2:00 a.m. that night. Several hours later Parks rose from his couch, put on his shoes and jacket, and departed, leaving the front door open–something he never did. He got into his car and drove to the townhouse of his parents-in-law, some twenty-three kilometres away. The journey, mostly by superhighway, customarily took Parks ten to fifteen minutes to drive. He entered the house using his key and carrying a tire iron, one of the tools he had in his car, along with a hatchet and two knives.

Denis Woods, Parks's father-in-law, woke to a choking sensation. He felt hands around his neck and had the impression that the person who was strangling him was also straddling his body, as he could feel weight around his waist. He called out to his wife, Barbara, for help but heard no response. He then passed out. Upstairs, the Woods children–Emma, Prudence, and Jonathan–were asleep. They awoke to the sound of a woman screaming. Both Emma and Prudence called downstairs to their mother. Just before the screaming sounds stopped, they heard animal or ape-like grunting noises. Emma and Prudence heard footsteps moving quickly up the stairs towards them and the ape-like noises getting louder. They both ran into a bedroom and closed the door. Suddenly, the footsteps retreated down the stairs. Shortly after, they heard the basement door slam shut. Fearful, the children jumped out the bedroom window, and escaped to a neighbour's house.

Ken Parks entered a police station at 4:45 a.m. and approached the front counter. He was dripping blood from severe lacerations to both his hands. The cuts went to the bone and severed the flexor tendons. First to the civilian telephone operator, and shortly after to several police officers, he said, "My God, I've just killed two people. My hands." One of the officers would later describe Ken's tone as one of amazement and realization when he made this statement. The scene at the police station was chaotic. He was immediately taken to a small office, where he gave the Woods's address. Throughout the time in the police station, Ken was extremely upset and distressed. He was variously described as crying, shaking, and very hyper. The officers, believing they could not stem the bleeding from his hands long enough to wait for an ambulance, decided to take him to the hospital in a police cruiser. During the two- or three-minute ride to the hospital, Parks kept repeating over and over again, "Why did I kill them? Why did I kill them?" He continued to cry and be most upset.

When the police arrived at the Woods's residence, Mrs. Woods's body was found in the TV room, outside the master bedroom. She had sustained a variety of serious injuries, one of which proved fatal. Her injuries included five stab wounds—one to the chest, which entered her heart, and four to the back; a skull fracture; other blunt force injuries to the head; and pressure fractures to several ribs. Mr. Woods was found by police, nauseous and dizzy, sitting on the basement stairs with severe lacerations to his head and upper back area.

At the hospital, Parks was overheard speaking aloud to himself: "I killed her parents," he mumbled. "I don't know why. I had a problem gambling. I woke up in the middle of the night. I don't know why. What the fuck did I do? What happened? I was sleeping on the couch. I just woke up. I had a dream. I had a knife in my hand. I was killing them. I choked them, and then I went to the police station. Don't worry about me, get them. How could I drive there and not know?" Throughout, he was extremely agitated and distressed. A treating physician described him as having a frightened "in-flight" appearance. Although Ken had no memory of having a dream, at the time he thought he might be in a dream or nightmare from which he would awaken.

Parks was transferred to Sunnybrook Hospital, where the police conducted their first extensive interview with him. During the interview, he became upset and began to sob heavily when he was told, for the first time, that the victim of the murder charge was his mother-in-law, Barbara Woods. As well, a strange story emerged from this interview. Parks's recollection after having fallen asleep on his couch was of being in the house of his parents-in-law and seeing Mrs Woods's face. Her eyes and mouth were open, and she had a "help me" expression on her face. She looked frightened. Although she sustained serious injuries all over her head, he recalled seeing no marks or blood on her face. At this time he heard the children yelling from the floor above. He began to run upstairs calling out, he recalled, "Kids, kids, kids." The children merely heard "animal grunting noises." He did not remember actually running up the stairs to the upper level, where the children were, but he remembered being on the landing at the top of the stairs and bracing himself. He never crossed the threshold into any of the rooms on that floor. He vaguely recalled trying the kitchen telephone, or thinking something about the telephone, and having a sense that the telephone was dead. The telephone may not have been used at all by him, but the phone was off the hook in the master bedroom, and a beeping sound could be heard. He could not recall leaving the townhouse or where his car was. He did not remember if he started his car or if it was already running. He drove to the nearby local police station, but he did not recall which of two possible routes he had taken to get there. At some point after he got into the car he saw a knife in his hand and threw it on the floor of the car. Although he had sustained serious injuries to his hands, he did not know how he got them and did not realize he had them until he got to the police station. Parks's memory of the period between waking and seeing his mother-in-law's face and arriving at the police station was fragmented and patchy. This interview took place before Parks ever spoke to a lawyer.

When I met Ken Parks, he was charged with the first-degree murder of Barbara Woods and the attempted murder of Denis Woods. He lay in a hospital room, his hands bandaged, filled with remorse and completely unable to cast light on the events in the early hours of May 24. I began to search and understand the events of the night by first turning to the circumstances of the surrounding days and his relationship with members of the Woods family and his own family. It was the first step in trying to fill the gap in Parks's recollection of falling asleep on his couch and awaking to see his mother-in-law's face, eyes and mouth open, with a "help me" expression.

Ken Parks, twenty-three years old at the time, was a huge man. He stood 6 foot 5 and weighed 280 pounds. His wife, Karen, the oldest child in the

Woods family, had been his high school sweetheart. They had married with the support and blessings of Barbara and Denis Woods. Parks described his relationship with Karen's parents as one of warm and mutual affection. Denis and Barbara Woods treated Ken as a son and, in all respects, he felt like a member of the family. He was particularly close to Barbara Woods, who amiably referred to him as a gentle giant. He could not recall an angry exchange that had ever passed between them. Karen's younger brothers and sisters were also close to Ken, seeing him as an attentive and playful older brother. Remarkably, Ken Parks's description of his relationship with the Woods family was confirmed by everyone I turned to in the months before trial. Despite the confusion and anger felt by Denis Woods and all the children, they never varied from this description of Ken Parks when they testified.

Parks's relationship with his wife, Karen, was more complex and troubled. As a young couple, they had initially done well. Parks had a good job at Revere Electric and had received several promotions. They had been able to buy their own home. Melissa, Ken and Karen's first child, was born in December and was five months old at the time of the incident. Despite this superficially idyllic picture, there were great strains on Ken and Karen's relationship.

In June 1986, one year before Barbara Woods's death, Parks had started to gamble. He first won some money when he went to the Queen's Plate with Karen for what seemed a pleasant Sunday diversion. However, he wanted to win again. Over the year his betting increased, and so did his losses. First, the Parks's savings were depleted. Then Parks turned to Revere Electric and stole $32,000 from the company, always hoping for the "big one" so he could pay it back. In March 1987 the company detected the theft and he was fired and charged. Only then did Karen realize that Parks had been gambling and that their savings were gone. Indeed, their future was in serious jeopardy. In the weeks following the discovery of the theft, the marriage was severely strained. Parks was unemployed and they considered selling their home to pay off the debt to his former employer. Parks promised to go to Gamblers Anonymous and to tell both his family and Barbara and Denis Woods about his gambling. The meeting with her family was set for that fateful day of May 24, 1987.

I was aware but initially failed to understand the significance of the fact that Parks was exhausted. For months, he was unable to sleep. His work had become demanding, often requiring him to put in ten to fifteen hours per day. His daughter had colic, which kept both parents up late trying to soothe her. The stress of his arrest and the accompanying marital discord kept him sleepless on the couch in the living room. On the night of Barbara Woods's death, Ken and Karen had talked and were committed to finding a solution to the problems they faced. They wanted to save their marriage, but the severe strains seriously threatened it.

As a young lawyer, I had become interested in and knowledgeable about the treatment of those not guilty by reason of insanity. I had prepared and argued the case *R. v. Swain,* in which we challenged the draconian and overly harsh treatment of mentally disordered offenders. We ultimately prevailed in the Supreme Court of Canada. While I knew that the defence of insanity had many potentially negative consequences, including potential lifetime confinement, in Parks's case it had to be explored. Even on the initial facts as I knew them, no meaningful explanation was available for Parks's presence in the Woods's home, or for the injuries suffered by the family, other than the fact that Parks somehow and for some reason had inflicted them.

From the first day, I endeavoured to shut the Crown out from my preparations and to go about the process of having Parks assessed in order to better understand what might have occurred. I started by making it clear to the police and the hospital that Parks was not to be seen by psychiatric staff beyond the brief initial contact I had not been able to stop.

I retained for the defence a senior psychiatrist at Sunnybrook, Dr. Ron Billings, to interview Parks and begin the assessment process. However, only the preliminary parts of the assessment were completed by the time Parks was scheduled to move to the detention centre. Other important examinations had not been undertaken and could not be readily completed without a court order to move him, which would alert the prosecution. Dr. Billings agreed that a full examination, including a neurological work-up, was necessary to see if any organic disease, such as a tumour or other lesion in the brain, was present. When Parks left the hospital, his chart contained the name of Dr. John Demeads, chair of the Department of Neurology. Conveniently, Dr. Demeads had also been retained by the defence. I wanted the blanket of solicitor/client privilege to fall over him.

In the months leading up to the trial, other experts were retained. At first they were retained as part of the effort to understand Parks and the events that had unfolded on May 24. Later, these experts were needed, tactically, to ensure there was full support for the ultimate conclusion they reached.

As our preparation went forward, Parks and I had to decide if he should apply for bail. Obviously, having a client out on bail is desirable, both for the client and for the preparation of a defence. However, I believed that no judge would release him without medical evidence to explain his conduct and assure the court that it would not happen again. Fortunately, Parks answered the bail question with a resounding no. As he grew to accept the evidence that he had caused the death of Barbara Woods, he became more horrified and afraid of what he was. He refused to consider an application for bail, fearing he would hurt someone else while unaware of what he was doing and unable to control his actions. This decision allowed me to continue preparing without having to disclose anything about Parks's defence to the prosecution. The initial group of experts, which now included a forensic psychiatrist, met to review their respective findings. By this time, no one doubted that Parks had suffered from something that caused his loss of memory for the events, assuming he had killed Barbara Woods. The neurological examination was negative. There was no tumour, lesion, or history of epilepsy. Similarly, the psychiatric evaluation disclosed no evidence of previous mental illness or any that had manifested itself while he was in custody. A transient psychotic depression was put forward as an initial hypothesis, but Parks's own words, "I fell asleep and woke to see her face," made me very uncomfortable with this diagnosis. So did the fact that this plea would lead to the insanity defence and years of confinement.

I turned to my spouse, Dr. Graham Turrall, a forensic psychologist who had seen Parks in jail, to assure me he was not suicidal. I had cut off access to Parks by the jail psychiatrist and needed to be assured that my client would not harm himself. I also wanted help with all the references to sleep. The thought was forming that sleep might itself be the key to these events. In 1982–83 my husband and I had spent a year in California, where I enrolled for a master of laws degree while he pursued postdoctoral studies at Stanford. He called the Sleep Disorder Laboratory there and we were surprised to learn that one of the world's leading experts in sleep disorder, Dr. Roger Broughton, was working in Ottawa.

Dr. Broughton tentatively agreed to become involved but needed access to Parks to run two sleep studies. I needed permission from the superintendent of the jail to put Parks in the infirmary so he could be wired to the necessary machines to study and evaluate the architecture of his sleep. Permission was granted, and one of Dr. Broughton's graduate students spent two nights in the detention centre infirmary. Dr. Broughton also requested that I find out if there was any history of sleep disorders, or parasomnias, in other members of Parks's family and that I ask Parks about his own sleep history.

I quickly learned that Parks had always been a deep sleeper, often requiring a physical shaking to wake up. Once awakened in the morning, he would experience a period of grogginess, lasting about half an hour. If addressed during this period, he would often mumble in response but would not recall it afterwards. He suffered from enuresis, or bed wetting, until he was in his early teens and had been observed to talk in his sleep at the time the enuresis ceased. He had been known to sit up in his sleep, and, on one occasion, when he was about twelve years old, he had been stopped from going out of a sixth-floor window in his sleep.

His family had a robust history of sleep disorders: sleepwalking (one grandfather, one brother, one first cousin, one more distant cousin); non-infantile enuresis (one brother, two uncles, two first cousins); sleep-talking (one grandfather, one brother, two first cousins, two great aunts, one uncle); night terrors (one grandfather, one uncle, one first cousin); and deep sleeping (one grandfather, one brother, two uncles, two first cousins). Parks had a genetic predisposition to sleepwalk. I was to learn later that Melissa, his daughter, also walked in her sleep. When the sleep studies were completed, Dr. Broughton called me and said they were classic examples of a sleepwalker.

With this information in hand, I convened a second meeting of the experts retained by the defence. This time Dr. Broughton presented conclusions that Parks was sleepwalking. After much discussion and examination of the data from the various disciplines, we agreed that everything fit this conclusion and everyone was prepared to defend it. While it is dangerous to permit experts to meet and discuss their findings, in this case I concluded that this approach was necessary to bring the disciplines together and to arrive at a conclusion by means of a process of differential diagnosis–the exclusion of other explanations.

I then sought the support of Dr. Frank Ervin, both a neurologist and a psychiatrist, who trained at Harvard and, for many years, ran the Los Angeles Neurological Institute before moving to Montreal. He is the elder statesman of the medical world in understanding the relationship between the brain and violence. The breadth of his experience is breathtaking, as is his intelligence. His other outstanding feature is his appearance, for he looks like paintings of Moses. He is the only witness I have ever seen who knows the questions of both the examiner and the cross-examiner in advance, even when they don't yet know them. Dr. Ervin came to Toronto, interviewed Parks, reviewed the data, and met with various members of Parks's family. He too was prepared to support the defence of somnambulism, or sleepwalking.

Parks, of course, never said he was sleepwalking. All he could say was that, after falling asleep, he awoke and saw his mother-in-law's face. Only the good faith and integrity of the team that worked with him allowed him to slowly accept this explanation for what had happened. His initial response was less enthusiastic. For a while he tried to hold on to the belief that someone must have broken into the Woods's home and that Barbara Woods must have called him for help. However, there was no evidence to support this theory. Accepting that he was sleepwalking also entailed accepting that some part of him could do terrible things completely outside his control. At first he was as incredulous of this theory as were the colleagues with whom I discussed the case.

I recognized the uphill battle. At the trial, I would first have to convince the jury that Parks was sleepwalking, then I would have to fight the legal battle that a sleepwalker was entitled to an absolute acquittal because sleepwalking was a form of non-insane automatism. I knew the Crown would seek to classify sleepwalking as a "disease of the mind" or "insane automatism," giving rise to a defence of not guilty by reason of insanity. The seeds of the temptation to cast the net broadly existed in the jurisprudence. Somnambulism as non-insane automatism existed more in theory than in the academic literature and arose only sporadically in cases in the common law world.

Two weeks before the trial I received a letter from the Crown asking me if the defence would be relying on medical evidence regarding psychiatric issues. I responded cautiously that no defence of insanity was being raised. My response reflected a concern with a decision in the Ontario Court of Appeal, *Regina v. Sweeny*, in which the court had ruled that if the accused raised the defence of insanity and declined to submit to a psychiatric examination by a psychiatrist appointed by the Crown, the trial judge could admit the evidence of the refusal and invite the jury to draw an adverse inference. I got no reply from the Crown and fretted about the possibility that my response could impair the defence, given that I had a wide array of medical experts to call. A few days later I wrote back to the Crown, saying I intended to call both medical and psychiatric evidence.

Up until this exchange of correspondence, I have no doubt that the Crown was anticipating a defence of insanity. On receipt of my letter, the Crown appointed Dr. Brian Butler and sought access to Parks. Dr. Butler was the only Crown-appointed psychiatrist I would have allowed to see Parks, otherwise, the risk of negative comment was not worth running. He was an intelligent and sensitive psychiatrist who would not dismiss sleepwalking as an explanation for Parks's conduct. As well, he was both a friend and a colleague I had worked with previously. When he called me, I laid out the family history of parasomnia. I learned several days later that he, too, had concluded that Parks was sleepwalking. It was the eve of the trial, and the Crown had no evidence to counter our defence.

On Monday, as the trial started and the jury was selected, I had one wish: I hoped the trial could proceed without the glare of publicity. I did not want the jury members to be discussing it with their respective friends and family or to be overwhelmed by a cynical press corps, knowing no admonition of the trial.

Here is where I owe a debt to Edward Greenspan. Uncharacteristically, Greenspan was in a provincial court defending what was really a domestic assault. His client, the husband, was accused of having done things that Greenspan regarded as a physical impossibility. He opted for the unusual approach of saying to the complainant, "Okay, show me." As a result, the two were locked in physical combat, rolling on the courtroom floor. The trial went on for days. Every member of the press corps covering the superior courts left the courthouse to watch Greenspan at the provincial court. Newspapers focused on the struggle. I was left alone, as was the trial of Ken Parks. No one returned until the defence was almost complete.

At trial, the evidence of the Crown was completely predictable. After a successful non-suit on first-degree murder, the trial proceeded on a charge of second-degree murder. The Crown's attack on the defence was two-pronged: the first to suggest that the defence was incredible; and the second to argue that somnambulism gave rise only to a defence of insanity, which should be the only defence left to the jury. The Crown's position forced me to call extensive evidence explaining not only what somnambulism is but also what it is not. To ensure that Ken Parks was acquitted, I needed to establish, as a matter of medical science, that somnambulism had no connection to either organic or functional mental disorders—and, further, that Parks did not suffer from them.

It was the unanimous opinion of the psychiatrists who testified that Parks had no history of mental illness and that he was not suffering from any mental illness—including neurosis, psychosis, or personality disorder—on May 24, 1987. They arrived at this conclusion after an extremely thorough differential diagnosis that encompassed the consideration and exclusion of the following possible mental illnesses: organic disease or disturbance (including temporal-lobe epilepsy, limbic seizures, frontal-lobe lesions, or drug- or alcohol-induced disease); depression or psychotic proportions; schizophrenia; paranoid state; fugue state; episodic dyscontrol syndrome; and anti-social personality disorder. As well, physical examinations, including neurological examinations, were negative, revealing no tumour, lesions, epilepsy, or any other disease of the brain or neurological system (except for the severed nerves in Parks's fingers).

I did not hesitate to use visual aids in the courtroom. When Dr. Broughton took the stand to explain the nature of sleep, he was armed with slides to show how sleep manifested itself in the human brain. When I asked for the courtroom lights to be dimmed, Justice Watt dryly asked where the popcorn was. I knew I faced a formidable task to convince the jury that a person could drive across the city and commit these horrendous acts while sleeping. Although, technically, I needed only to raise a reasonable doubt, the burden was greater than that.

Dr. Broughton testified that sleep, a universal phenomenon for human beings, is a behavioural state of relative inactivity and relative withdrawal from environmental stimuli. From a physiological perspective, however, the brain remains active. There are two basic forms of sleep: REM and non-REM. Wakefulness, REM sleep, and non-REM sleep are three different electrochemical configurations of the brain, and the two forms of sleep are as different from each other as they are from wakefulness. Within non-REM sleep there are four levels of depth: "deep" sleep (also called "delta," "slow-wave," or "stage 3 and 4" sleep) and "light" sleep (or "stage 1 and 2" sleep).

Sleep is periodic, going through cycles of approximately one and a half hours in duration. Most deep sleep normally occurs in the first two cycles of a sleep. A cycle consists of shifts of deep sleep, to light sleep, to REM sleep.

People usually waken with a shift from light non-REM sleep to wakefulness. When they shift from stage 3 or 4 non-REM sleep to wakefulness, they may be confused or disoriented and do inappropriate things, being "drunk with pressure to remain in sleep."

Dr. Broughton testified that sleepwalking is an intensified and prolonged period of partial arousal in stage 3 and 4 non-REM sleep in which the person behaves automatically, having the ability to move around and perform tasks (thus appearing to be awake), but not having the ability to think (which makes the person unresponsive and indicates that he is asleep). The sleepwalker is both subjectively and physiologically asleep at such time. Because a sleepwalker is asleep, he has amnesia of the sleepwalking event. Although the sleepwalker can perform complex tasks, they are done automatically and without conscious control or purpose. Sleepwalking occurs at least once in 2 to 2.5 percent of the adult population and is virtually universal in young children. While aggression during sleepwalking is rare, it is a well-known phenomenon. However, it has never been known to occur to the same person twice.

Dr. Ervin testified that everyone shifts through stages of sleep cycles. These shifts are no more than the electrochemical reorganization of the brain, akin to putting a new program into a computer, and they are not only usual but are also necessary and healthy. One possible organization of the brain is for the cortex to be in the equivalent of a coma while those parts allowing sensory input and motor skills are active. This physiologic organization of the brain allows automatic movement while asleep (sleepwalking). It is not pathological but, rather, an organization of the brain into which anyone may shift. In cross-examination, Dr. Ervin testified that he did not have or know of a tenable hypothesis to differentiate neurologically between the sleepwalker who has a violent episode and one who does not.

Sleepwalking is more likely to occur in those who are deep sleepers (because sleepwalking occurs out of a deep sleep) and who have a fragmented sleep (because such fragmentation increases the likelihood of a shift in the brain's organization). Thus, through the study of a person and his family, since these personal features are passed genetically, we can determine if a person is more predisposed to sleepwalk than the average person. As well, sleepwalking is part of a cluster of sleep disorders known as parasomnias (sleepwalking, sleep talking, night terrors, and non-infantile enuresis), and a personal and/or family history of parasomnias will indicate a predisposition to sleepwalk.

However, these predisposing factors are not determinative. A person with them may never sleepwalk. Conversely, a person without them may sleepwalk, since the capacity to shift into this state is universal. Certain immediate triggering factors increase the likelihood of a sleepwalking event: those increasing deep sleep (such as sleep deprivation and excessive exercise), and those tending to fragment sleep (stress, alcohol, drugs, noise, pain, or bodily discomfort).

During a sleepwalking event, a sleepwalker cannot think or plan because the cortex of the brain is effectively in a coma—whether the person is in a normal deep sleep or a partial arousal from deep sleep leading to a sleepwalking episode. The person has no motivational mind, and observed behaviour is automatic. Thus, during a sleepwalking episode, because there is no mentation, the sleepwalker has no conscious control over activity. As well, he is unmotivated, unaware of his actions, and not consciously responsive to the environment. Further, it is impossible to plan to sleepwalk or carry out a particular action while sleepwalking before going to sleep.

The Crown tried to push sleepwalking into the insanity category. Dr. Broughton admitted during cross-examination that sleepwalking has occasionally been described as a dissociation state and that it superficially appeared to share certain features with psychosis—such as dissociation from reality, impaired responsiveness, or inability to tell right from wrong. He stated, however, that none of these features were diagnostic of psychosis and that all occur in a large number of medical conditions.

Medical intervention in the treatment of sleepwalking is minimal. People reduce the risk of sleepwalking primarily through sleep hygiene: the reduction of predisposing factors of deep sleep (through proper rest and the avoidance of excessive exercise) and sleep fragmentation (through reduction of stress, consumption of alcohol and noise). Although in some circumstances medication may be administered to induce sleep and thus to reduce sleep deprivation, no in-patient treatment is required for any aspect of sleep hygiene.

All five experts testified that from the perspective of their respective disciplines (neurology, sleep, clinical psychiatry, neuro-psychiatry), sleepwalking was not an organic disease or mental illness. Further, they all testified that it was not in any way likened to organic disease or mental illness, and, in any event, all five testified that Parks did not suffer from any organic disease or mental illness. The Crown called no reply evidence to contradict these opinions.

Furthermore, in Dr. Broughton's opinion, the probability of Parks having another violent somnambulistic episode was "infinitesimal," "not statistically significant," and "absolutely improbable." He stated that for such an episode to occur, there would have to be a recurrence of the constellation of precipitating factors that had occurred in the incident before the court. The only preventive action against the infinitesimal risk that he recommended for Parks was simple sleep hygiene. The Crown called no reply evidence to contradict these opinions.

In concluding that the defence of insanity would not be left to the jury, Justice Watt held:

In the circumstances of the present case, it is doubtful whether the sleep disorder from which the accused suffers would constitute a disease of the mind under s-s. 16(2) in accordance with the general principle. From a medical point of view, the evidence establishes that the disorder is not characterized as a mental illness, disorder or disease of the mind. It is not associated with, casually related to nor derived from any such source. Crown Counsel adduced no evidence to the contrary, although a well-known forensic psychiatrist and, it would appear, a sleep disorder expert, were seated at the counsel table during the testimony of the defence expert. Whilst it is plainly not desirable from the perspective of criminal law policy that exemption from criminal responsibility be extended unreasonably to any and all types of disorder from which an accused may suffer, and, further, that the public be protected by the control and treatment of persons who have caused serious harm whilst in a disordered state, it would not seem consonant with sound criminal law policy to force into the notion "disease of mind," hence legal insanity, and the stigmatization and confinement associated with a special verdict, a person who suffers from a sleep disorder whose behaviour whilst in a awakened state is otherwise socially acceptable. It is no doubt true that proneness to recur is not determinative of whether a condition is or may be a disease of the mind within s-s. 16(2) of the Criminal Code, but, as a matter of criminal law policy, the absence of a recorded instance of recidivistic somnambulistic violence may lend further support to the inappropriateness of characterizing a sleep disorder as a "disease of the mind." It would seem strange to a reasonable person that one who committed what otherwise would be a crime in a somnambulistic state should be stigmatized as insane and subject,

theoretically at least, to indefinite confinement in a psychiatric institution, to receive instruction in good sleep hygiene. It may well seem
equally incomprehensible to a reasonable person that one who kills
in his sleep should not escape all criminal responsibility. There may
be a number of appropriate responses to the legitimate state interest in the control and the treatment of those who have caused serious harm whilst in a somnambulistic state, but mis-characterization
of the disorder as a disease of the mind and the use of the blunt
instrument of indefinite confinement by warrant under special verdict of not guilty by reasons of insanity is not one of them. For these
reasons the jury will be instructed on the defence of non-insane
automatism and not insanity or insane automatism.

After the charge to the jury was completed, the members retired and
deliberated for ten hours. In the evening, they returned a verdict of not guilty.
Ken Parks remained in custody because he had no bail on either his attempted murder charge pertaining to Denis Woods or the $32,000 fraud, which was
still outstanding. However, several days later Parks received bail on both
charges. The wait to see if the Crown would appeal was full of anguish for
both Ken and Karen Parks. By testifying on Ken's behalf during the trial,
Karen had lost the support of most of her family. As a couple, they faced a
long and difficult road to deal with the issues these events had raised. On the
twenty-ninth day, the Crown filed its Notice of Appeal. It was alleged that
Justice Watt erred and should have found that somnambulism was a disease
of the mind, giving rise to the defence of not guilty by reason of insanity. The
prosecution requested that the Court of Appeal substitute a verdict of not
guilty by reason of insanity or, alternatively, order a new trial. At least the factual issue of somnambulism was off the table in the appeal. The question now
was the legal effect of this factual conclusion.

Some weeks later, Park once again appeared before Justice Watt on the
charge of attempted murder. Both the Crown and the defence agreed to apply
the evidence from the earlier trial. Justice Watt entered an acquittal on the
attempted murder charge.

The appeal for Ken Parks's acquittal took a long time to hear. The battle lines were clearly drawn. Did Justice Watt err by refusing to leave the
defence of insanity to the jury? Ought he to have characterized somnambulism as a disease of the mind, a question of law on which he was obliged to

rule? If somnambulism was a disease of the mind, only insanity should have been left to the jury: automatism is subsumed in the defence of insanity if the unconscious and involuntary actions can be traced to or are rooted in a disease of the mind.

It was not without difficulty that the Court of Appeal dismissed the Crown's appeal. The court held that in order for there to be a disease of the mind within section 16 of the *Criminal Code*, there must be a causal link between the illness or the disorder and the abnormal faculties of reason, memory, or understanding. While concluding that Ken Parks's mind was impaired, the court concluded that the evidence overwhelmingly established that the cause of the impairment was sleep. The sleepwalking did not cause the impairment.

The natural tendency to widen the net was resisted, but the Court of Appeal found the result unsettling. Justice Galligan observed:

> This case is extremely troubling. The facts are so extreme that it stretches credulity to think a person could perform all of those apparently deliberate acts over such an extended period of time without volition or consciousness, However, an appellate court must guard against temptation to usurp the jury's function of finding the facts. I must also guard against any temptation to eliminate or limit a defence recognized by law because of the unsympathetic factual context in which the defence is presented for review. Sleepwalking is a category of non-insane automatism, which the law recognizes as a defence entitling an accused to an outright acquittal. There was uncontradicted testimony, which supported the defence in this case. That evidence was either accepted by the members of the jury or at the very least it raised reasonable doubt in their minds. The jury was carefully and accurately instructed in all aspects of the case by the trial judge. The wisdom of the jury's verdict cannot be the subject of the review in this court.

The Crown was granted leave to appeal to the Supreme Court of Canada. The Supreme Court of Canada unanimously confirmed the decision of the Court of Appeal that the trial judge was correct in leaving only the defence of non-insane automatism. Again, this decision was reached with some difficulty by at least two members of the court. Chief Justice Lamer and

Justice Cory, while upholding the acquittal, would have referred the matter back to the trial judge to decide whether to order Ken Parks to enter a common law peace bond, the conditions of which, the chief justice noted, should not violate section 7 of the *Charter of Rights and Freedoms*. The other members of the court declined this invitation, noting a restriction on liberty was incompatible with an acquittal.

Today, Ken Parks resides outside Toronto and is a productive employee, a father, and a husband. He has encountered no further difficulties with the law.

Automatism–Legitimate Defence or Legalized Irresponsibility: *R. v. Joudrie*

NOEL C. O'BRIEN, QC

1998

On January 21, 1995, Dorothy Joudrie, without the slightest suggestion of provocation, reached out towards her estranged husband with a small-calibre handgun and fired six bullets into his body. A year and a half later a jury concluded that Mrs. Joudrie was "not criminally responsible" for the attack. She relied on an extremely controversial defence known as automatism.

As a defence, automatism has a tendency to raise more than controversy. It often gives rise to outright public condemnation and, in some cases, community outrage. This type of reaction may be understandable, given the results of high-profile cases such as *R. v. Parks* and, more recently, *R. v. Joudrie*. When an accused murders or attempts to murder another human being, it no doubt offends the ordinary person's sense of justice to see the admitted perpetrator go free based on what appears to be a simple claim of sleepwalking or disassociation. Indeed, Justice Dickson, in *R. v. Rabey*, admitted to the potential for the defence of automatism to severely strain the credibility of the criminal justice system, particularly in regard to the fact that "automatism as a defence is easily feigned." Automatism has been condemned by some as legalized irresponsibility. Others simply shrug off the defence as an easy way out for those fortunate few who are wealthy enough to buy their own form of justice. Is this cynical view truly justified?

Do lawyers really believe that automatism actually exists, or are we simply feeding off eager psychiatrists who appear more than willing to promote our self-serving theories and satisfy our pursuit of a successful defence for our client? Is the defence of automatism a fraud on the judicial system and the public at large for which lawyers are responsible, or can we justify it on the basis that the defence is, for the most part, simply misunderstood? Do lawyers consciously or subconsciously provide clients with the necessary fodder to feed the psychiatrist with the material to form the foundation for this defence? Is the public correct in its apparent assessment that automatism, as a defence, promotes nothing less than a complete abdication of the require-ment that all citizens bear personal responsibility for their actions? These types of questions arise naturally from cases such as *R. v. Joudrie* in which the defence of automatism is advanced.

There is little question that the jury verdict that Mrs. Joudrie was not criminally responsible for her actions, although applauded by some, was for the most part met with disdain and outrage. With so much criticism, I asked myself why the community reacted this way to a verdict that I found emi-nently fair. Having been defence counsel in almost sixty murder cases, I am neither timid nor reluctant in advancing all legal defences available to my client, no matter how reprehensible the crime. My interest in this case lay more in the possible reasons underlying such an adverse reaction to the Joudrie verdict and the defence of automatism. Was it because the media por-trayed her as a "wealthy socialite" well equipped to buy herself a successful defence? Was it a natural reaction from those who feel that there is a justice system for those who have money and a different one for those who do not? Was it simply because the public was inadequately informed on the legal intri-cacies of a defence that, by its very nature, is complex and difficult to com-prehend even by those who are schooled in both the medical and the legal fields? Or was it because the public is right and the criminal justice system is lax in ensuring that all offenders must be held accountable for their actions?

A taste of the public reaction can be found in the headline of one of Calgary's leading newspapers, which unambiguously read "Outrage" follow-ing the Joudrie verdict. The newspaper claimed that the majority of readers who responded to the newspaper poll considered the case to be a "gross mis-carriage of justice." The *Globe and Mail* stated that the Joudrie verdict "raises issues as to whether there were special systems of justice for the rich and for battered women." Although those who studied the intricacies of the case in more detail sprinkled the editorials with some support, the prevailing automatic reaction was that the defence of automatism was a sham and that the justice system failed.

As is to be expected, gross overstatements appeared in numerous editorials. One commentator in a Calgary newspaper stated, "If you are a member of a predetermined oppressed group, women, natives, gays, whatever, then you can't do anything wrong. Whatever you are charged with, you are innocent." This form of hysteria is not unexpected in controversial cases but, in my view, it does mislead the public on important judicial issues.

Criticism even arose from the most unlikely of sources. One law professor from an Ontario university, for example, suggested that the automatism defence was "symptomatic of an overall trend toward legalized irresponsibility." He went so far as to suggest that this type of defence, along with the *Charter of Rights and Freedoms*, poses a threat to society in that it eventually leads to the loss of the moral authority to punish transgressors. He stated that "this trend leads not to tolerance, but to tyranny." Another legal columnist, a lawyer writing in the *Canadian Lawyer Magazine*, condemned what she perceived to be the court's increasing sympathy for allowing claims of diminished responsibility—a trend that is leading to "general moral abdication."

My purpose in this essay is to consider the adverse comments made on this case in an effort to determine whether some of them have merit. Was Dorothy Joudrie actually in a dissociative state when she shot her husband or was it all a sham? I can never know for sure, and all I can do is to speak of what information was available to me, the psychiatrists, and the court. Each reader will have to decide if this form of defence is founded on valid medical opinions and solid legal principles or, rather, is a deceitful sham.

Despite the evidence of a history of physical and mental abuse towards Mrs. Joudrie, there was no public support from any women's groups or from women in general for my client. Was this because she did not fit within the mythical stereotype of a battered woman, one that typifies such a person as a fragile, economically dependent spouse? Our collective experience in the criminal justice system reminds us that abused women come from all socioeconomic groups and that spousal abuse knows no boundaries. Many women who have successful careers and fall within various age groups, educational backgrounds, and socioeconomic status have fallen victim to abusive relationships. I am not suggesting that Dorothy Joudrie should have been a poster woman for battered women, but I find the apparent lack of understanding of the long-term psychological effects of spousal abuse somewhat troubling. Perhaps, as a result of recent trends in our judicial system to focus on some of these issues, those of us who work in the justice system are, by necessity, exposed to the falsification of many long-standing myths about battered women, while the population at large remains uninformed or uninterested.

On the face of things, Dorothy Joudrie appeared to be self-confident, rich, and well connected to the most powerful people in this country. In public she was vociferous and in control. She was not the type of person we normally perceive as a victim. Perhaps what gave rise to many misconceptions was the inability of the commentators on the trial to have the opportunity to examine this case in the same manner and to the same degree as the jury.

* * *

Dorothy Joudrie was born in 1935 into a middle-class family in Camrose, Alberta. She was extremely close to her gentle and loving father, who was a professor at the University of Alberta. She met her future husband, Earl Joudrie, when she was fifteen years old and fell immediately in love. The two of them dated each other throughout high school and university. They were truly inseparable. She was never to love any other man. On August 17, 1957, Dorothy and Earl were married in Edmonton, Alberta, in a traditional, if not lavish, wedding ceremony. Nobody doubted that Dorothy would honour her vow until death do us part.

Earl was tough, intelligent, and talented. He came from more humble beginnings than Dorothy but was a self-starter and highly motivated. It was apparent to all who knew him that he was destined to be successful in any venture he tackled. He rose through the corporate ranks to become president or chairman of major corporations such as Ashland Oil, Dome Canada, Encore Energy, Algoma Steel, Gulf Canada, Canadian Tire, and others. His resilience and reputation for toughness made me fully aware of the difficult task I would face in cross-examination. I have to say that, overall, Mr. Joudrie earned my respect for the manner in which he faced the opening up of distasteful aspects of his life with Dorothy. Indeed, it was Earl who rejected the RCMP offer to protect him from the hordes of media during the course of the trial, and he faced the issues with which he was confronted head-on in delivering his evidence. In the end, Mr. Joudrie proved to be a very important witness in advancing our defence.

The lives of Dorothy and Earl Joudrie, and their whole family, were opened up for public consumption during the course of the trial. The perfect marriage projected by the couple was anything but. Systematic abuse interspersed with wonderful times resulted in an unusual, if not bizarre, relationship. Any legal analyst might ask the question why, if Dorothy was not acting out in self-defence or provocation, any of the historical episodes of abuse by Earl, most of which were many years in the past, would bear upon any possible issue at the trial? To answer that question, we have to make an attempt to understand how this form of evidence relates to the defence of automatism. In my view, the evidence was not only relevant but crucial to the defence.

The law recognizes that events cannot be examined in a vacuum. The mental state of an accused is of fundamental importance to the degree of criminal liability. Furthermore, this mental state can be significantly affected by past events. Madam Justice Wilson, in *R. v. Lavalee,* stated: "Given the relational context in which the violence occurs, the mental state of an accused at the critical moment she pulls the trigger cannot be understood except in terms of the cumulative effect of months or years of brutality."

Psychiatric studies have now established that battered women typically suffer guilt, yet at the same time deny anger and loathing. According to this theory, these women have been socialized into the belief that they have been doing something wrong to cause their husband to act violently towards them. Although the woman presents a passive face to the world, she experiences enormous amounts of severe stress, anxiety, and anger. Complex psychological reasons, which can be founded on social, economic, and legal issues, explain why a woman remains in an abusive relationship. Typically, cycles of violence are interrupted with contrite and loving behaviour by the abusive spouse, complicating the eventual psychological make-up of the party being abused. Traditionalists, such as Dorothy Joudrie, survive only through living a life of denial and by painting a false image of the marriage to the world. They remain passive, quiet, and even defensive of the marriage at all costs.

In Dorothy Joudrie's case, the psychological and emotional abuse, according to psychiatrists, led to a form of massive denial and repression that ultimately led to a further complication–the use of alcohol. This combination, as the psychiatrists explained, along with other factors to be discussed, ultimately led to a dissociative state, one that supported the defence of automatism.

The evidence at the trial indicated that Earl Joudrie was a jealous man even during their courtship. However, these early signs of hostility and aggression were not enough to deter Dorothy from marrying Earl. Violence in the marriage began to escalate in the 1960s and 1970s. The couple adopted one child, then went on to have three children of their own. Dorothy recounted one episode where she alleged that Earl struck her in the stomach while she was pregnant with her first child.

Earl Joudrie, in his evidence, readily accepted responsibility for many of the acts of violence. Mrs. Joudrie testified to having been hospitalized on three occasions. Her nose had been broken, her eyes had been blackened, and her ribs had been bruised. She testified that on one occasion Earl kicked her while she lay on the ground during an episode that her parents unfortunately witnessed.

Perhaps the most compelling evidence of the abuse in the relationship was given by Elizabeth Griffiths, who moved into the Joudrie household while they were living in Toronto in 1973. Although Dorothy had had no contact with Elizabeth for many years, Ms. Griffiths contacted my office as a result of the wide publicity the Joudrie case had received. I don't think I have ever met a more concerned and honest witness in my career as defence counsel.

It was difficult for Crown counsel to cross-examine Ms. Griffiths on her chilling account of her observations because it was obvious from the manner of her delivery that everything she said was true. Ms. Griffiths lived with the Joudries as a nanny to their four children. She appreciated the warm welcome Dorothy gave her when she moved in. She reflected on Mr. Joudrie's sporadic involvement with his family because of his preoccupation with his upward march through the ranks of the corporate world. Earl himself during cross-examination confirmed this fact by his inability even to remember Ms. Griffiths, who had lived in his household for two years. Ms. Griffiths, in gripping testimony, said that on one occasion she witnessed Earl push Dorothy so hard that he sent her flying over a kitchen chair. Dorothy just picked herself up and tried to proceed as though nothing had happened. She testified about another occasion when Dorothy and the children were at the dinner table and Earl arrived home late. She said that Earl grabbed Dorothy by the hair and dragged her from her chair and into the living room, where he began to beat her. The children were horrified, one of them screaming uncontrollably with his eyes tightly shut. On that occasion, Ms. Griffiths called the police.

However, as was typical at the time, Dorothy refused to press charges against Earl, and the authorities went away.

Earl Joudrie testified that after a violent episode in Ashland, Kentucky, he realized that the acts of brutality would have to stop. In reference to the same incident, Dorothy testified that Earl had come home from a business trip to Europe. He arrived late in the evening on the corporate jet. She said he came into the house with a black look on his face. Her mother and father were visiting at the time. That evening she suffered an intolerable beating to her arms, legs, and ribs. She could not walk up the stairs to her bedroom. She recalled looking up the stairs to see her parents staring down at her. Nothing was said. The next day, Earl arranged for her parents to depart on the private corporate plane, and he took Dorothy to the hospital to have her examined for broken bones. Earl's recognition that this violence had to come to an end was admirable, but it appears that the physical violence was simply replaced by the emotional abuse of violent outbursts of temper and anger. On these occasions he punched holes in the walls and doors. To paraphrase the somewhat ironic view expressed by Mr. Joudrie in his evidence, he did a lot of wall damage, but no Dorothy damage.

However, according to the psychiatrists, the fact of the matter appeared to be the opposite. The emotional abuse led to alcohol dependency for Dorothy Joudrie. Although she was able to involve herself in numerous activities, including the Children's Hospital Aid Society, the Young Naturalist Foundation, and the International Olympic Committee, she took to excessive consumption of alcohol, usually in the privacy of her own home. Even her friends and business associates were unaware of the degree of her alcohol use and were kept in the dark, just as they had been denied information about the violence in the marriage. Whatever damage Dorothy was suffering, she was not allowing even a hint of it to escape, so as to maintain the mythical image of a happy marriage.

Perhaps the most compelling evidence led at the trial of this massive denial came in the guise of the traditional Christmas letter that Dorothy sent to some two hundred friends and relatives around the globe. As she eagerly expressed in these letters, Dorothy and Earl, on the face of things at least, led glamorous lives. Among their friends were a former prime minister, a premier, and the most powerful corporate moguls in America. They made an annual trek to the Kentucky Derby, and they attended numerous social func-

tions in the fast-paced corporate world. These events brought them into contact with an enormous array of associates, and Dorothy continued to corre-
spond with them at least once a year through the Christmas letter.

Even during the most horrific years, when life in the Joudrie household
was described as hell, the Christmas letter always presented a picture that
could only be described as an idyllic life. Each year Dorothy would recount
the achievements of Earl and her children, focusing on how wonderful life
was. The reality, of course, was just the opposite. To make things even worse,
her progressive alcohol dependency fed the denial she was experiencing.

There is no doubt that Dorothy enjoyed being Mrs. Earl Joudrie. An
enormous psychological bond between her and Earl made it devastating for
her when they separated in 1989. Perhaps more devastating than the break-
up itself was the continued contact between them, one that included the
exchange of birthday and Christmas presents and sham appearances at some
social events. This contact led to denial by Dorothy that the marriage could
ever end. She continued to focus on the lifelong dream that she and Earl had
often discussed in the past: to retire and travel the world until death parted
them. This mental state persisted even when Dorothy learned that Earl was
taking a position in Ontario and moving to Toronto. He did not tell her of
this move himself–his secretary informed her.

Despite their separation, during Christmas of 1991 Earl sent a
Christmas card to Dorothy in which he stated, "I really do miss you." Dorothy
continued to cling to the hope that their marriage would never end. Another
crushing blow came shortly after, when she received a birthday card from Earl
in which he announced that he was moving in with Dorothy's young cousin,
Lynne Manning, whom Earl and Dorothy had babysat as a child. It was obvious to any objective on-looker that the marriage had come to an end.
However, at this stage in her life, Dorothy lived in complete denial, and the
prospect of divorce was simply unthinkable. She used the successive weddings
of her children to put off any discussion of divorce with Earl.

During this period, Earl was generous towards Dorothy from a financial
point of view. The financial settlements made Dorothy entirely independent
economically, and she resided in a high-end condominium on an exclusive
golf course. She also owned a nice home in Phoenix, Arizona, where she spent
a good part of the winter months. Indeed, it was her travelling alone to
Phoenix that prompted her to purchase the .25-calibre Berretta, three years

before the shooting. Recent hijackings in California and Arizona of older women travelling alone prompted Dorothy to accept the advice of her friends to purchase the small firearm for her protection. At the trial, there was no serious challenge to the legitimacy of her buying this handgun, for she had obtained the proper documentation and records pursuant to the laws of Arizona. As is routine in Phoenix, she was provided with a brief training course on the use of the firearm and told by the store owner that keeping an unloaded firearm was a useless exercise.

The Crown did not mount any significant challenge to Dorothy's explanation of the way the firearm made its way to Calgary. In the previous year, she said, she forgot to remove it from under the seat of her vehicle before returning home in May from Phoenix. She realized that the gun was there only when she was cleaning the car, which she had sold, and she took it into her condominium. She placed it in a drawer in her bedroom, concealed in a small fanny pack. There it remained untouched until Dorothy retrieved it at some unexplored moment before she shot her husband.

Saturday morning, January 21, 1995, was a brilliantly clear and sunny day. Dorothy went to get her hair done, which was routine for her. She had previously spent some time searching for a document related to the matrimonial home, which Earl had requested for insurance purposes. She was expecting Earl to arrive at her condominium at some point that morning, although no specific time had been agreed upon. Dorothy had located the document of interest for Earl and, in addition, she made a copy of an album of pictures of Earl as a young man, which she thought he might enjoy. More interesting, given what occurred later, she had also organized copies of the Christmas letters provided to their friends over many years and she presented her husband with a nicely bound copy of their wedding photos, taken almost forty years before.

By all accounts, the meeting that morning in Dorothy's condominium between Earl and her was a pleasant one. There was no hostility, and the meeting was quiet and subdued, although Earl expressed his view that there was an air of sadness in the conversation. Earl suggested that Dorothy appeared to be somewhat puzzled by the discussions he had with her regarding the ongoing divorce proceedings. When she asked Earl if he still wanted a divorce, he responded affirmatively. She replied, "I am alone and you have someone." Earl politely refused a second cup of coffee and indicated that he wished to leave, as he had to attend to other commitments.

Dorothy asked Earl to walk out through the door leading into the attached garage, a request that was not entirely uncommon given her pride in the white carpeting leading to the front door. According to the Crown's theory, Dorothy had a much more nefarious purpose in mind. Earl left the kitchen, exiting through the small laundry room, and was stepping down the stairs into the garage when he was suddenly stunned by what he described as a "whack across his back which felt like a shovel or a 2 x 4." As he fell to the ground, he turned to face Dorothy, who was now armed with a .25-calibre Berretta handgun. She fired two more shots into him before he even hit the floor. She calmly walked up to him and shot him three more times. During one of those shots, she bent over him and placed the gun approximately one inch above his chest near his heart and fired. Miraculously, the bullet deflected off a rib and penetrated his shoulder. For reasons explicable only by good fortune, Earl not only survived but never even lost consciousness. Dorothy had one bullet left in the Berretta. She didn't use it.

Where did the gun come from? When did she retrieve it from the bedroom? How was it readily available? Dorothy consistently claimed she had no recollection. Was the obvious retrieval of the firearm at some point before the shooting consistent with the defence of automatism? Some of the media criticized the Crown for not being more emphatic in exploring this issue at the trial during cross-examination. The questions, if asked, would no doubt have raised some problematic issues on the applicability of automatism, but I doubt that Dorothy Joudrie could have provided the Crown with answers. Earl Joudrie was not asked whether Dorothy had followed him directly from the kitchen, or whether she had the opportunity to go to the bedroom to get the gun during the time it took for his short walk to the steps leading to the attached garage. It remains one of the more perplexing questions left unanswered by the trial.

Ironically, the fact that Earl survived the incident and never lost consciousness strengthened the defence of automatism. Earl, despite having been shot six times, was somehow able to talk Dorothy back into reality. Remarkably calm, Earl spoke to Dorothy with some admonishment while at the same time avoiding further incitement. His clear recollection of the events after the shooting was one of the most fascinating elements of this trial. Earl described Dorothy as "calm" and "almost detached." He described her tone of voice as being one he had never heard in their forty years of marriage. Her demeanour was "cold and controlled," he said, and "like a person I had never known." He recalled vividly that Dorothy displayed no emotion in the way she spoke, almost as though she were "a person speaking from another place." He described the dialogue he had with her after the shooting as a "weird conversation." Dorothy never expressed rage but, rather, a peculiar calmness. With unprecedented coldness, she spoke of Earl's last will and testament in response to his plea for aid. She told him that she would load him up into the car and, in her words, "dump you off in a ditch someplace." She asked but one question: "How long is it going to take you to die?" It remains unclear whether Dorothy was aware that another bullet remained in the gun she held in her hand.

Whether prompted by Earl's persistent demands for help or by an inexplicable reversal of emotions, Dorothy appeared to come out of her state with the words, "Oh my God, what have I done?" Earl described her as having a "new voice, more like Dorothy's voice, plaintive and frightened." Dorothy followed all of Earl's instructions regarding telephoning 9-1-1. The 9-1-1 calls were taped by the police and were consistent with the fact that she had no knowledge she had shot him. She was unable to describe where he had been shot or how many times. In several calls made to 9-1-1, Dorothy expressed her characteristic impatience in berating the paramedics for their delay in arriving at her residence: "He's going to die if they don't get here," she stated. The ambulance personnel would not enter without the police, the police would not enter without back-up, and Earl was dying in the meantime. At some point Dorothy replaced the handgun in her dresser drawer in the bedroom and cleaned up some of the expended cartridges from the floor of the garage. She was unable to recall these actions.

The police officers who arrived at the scene described Dorothy Joudrie as "disorientated" and indicated that "she didn't seem to comprehend the questions immediately at the time." She seemed to be "just wandering." One experienced police officer testified that she had the "air of someone who had suffered or experienced a traumatic event" and was far from a normal person. When asked what had happened, Dorothy simply responded that her husband had told her not to say anything to the police. The police told Dorothy that the calibre of the firearm could be important information for the paramedics treating Earl, so she quietly led an officer to the gun hidden in her bedroom.

In the meantime, a paramedic asked Earl, "Have you been shot?" Indeed, he had, and Earl was hurriedly dispatched by an air ambulance helicopter to a local Calgary hospital. He remained hospitalized for eighteen days and, on discharge, left with four of the bullets remaining in his body. As Earl was being flown to the hospital, Dorothy was arrested and taken into custody by the RCMP. They brought her to a detachment office in Cochrane, a small community just west of Calgary. Her daughter Carolyn arrived at the detachment and described her mother as being a "different person." She testified that there was a "kind of calm about her" that was almost "surreal." Carolyn was upset at her mother's apparent indifference about the near killing of her father, evident in Dorothy's concern over her ability to attend some upcoming social events. In my view, Dorothy had not even begun to appreciate the enormity of the situation, and her reactions were entirely consistent with the defence we ultimately advanced.

Within a few hours of the shooting, Dorothy Joudrie's divorce lawyer, Ron Foster, contacted me. It was an unusually warm Saturday in January, and I was reluctant to abandon some planned leisure time to respond to another shooting. My career to date had involved several major criminal investigations, many of which had achieved a very high profile. Nothing, however, prepared me for the onslaught of attention that the media focused on this case.

When I arrived at the RCMP detachment a few hours after the shooting, I was met by what appeared to me to be a white-haired, grandmotherly woman who seemed emptied of emotion and very much out of place. Dorothy was a far cry from the typical person lawyers meet in those circumstances. I immediately noted that she was calm, somewhat aloof, and breathing heavily. At this point I was totally unaware of the complexity of her psychological make-up.

The first remarkable feature was her apparent lack of memory of the shooting. As defence counsel, we have all heard this claim before and we approach it with some degree of scepticism. However, her calm disbelief of the predicament she found herself in reinforced the credibility of her claim. She exhibited an enormous degree of genuineness in asking a police officer who was present, "Why can't I remember?"

The second remarkable feature of my initial interview with Mrs. Joudrie was the revelation of spousal abuse. Dorothy's divorce lawyer was present during the course of our meeting. I asked her outright whether she had ever been abused by Earl. Her positive response caused her divorce lawyer to gasp in surprise. Although he had dealt with her for the past five years in representing her interests in the divorce proceedings, including numerous motions before the courts, it was the first time that she had revealed to him the litany of abuse that would be confirmed in subsequent proceedings. Before this stage in her life, Dorothy had not confided in anyone, even her closest friends, that she had been subjected to spousal abuse. I recall a surprised Mr. Foster seeking confirmation of this revelation from some of the Joudrie children who were beginning to arrive at the police detachment. At this early point in my defence of Mrs. Joudrie, I still did not appreciate the significance of the peculiar form of massive denial she suffered and how it might bear on my subsequent defence. Despite the revelation of previous spousal abuse, it was readily apparent that the shooting episode with which I was dealing was not precipitated by any immediate act of violence on the part of Earl Joudrie.

My immediate attention was directed towards Dorothy's state of mind, and I requested that the RCMP perform a breathalyzer test to measure any possible alcohol consumption. Some three hours after the shooting, the alcohol level in Dorothy's blood was approximately 40 milligrams, which was not enough for a viable defence of drunkenness but sufficient to raise questions in my mind, considering that the shooting took place early on Saturday morning. It was clear I had only begun to scratch the surface of this very complex woman.

Much of the public reaction to the final verdict of not being criminally responsible focused on the suggestion that there was a justice system for the wealthy that differed from the justice system provided to the less fortunate. In some respects, this suspicion proved true. Dorothy had sufficient wealth to enable her to afford the necessary medical assessments required to advance her extremely complicated defence. I must concede that our justice system provides an advantage to those who can afford it. However, Dorothy did not buy justice. She was merely in a financial position to obtain the type of justice every citizen of this country should be able to get. It didn't take me long to realize that, to assist this woman who just put six bullets into the body of her husband, I would need a detailed examination by a number of psychiatrists of a bizarre forty-year relationship. There is no question that because Mrs. Joudrie was in a position to afford such a full and complete assessment, her chances of success in the defence of the charges against her, through the use of the defence of automatism, were advanced.

Before we submitted Mrs. Joudrie to a battery of psychiatric and psy-chological assessments, I felt we had to tackle three fundamental issues. First, it was necessary to have her released immediately on bail. To accomplish that, we were able to hire our own psychiatrist to make a quick assessment to sat-isfy the Crown that she could be released into the community without further risk. I met with the Joudrie children the day after the shooting and we worked out a set of reasonable conditions for her release that the prosecutor might accept. It worked. The following day in provincial court, where Dorothy faced formal charges of attempted murder and using a firearm in the commission of an offence, the court agreed to her release.

With Dorothy's release from jail accomplished, the second important issue that had to be dealt with immediately was the issue of alcohol depend-ency. Again, because of her financial situation, Mrs. Joudrie was able to attend the Betty Ford Clinic in California for a period of twenty-eight days. Although the defence of automatism did not loom large in my mind at this early stage, it was evident that any form of success in Dorothy's defence would necessitate sobriety on her part. Her stay at the clinic proved pivotal in her subsequent success in abstaining from alcohol.

The third pressing issue that had to be dealt with immediately was her divorce from Earl Joudrie. For the past five years, Mrs. Joudrie would not con-sider the prospect of divorce, conjuring up new delay tactics at every turn. She could not face it in the past, but her newly found legal predicament demand-ed a quick and decisive break from Earl. The divorce went through almost immediately.

Mrs. Joudrie was then faced with the prospect of a number of psychi-atric assessments, to which she willingly submitted. The first was with Dr. Lenor Walker, the renowned author of *The Battered Woman*. In order to make sense of Dorothy's state of mind at the time of the shooting, it was important for me to understand the long-term effects of mental and physical abuse and how they would contribute to the degree of stress, anxiety, and denial of the accused. This assessment proved to be most important for the existence of a dissociative state, one that ultimately led to the defence of "automatism."

The result of the assessment was clear. Dorothy was a battered woman in every sense of that term. One thing, however, concerned me. Dr. Walker, using her expertise from her studies of spousal abuse, attempted to put a self-defence spin on the circumstances of the actual shooting. I could not agree. This case was not self-defence, and I was convinced that any attempt to make it so would result in miserable failure. No reasonable jury would have accepted that Dorothy had any apprehension of danger to herself, real or imagined, when she shot Earl. In my opinion, Dorothy's mental state was a great deal more complex than that. There was nothing in her recounting of the events or the information provided to me that indicated she had an apprehension of violence at the time of the incident. Indeed, the evidence indicated quite the opposite. I would not attempt to advance self-defence because it was doomed to failure.

In medical terms, a dissociative state is a disruption in the brain of the normal integration of activities such as memory, awareness, and response to the environment. Conscious awareness is eliminated to such a degree that it cannot be said that a person's actions are voluntary. Dissociative state is a medical term, not a legal one. It is this medical state, however, that can lead to a legal state of automatism by creating doubt that the accused's acts were voluntary, which, in turn, may result in a finding of non-culpability.

Although Dorothy was always consistent in her lack of recollection of the actual shooting, it was the evidence that began to surface at the preliminary inquiry that gave birth to the real prospect that this case could be a legitimate one of automatism. Self-reported memory loss by those charged with serious crimes is nothing new, and that standing alone provided little basis for hope of a successful defence. However, when Earl Joudrie described the events in the manner discussed earlier, it became apparent that this case did not simply concern an accused not wishing to remember her crime. The various accounts of the police observations fuelled the focus towards the defence of automatism.

After her release, Dorothy began to receive therapy from a Calgary psychiatrist, Dr. Alan Weston. He concluded that although she suffered from no formal mental disorder or psychotic illness, she appeared to have been living a life of massive denial, particularly as it related to her marriage. In Dr. Weston's view, corroborated by the evidence led at the preliminary inquiry, Mrs. Joudrie suffered from a dissociative state that rendered her incapable of engaging in the voluntary and conscious act of shooting her husband.

I wanted further back-up for that opinion, so I searched out the most able psychiatrist I could find. I knew of Dr. Roy O'Shaughnessy by reputation as a well-respected psychiatrist in Vancouver, BC. He met with Dorothy and, after a detailed study of the evidence, the witness statements, and psychiatric tests, we had our supporting assessment. His confidence and intellectual approach on the witness stand would prove invaluable to the defence. A valiant attempt by the Crown to cross-examine him proved fruitless.

The evidence led at trial disposed of some of the myths around a dissociative state. This condition can occur in both normal people and those with a mental illness. In addition, purposeful or goal-orientated behaviour does occur during the course of a dissociative state. Obtaining a firearm and shooting her husband were not inconsistent with Dorothy Joudrie being in this mental state. Another myth was destroyed by the evidence of Dr. O'Shaughnessy, who testified that memories of things previous to a dissociative state are not lost during the state itself. In other words, Dorothy would have known where the gun was in order to retrieve it. The evidence of the psychiatrists indicated that a dissociative state is usually accompanied by inappropriate mood and calm detachment as opposed to excitement. The onset of the dissociative state by a precipitating event is rapid, and the offset is more gradual. Partial or complete memory loss may occur during that state. There is a complete lack of awareness of one's actions.

Public scepticism of such a state of mind was not unexpected. The evidence led on the issue was detailed and complex. The jury was given a great deal of detail from the psychiatrists relating to the elements they look for in order to become convinced that a person suffered a dissociative state. The psychiatric opinion was not based on simple self-reporting. A psychiatrist must ask whether the diagnosis makes clinical sense by looking at the individual psychological make-up of the accused. Was there a potential precipitating event that caused the dissociative state? Was there any predisposition to the occurrence of a dissociative state? What were the psychological make-up, patterns of behaviour, and background history of the accused? A legitimate assessment of the accused's credibility or deceitfulness assists the psychiatrist in coming to his opinion. Most important, the psychiatrist must consider the observations before, during, and after the event by other parties who may have witnessed the accused at or near the time of the event.

Dr. O'Shaugnessy expressed the view that the psychological predisposition for a dissociative state existed in Dorothy Joudrie because of her massive denial. She never came to accept the enormous dysfunction in the marriage. She was a traditionalist who, despite a cycle of violence, led a life denying the abusive relationship. He indicated that her identity became that of Mrs. Earl

Joudrie and that it was clear to him that the theme represented in the Christmas letters sent out each year was radically different from the reality of the marriage. Her denial continued right up until the shooting of January 21, 1995. He said the excessive and addictive consumption of alcohol simply encouraged and fed the denial. In his opinion, an enormous reservoir of emotions was built up as a result of this denial, which prevented Dorothy from addressing any of these issues. This reservoir included resentment, hurt, anger, sadness, stress, and anxiety. These emotions went unrecognized throughout the marriage, and the use of alcohol helped her avoid resolving the many issues she should have been facing in life.

Dr. O'Shaughnessy explained to the jury that although an emotional outburst might be expected from someone with such a history, the real paradox supporting the dissociative state was her calm detachment in the shooting of Mr. Joudrie. Dr. O'Shaughnessy thought that the decades of denial collided head-on with the final realization, on January 21, 1995, that the marriage was over, yet her emotions remained inconsistent with the event of the shooting itself. There simply was no outpouring of rage.

Although recent amendments to the *Criminal Code* have frowned on the distinction between insane automatism and non-insane automatism, it is essential to the defence of automatism to understand the difference between the legal implications for an accused person whose dissociative state is precipitated by a mental disorder and one that results from some other means. Section 16 of the *Criminal Code* no longer deals with terminology such as insanity. An accused person who is incapable of appreciating the nature and quality of his acts or of knowing that it was wrong by virtue of his suffering from a mental disorder is now found not criminally responsible. If a dissociative state that leads to an automatism defence is based on a mental disorder, the verdict is properly not criminally responsible under section 16. If, however, the dissociative state can somehow fall outside the scope of a mental disorder–for example, from a concussion or a blow to the head–then the accused is to be acquitted outright. A mental disorder is defined in the *Criminal Code* under section 2 as a disease of the mind. This definition raises issues of law on which psychiatrists are reluctant to engage. A psychiatrist may venture an opinion on the psychiatric state of the accused, but it is up to the trial judge to determine if that evidence, as a matter of law, will support a finding of a disease of the mind for the purpose of section 16 of the *Criminal*

Code. This system led to a number of complexities in the Joudrie case. Under what category should her case fall? Would the trial judge be open to putting both categories of automatism to the jury?

In the months leading up to the trial, we made no attempt to keep the fact that our defence would be one of automatism secret from the Crown. In fact, we made it known to the prosecution. I sensed that the Crown view of the defence was akin to the opinion of one Lord Justice in the House of Lords who stated: "Automatism is nothing more than a quagmire relied upon rarely and only by those in desperate need of a defence." Despite the misgivings, it remains a defence that required some response from the prosecution to prove that Mrs. Joudrie had an operating mind at the time of the shooting. I confess to being somewhat surprised that the Crown's psychiatrist did not get involved until late in the game. A few days before the trial was set to commence, we received a request from the Crown to present Mrs. Joudrie to their psychiatrist, Dr. Arboleda-Florez, for assessment so they could obtain their own opinion as to whether she suffered from a dissociative state at the time of the shooting. This request caused us to consider the pros and cons associated with such a demand. Should we present Mrs. Joudrie, who was suffering from significant anxiety before the trial, to the Crown psychiatrist for assessment? A refusal could have a devastating effect on the credibility of the defence. Although Mrs. Joudrie's refusal to comply with the Crown request, as a matter of law, could not result in an adverse inference being drawn against her, the reality of the situation was entirely different.

In *R. v. Stevenson,* the court held that the jury, in assessing the Crown's expert evidence opinion, could properly consider the refusal of the accused to discuss the offence with the Crown's expert. Under these circumstances, we opted to allow the belated assessment. I believe any other decision would have had disastrous results. I would rather be in the position of cross-examining the Crown psychiatrist on a conflicting opinion than give the jury the appearance that our defence could not withstand any scrutiny. In retrospect, I believe our strategy of being completely open with the Crown's office worked to our advantage.

With understandable anxiety, just one day before the jury was to be selected for her trial, Dorothy submitted herself to an intensive and exhaustive assessment by the Crown psychiatrist. The trial was scheduled to proceed on Monday, April 27, 1996. On the Sunday afternoon, literally only hours before the trial commenced, I was provided with a four-page report from Dr. Arboleda-Florez, which was non-committal on the issue of automatism. Although the doctor's opinion did not provide overt support for the opinions we had obtained from our own psychiatrist, it did not directly contradict those assessments either. Dr. Arboleda-Florez was clearly sitting on the fence. He had decided to reserve any conclusive opinion until he heard the testimony of our experts, Dorothy, and the other witnesses who had come in contact with her at or near the time of the shooting. His indecision must have created an impossible dilemma for the Crown as the trial began.

The following morning, the Crown counsel, Jerry Selinger, opened to the jury with the assertion that Mrs. Joudrie purchased a firearm well in advance of the shooting and planned to kill Mr. Joudrie because he had left her for her younger cousin. There is no question that, in the opinion of the Crown, the dissociative state argument was a sham to hide her true resolve and intent. The Crown had hopes that Dr. Arboleda-Flores would eventually discount the automatism defence once he had the opportunity to study the evidence yet to be led before the jury. Nevertheless, the Crown had an expert witness who was not committing himself as to whether Mrs. Joudrie acted with volition in her attack on her husband. As defence counsel, I could not have asked for a better way to start the trial.

Dr. Arboleda-Florez was permitted to remain in the courtroom, along with the other experts, to hear not only the psychiatric evidence of Dr. O'Shaughnessy and Dr. Weston but also the evidence of Dorothy Joudrie herself. The case for the Crown deteriorated when Dr. Arboleda-Florez announced that, after hearing the testimony, he agreed with the assessment that Mrs. Joudrie was in a dissociative state. However, he ventured further and opined that her mental state was probably the result of a mental disorder, perhaps a result of organic brain damage due to alcohol consumption. This turn of events clearly gave the defence an enormous advantage because we were able to argue an either/or proposition for a full acquittal or for a "not criminally responsible" verdict. It placed the Crown counsel in a contradictory position because his primary prosecution held that there was no dissociative state whatsoever, yet his own medical expert opinion discounted that argument. Mr. Selinger startled me, however, with his announcement that he had decided not to call Dr. Arboleda-Florez as a witness in the trial. Needless to say, I was disappointed by this news. It was my belief that the Crown had an ethical obligation to present this evidence before the jury even though it did not support his own case, particularly since Dorothy had complied with the Crown's request to be examined by his expert. The Crown certainly had no argument to advance that this witness was not credible or reliable and, in my view, he had a duty to produce him. After considerable discussion, Mr. Selinger, who I have always known as a prosecutor with the highest degree of ethics, changed his mind and placed the Crown psychiatrist on the stand.

The defence was now in the enviable position of simply maintaining that this was a case of automatism simplicities, which must either be disproved by the Crown or lead to an acquittal. We could remain comfortable as we observed the Crown advance contradictory theories that Dorothy Joudrie made a well-planned attempt to execute Earl or, alternatively, on a balance of probabilities, that she suffered from a mental disorder. The result was an extremely complex jury charge on these issues which I believe worked to our advantage.

After a lengthy but well-balanced and fair charge to the jury by Mr. Justice Arthur Lutz, the case lay in the hands of an eleven-woman, one-man jury. I have been questioned many times over the constitution of the jury, which to an objective observer clearly appeared to be stacked with women. However, as any person schooled in jury selection knows, the defence and the Crown had an equal number of peremptory challenges (twelve in this case). Did we want more women than men on the jury and, if so, how did we get such a high number of female jurors selected to hear the trial?

There is no question that I wished to have as many women on the jury as possible. I used all my peremptory challenges to ensure that the first six persons on the jury were women, so I had at least an equal balance. Mere chance then took over and added five more women to the jury. Without any empirical data to support my thinking, my previous jury trial experience has led me to believe that women make better jurors. I am convinced that women jurors will approach the issues at hand with open-minded, rational thinking, directed towards achieving justice as defined by the law. The public reaction to the verdict may well have proved wrong my theory that women would be more sympathetic towards Mrs. Joudrie than men. Nevertheless, at the time I was delighted to have the jury composed almost entirely of women.

The jury was sequestered for two nights to agree on a verdict. Given the amount of media attention surrounding the verdict, the jury must have faced an enormous degree of pressure in its deliberations. Up until the sequestration of the jury at the end of the trial, the jurors were exposed to press reports and editorials that, for the most part, demanded accountability and personal responsibility for acts of violence. Indeed, just days before the jury was to commence its deliberations, the *Calgary Herald* ran a front-page story focused on the accomplishments of Earl Joudrie in the corporate world, followed with a litany of accolades from people ranging from the former premier of Alberta to other well-known and accomplished businessmen. I thought it in poor taste, considering the timing of the story.

Despite it all, the jury returned its verdict of not criminally responsible. Clearly, the jury accepted the fact that Dorothy had slipped into a state of disassociation at the time of the shooting and had not been acting in a conscious manner. Although the verdict might be tantamount to a not guilty verdict, it was somewhat qualified by the legal requirement that she submit herself for assessment before the Alberta Board of Review. This board is designed and constituted under the *Criminal Code* to ensure that the safety of the community is not compromised.

As in most cases, it was easy to be an armchair critic about the verdict, and there was no shortage of those willing to express their opinion on the Joudrie verdict. However, none of these people were in the position of the jurors, who had the detailed circumstances of this very complex case placed before them.

One juror spoke to the media in response to the public sentiment expressed by the majority and explained that the jury members did not come to a hasty judgement but, rather, spent a considerable amount of time thinking about the appropriate verdict. She found that the comments from the street were difficult to understand. I felt a great deal of empathy for her and the other jurors, who were presented with a difficult task and then second-guessed by those who offered opinions with little understanding of the evidence or the law.

I believe that the reaction of the majority to the not criminally responsible verdict demonstrates that the public is generally misinformed on legal principles, misunderstands the underlying facts of the case, and mistrusts the justice system. Even the people who supported the judgment seemed to do so for the wrong reasons. The verdict had nothing to do with revenge for past wrongs to Mrs. Joudrie. The vast majority of expressed opinion held that the verdict ought to be condemned for promoting a disregard for personal responsibility. But is that criticism really justified?

The defence of automatism has arisen more frequently in recent judicial history because of advances made in the study of psychiatry. In *R. v. K.*, the defence was defined as follows: "Automatism is a term used to describe unconscious, involuntary behaviour, the state of a person who, though capable of action, is not conscious of what he is doing. It means an unconscious, involuntary act where the mind does not go with what is being done."

By its very nature, the defence prompted calls for policy considerations in its application, not only because it was new to the justice system but also because it appeared to create an easy escape from personal responsibility. Such a concern was voiced by Justice Dickson in *R. v. Rabey*: "There are undoubtedly policy considerations to be considered. Automatism as a defence is easily feigned. It is said the credibility of our criminal justice system will be severely strained if a person who has committed a violent act is allowed an absolute acquittal on a plea of automatism arising from a psychological blow." Although automatism is very much an evolving defence, the Alberta Court of Appeal in *R. v. Honish* held that broadening the scope of the defence must address not only the medical components involved but also the policy components. In other words, it involves addressing personal responsibility along with the other underlying principles of criminal law.

In my view, the courts and Parliament have attended in a balanced way to the often-competing principles of law that underlie this defence. Automatism holds a unique position in our law in that, in many respects, it is not a defence per se. As a general rule, the Crown must prove both *mens rea* (intent) and *actus reus* (action) to obtain a conviction for a criminal offence. The *actus reus* of an offence means that the action was a voluntary one, made with conscious volition. The onus is on the Crown to prove that the act of the accused was a voluntary one. One of the fundamental principles of justice is that the aim of criminal law is to punish only those persons who can be described as morally blameworthy. The law should not punish those who are without fault. At the same time, another well-recognized goal of our justice system holds that the purpose and function of the law are directed towards the protection of the public. In some instances, and in particular cases involving the defence of automatism, these principles may appear to conflict and compete with each other.

Automatism is a legal term, not a medical one. It is behaviour performed in a state of mental unconsciousness without full awareness and with the absence of volition. In my view, the law attempts to recognize that the state of mind leading to automatism may have been precipitated by the accused himself through some fault of his own and, as such, different considerations should apply for policy reasons to give effect to the requirement of personal responsibility. Mistaken public perception on the defence of automatism arises from the mistaken belief that the law somehow ignores the issue of whether the accused contributed to the mental state giving rise to the defence.

There appear to be three recognized categories of automatism, all of which will result in different verdicts based on the personal responsibility of the offender. They can be categorized as follow:

- *Automatism without mental disorder:* If a person is in a dissociative state which is not precipitated by a mental disorder or disease of the mind and which has not been precipitated through his own fault by either self-inducing the state or through his negligence, then the offender is entitled to a full acquittal. An obvious example is a person who suffers from a concussion and commits a criminal act without volition.

- *Automatism with mental disorder:* In this category, the state of mind is precipitated by a disease of the mind, as interpreted by the law. There may be a lack of fault or moral blameworthiness attached to the factors that precipitated the automatism, but the law, through legislation, recognizes its obligation towards the protection of the public. In this regard, the verdict of acquittal is qualified and described as not criminally responsible. The focus of the legislation under the Criminal Code is to ensure that the offender does not present a significant threat to the community. The Criminal Code provides for the process of treatment and possible eventual reintegration into the community.

- *Self-induced automatism:* The common law has long recognized that self-induced acts leading to a state of automatism will not lead to a full acquittal. This point was made by Justice LaForest in *R. v. Parks*, adopting a previous statement of Justice Dickson in *R. v. Rabey:* "In principle, the defence of automatism should be available whenever there is evidence of unconsciousness throughout the commission of the crime that cannot be attributed to fault or negligence on his part."

Whether any self-induced state, such as voluntary intoxication, that leads to a state of mind akin to automatism should ever be a defence to general intent offences was the subject of an interesting debate in *R. v. Daviault,* where the common law rule was somewhat altered. This change was met immediately with a legislative response that, for the most part, eliminated such a defence.

Overall, the law has attempted to address issues of personal responsibility in the evolving defence of automatism. Considering the three categories of automatism outlined above, different verdicts would result from the same act of an accused based almost entirely on the issue of his or her personal responsibility. For example, if an accused person attacked his neighbour and was subsequently charged with an assault, he would be fully acquitted if the evidence established that his actions were involuntary because of automatism caused by a concussion. If the automatism resulted from a psychotic episode, however, the verdict would be one of not criminally responsible, pursuant to section 16 of the *Criminal Code.* The accused would not stand convicted, though provisions are in place to protect the safety of the community. Finally, if the accused was in a state of mind akin to automatism precipitated by gross intoxication due to voluntary consumption of alcohol, both common law and section 33.1 of the *Criminal Code* would negate the defence. Clearly the law attempts to address the need for personal responsibility in balancing the application and availability of the defence of automatism. In my view, the criticism directed towards the verdict and the law in general is misguided because of its failure to consider these distinctions.

The most difficult task facing a jury, or a judge alone, is not so much understanding the difference among the categories of automatism but determining which category applies to the accused in the case. Many variables are involved in determining what precipitated the state of mind leading to the involuntary behaviour of the accused, and these questions are difficult to answer.

In the case of Dorothy Joudrie, some would argue that her state of mind was precipitated by her own voluntary decision to consume alcohol and, through a series of free choices, she became the author of her own psychological make-up. At the trial, however, it was argued that the external actions of her husband, Earl Joudrie, over decades of abuse, precipitated her ultimate state of mind, leading to the defence of automatism. The issues become even more complicated in determining whether the automatism arose as a result of a disease of the mind, and should therefore be dealt with under section 16 of the *Criminal Code,* or whether it falls within the category previously described as non-insane automatism. The consequences flowing from the various verdicts are, of course, entirely different.

In Dorothy Joudrie's case, the trial judge put both options to the jury. If they rejected the Crown theory that Dorothy was acting out a pre-formed intent to kill Earl and found that she was indeed in a dissociative state at the time of the shooting, then they would have to determine what verdict was appropriate, having regard to the evidence before them. If her unusual state arose from a form of psychological blow or from a mental disorder, then they were to bring back a verdict of not criminally responsible under section 16 of the *Criminal Code.* If they concluded that there was no mental disorder, then she would be entitled to a full acquittal.

In cases such as these, complexities arise before a jury because disease of the mind and mental disorder are legal rather than medical concepts. Imported into the definition of disease of the mind are not only the medical components, which often change from day to day, but also policy components added into the equation by the courts. The courts use analytical tools to determine whether the accused was suffering from a disease of the mind. In *R. v. Rabey*, the court appeared to favour the use of what has been called the "internal/external theory," one based on generalized conclusions as to whether the state of mind was precipitated by the internal psychological make-up of the accused or by some external source that resulted in the state of automatism. Another form of analysis used in attempting to define what a "disease of the mind" might include is the "prone to recur" test, which focuses on whether the state of mind that led to violence is likely to occur again. This method concerns itself with the likelihood of a continuing danger to society. The general trend since *R. v. Parks* is to consider these tests as analytical tools only and to determine, on a case-by-case basis, whether the particular state of mind in the case before the court amounts to a disease of the mind.

In Dorothy Joudrie's case, I can only speculate as to the daunting task it was for the jury to apply the complexities of these definitions, along with the differing and opposing burdens of proof attached to them. We can only surmise that the jury relied on the application of common sense.

When the jury returned a verdict of not criminally responsible for Mrs. Joudrie, we were elated. Because she had been released from custody since her charge, and the presiding trial judge, after the verdict, had no hesitation in permitting her simply to go the Alberta Hospital Edmonton on a voluntary basis for assessment, we anticipated an uneventful assessment by the Provincial Board of Review.

Part XX.1 of the *Criminal Code* is a legislative response to a recent criticism by the Supreme Court of Canada of the treatment of people previously found not guilty by reason of insanity. It recognizes that the accused has been found not criminally responsible and goes to great lengths to secure the liberty and dignity of the person. Interim release orders in effect at the time of the verdict remain in effect until a board of review makes a disposition. The *Criminal Code* provides that the board must hold a hearing within forty-five days of the verdict to determine whether the party is not a significant threat to the safety of the public. If such an opinion can be made, the party must be absolutely discharged from the jurisdiction of the board and may carry on as any other acquitted person. If such an opinion cannot be made, the party is entitled to the least onerous and least restrictive disposition available, which normally comes in the form of a conditional discharge. Detention in a psychiatric facility is, by law, clearly a last resort reserved for those who truly pose a danger to others. The judicial pronouncements to date on this new legislation confirm that these provisions are neither penal in purpose or effect nor geared towards retribution. In addition, these sections of the *Criminal Code* do not place any practical burden on the accused to establish entitlement to an absolute discharge. Although the purpose of the new legislation dealing with those who have been found not criminally responsible is well meaning in its focus, the vagueness attached to it creates some legitimate concerns that have prompted constitutional challenges in our courts. Frankly stated, and for this reason, my experience before the Alberta Board of Review in this case was less than satisfying. Indeed, it gave rise to considerable concerns on my part.

As lawyers, we are used to the adversarial process and have become accustomed to, and perhaps even take for granted, the independence and impartiality of the courts. There is consistency in the rules of evidence and in the application of procedure. Although I can understand the need for an informal process where circumstances permit in matters before the Alberta Board of Review, I was disappointed by the apparent lack of rules or regulations on practice and procedure before the board. The *Criminal Code* provided the authority to the board to create such rules, yet nothing of this nature exists to promote consistency in its hearings.

Mrs. Joudrie attended the Alberta Hospital Edmonton on her own volition and spent approximately two weeks cooperating in extensive testing and assessments. The matter came before the Board of Review on May 2, 1996. To my surprise, we were met with a position by the hospital that Dorothy be kept there for further assessment. In my view, this stay was unnecessary, particularly as this form of assessment could easily have been done on an out-patient basis. By this point, Dorothy had completed the Betty Ford program and was in regular attendance at Alcoholics Anonymous. She was being counselled by a respected psychologist and, despite the pressures of the trial, was well on the road to a healthy lifestyle. Her experience in the Alberta Hospital Edmonton quickly undid the progress she had worked so hard to maintain.

During the in-patient assessment procedure, Mrs. Joudrie received no treatment whatsoever. The psychiatric assessment was extremely confrontational, and staff members of the hospital appeared to have their own agenda. The psychiatrist assigned to Dorothy's case immediately challenged the verdict of the jury because of her scepticism of the defence. It quickly became apparent to me that Dorothy would have to fight to get released from the hospital. There is no question that politics played a major role in the treatment of Mrs. Joudrie, and we had to hire a plethora of our own psychiatrists to rebut the strange and subsequently refuted diagnosis originally presented before the Board of Review. For example, the hospital team would make a clinical diagnosis suggesting various disorders, and, in turn, Dorothy's own doctors would challenge the diagnosis. Then the hospital's diagnosis would not be mentioned again. Diagnoses such as hypomania, narcissistic personality disorder, and organic brain disorder all retreated as quickly as they were advanced. My personal confidence in anything the hospital team put forward was absolutely shattered.

Some recent case law suggests that the review hearings following a not criminally insane verdict are non-adversarial. I am at a loss to understand that view. The hospital wished to have the board confine Dorothy, and she wished to retain her liberty. The very nature of the differing positions necessitated an adversarial process. It was clear to Dorothy at least that the hospital did not have her best interests in mind. Given that the liberty of the patient was at risk, there appeared to be no safeguards to protect her against infringements of her liberty. We were met with a complete lack of disclosure of anything meaningful: none of the evidence before the board was given under oath, personality conflicts between Mrs. Joudrie and some of the staff appeared to play an unnecessary role in opinions being provided, and considerable hearsay evidence was given, often without indicating the source. When we asked for the sources of the information, we were simply told, "We have our sources."

When it became apparent that the Alberta Hospital Edmonton was reluctant to complete the assessment, we attempted to have an early review. I made a written application to the Board of Review, one the *Criminal Code* provides for. I sought to make personal representations for the early review before the board, but I did not even receive a response to the application. Yet there was communication between the board and the team psychiatrist regarding the progress of Dorothy's assessment, and a date was set for a review, without regard to any input from Dorothy or her counsel. I also found that the team management approach to treatment gave rise to some serious concerns that the professional opinions of some the doctors were being influenced by the rest of the team. I was receiving off-the-record opinions from some of the team members that did not reflect the official position being advanced by the team psychiatrist.

Meantime, Dorothy's health began to suffer, though she continued to cooperate with all the assessments. An outside neurologist hired by the hospital stepped in and advised Dorothy that a risky augmented CAT scan ordered by the hospital was going too far and was not necessary. The hospital did not proceed with that test. On one occasion Mrs. Joudrie was assaulted in the hospital, resulting in her nose being broken. Hospital staff trivialized the event, even though it traumatized Dorothy. However, she refused to make an issue of it, nor would she tolerate the offending patient being charged with assault.

Because the opinions of the hospital team were being challenged, the process became adversarial. We cross-examined the psychiatrist for the hospital on the issue of hospital records, and they were reluctantly released to us. Through it all, I felt that counsel was merely tolerated in the process, although, eventually, the psychiatric opinions advanced by our privately retained doctors were accepted as entirely accurate.

After several days of hearings over a period of five months, coupled with enormous financial costs to Mrs. Joudrie, she was reluctantly released from the hospital. Her stay in the hospital took its toll. In the last month alone she mysteriously lost thirty-five pounds. She returned to Calgary from the hospital in a deplorable condition. Although happy to be reunited with friends, she quickly lost another thirty pounds and was admitted to a Calgary hospital. I was convinced that she would not live to see Christmas. She was immediately diagnosed with a dangerous thyroid condition known as Graves disease. Despite her obvious symptoms, this medical condition escaped any notice during her stay at Alberta Hospital Edmonton. Dorothy recovered, only to be faced with a bout of breast cancer. Fortunately, she overcame that too. Mrs. Joudrie surprised all who came in contact with her after leaving the Alberta Hospital Edmonton with her ability to face every hurdle she confronted, while always exhibiting a wonderful sense of humour.

A further concern arose in my mind over the manner in which the subsequent review hearings were conducted. Successive hearings were held to determine whether an absolute discharge should be granted to Mrs. Joudrie, with the major issue being the ability of the Board of Review to formulate an opinion that Dorothy is not a significant threat to the safety of the community. Throughout these hearings we were never provided with any direction by the board about the issues they wanted addressed in order to move the process along towards an absolute discharge. In fact, we were left to speculate from one hearing to the next about the issues that might be of concern to the board. For example, one board member at an earlier hearing suggested possible organic brain impairment from alcoholism, so steps were taken to address that issue. Instead of the board following up that concern with a request for appropriate testing, it was left to Dorothy to hire a neuro-psychologist at her own expense to establish that she did not suffer from any cognitive brain dysfunction. My concern is for those parties who are unable, for financial reasons, to address issues that might be of concern to the board, when the board itself should be taking the initiative to have the appropriate assessments made. This onus ought not to be placed on the individual. The financial cost to Mrs. Joudrie to establish to the board that she was not a significant threat was huge. The law may state in principle that there is no burden on any of the parties in a review hearing before the board, but, practicably speaking, the reality is quite the opposite.

The law requires that Mrs. Joudrie be absolutely discharged from the jurisdiction of the Board of Review once it is found that she is not a significant threat to the safety of the public. The shooting of Earl Joudrie was the result of a convergence of varied and complicated issues most unlikely to be repeated in her life. By this time, Dorothy was clearly not the same person she was in January 1995. She faced life's tribulations without denial, and she had deep insight into the issues that had created this tragedy. She had worked hard to get to that state. Finally, on October 20, 1998, Dorothy Joudrie was granted an absolute discharge by the Alberta Board of Review.

Was this case all just a sham? Is the automatism defence nothing more than a hoax and a fraud on the justice system? Does it simply afford those criminals who can pay for the defence a way to escape personal responsibility and accountability? Even after having conducted the defence of Mrs. Joudrie, I am not certain I can offer an answer to these questions. We all have to formulate our own opinions based on the information we have at hand, but it is enough for me that the jury in this case, representing the community as a whole, found that Dorothy Joudrie was not criminally responsible.

concern for health care and the well being of his patients. Seven representatives of the community, ranging from North Bay's perennial citizen of the year–Sister Smith, a nun who had been the Executive Director of St. Joseph's Hospital–to patients and colleagues in the medical profession, were united in their view that the allegations were totally inconsistent with Dr. Mohan's character. These testaments could support Dr. Mohan's testimonial trustworthiness at trial and, at least to some extent, addressed the unlikelihood that he might commit such an offence. Character evidence was an essential aspect of the arsenal that could be mounted in his favour. Although George Bernard Shaw observed that his reputation grew with every failure, the reality of reputation is that, although it is easily lost, it is most difficult to acquire. Few men or women who I have represented in my career have been able to rely on such impressive evidence of reputation as Dr. Mohan.

However, I wasn't prepared to risk total reliance on Dr. Mohan's passionate and categorical denial, supported by his general reputation in the community. I wasn't satisfied that we had done enough to marshal the most effective defence available. With Dr. Mohan's concurrence, we sought an opinion and an assessment from a distinguished psychiatrist, Dr. R.W. Hill. Dr. Hill has an impressive curriculum vitae. Between 1974 and 1982 he had been a staff psychiatrist and, later, director of the Forensic In-Patient Service at Toronto's Clarke Institute of Psychiatry, where he and a colleague had assessed hundreds of persons charged with sex-related crimes. He had testified for both the defence and the Crown across the country, he was a consultant at the Oakridge Unit of the Mental Health Centre at Penetanguishene, and he was a consultant to Corrections Canada and to the Ministry of Correctional Services in Ontario. He was a teacher and scholar who was obviously current in all the relevant literature. I sought Dr. Hill's assistance with two issues. First, did Dr. Mohan reveal any trait of personality or psychological inclination to engage in the sexual improprieties alleged? Second, did an individual who committed the acts alleged by the complainants belong in a select group of individuals characterized by some psychiatric aberration? I hoped to limit the possible perpetrator to a defined group with distinguishing characteristics and to exclude Dr. Mohan from that select group.

After a mistrial at North Bay, caused by a juror's failure to disclose that he was a friend of one of the complainant's families, the fourth complaint emerged. Its similarity to the other allegations led the Crown to seek joinder;

The Mystique of Science: The Influence of Experts on the Administration of Criminal Justice

BRIAN H. GREENSPAN

1995

Among the recent cases I have been involved with that illustrate an important issue in criminal law, the one that is of great current significant is the use, abuse, and influence of experts in the criminal trial process. To my great dismay, however, the most obvious case in this category was the matter of Dr. Chikmaglur Mohan–a case in which I had been unsuccessful. I immediately looked for another issue, but the best examples all seemed to end in defeat–resoundingly public and reported defeats. In one of the few selfless gestures of my career, I've therefore retreated to *Mohan*. This decision, I assure you, was not dictated by modesty or humility but was simply what was required. Nevertheless, I present to you a profile of a defeat. After all, only Earl Stanley Gardner could conceivably ascribe to a defence lawyer the nonsense that "I never take a case unless I'm convinced my client was incapable of committing the crime charged."

The *Mohan* case is instructive on a variety of levels, and it raises an important practical cautionary note with respect to the abdication of the fact-finding process to a reliance on opinion. Mohan confronts head-on the emergence of unscientific science.

On a personal, professional level, this case was only one of the three conviction appeals of the more than twelve hundred appeals I have argued in the Court of Appeal for Ontario in which I acted as both trial and appellate counsel. It is the only matter in my career in which I was trial counsel, counsel in the Court of Appeal, and counsel in the Supreme Court of Canada.

Einstein said that "The whole of science is nothing more than a refinement of everyday thinking." If that were true, we would never need experts in a criminal trial, nor would expert opinion be admissible. The fundamental threshold for the introduction of opinion evidence is to furnish the court with scientific information that is likely to be outside the experience and knowledge of the trier of fact. If, on the proven facts, a judge or a jury can form its own conclusions without help, then the opinion of the expert is unnecessary. However, until recently, and indeed until *Mohan*, the Supreme Court has been generous in its acceptance of expert testimony and in liberally interpreting the relevance of this testimony to material issues. Professor Thayer observed that this determination of relevancy is "an affair of logic and experience, and not at all of law." The judgment of the Supreme Court of Canada in *Mohan* signals a more cautious approach, particularly with respect to novel scientific evidence.

It was not the intention of the defence in the case of Dr. Mohan either to establish precedent or to advance psychiatric insight. In the course of the past decade there has been an expansion of the use of expert evidence in criminal cases in non-traditional areas involving aspects of psychiatry, psychology, and other behavioural sciences. The emergence of "syndrome" evidence, and the cottage industry of purported experts it has spawned, has become a common feature of criminal trials. As a defence response, there has been an increasing development of "profile" evidence directed at demonstrating that the accused's characteristics are incompatible with the commission of the alleged offence.

The emergence of sexual abuse prosecutions as almost commonplace and the increasing allegations by both children and adults who claim recall of childhood victimization have led the prosecution and the defence to seek support for their positions from those trained in the behavioural sciences. In the context of that dynamic, I undertook the defence of Dr. Chikmaglur Mohan in 1989.

When I entered the case, Dr. Mohan had already been committed for trial for three of the four complaints he ultimately faced. He was a highly regarded physician who specialized in pediatric medicine in the community of North Bay and was also chief of pediatrics at both local hospitals. Dr.

Mohan treated approximately 1,500 patients a year, in his own offi hospital, and over 3,000 patient files were stored at his office.

Four complainants who were former adolescent patients eac that Dr. Mohan had engaged in sexual improprieties in the course of examinations. The claimed misconduct was extremely serious and vaginal and breast examinations and the use of sexually inappropr guage. Dr. Mohan categorically denied the allegations and ultimately that he had not even conducted the alleged examinations. He said t examinations would not have been medically appropriate, given the concerns and complaints.

An initial review of the Crown disclosure and the transcript of liminary hearing made it readily apparent that the most persuasive ar ful aspect of the Crown's case was in strength of numbers. The fii plainant had alleged that, during the course of several examinations July 1987 and May 1988, Dr. Mohan had engaged in intrusive pelvic nations. Following this complaint, Dr. Mohan had been charged and of that allegation widely circulated in the local media in North Bay. ond and the third complainants, who alleged similar conduct in tl time frame, came forward after learning of the first allegation. Howe specific details of the improprieties had never been expressly reporte in the electronic or the print media. The fourth complaint lacked tl independence, as that complainant had come forward following a mi which the specific details of the improprieties had been reported. It w fair to suggest that the age, time frame, and nature of the allegations of the complainants were strikingly similar and that the fourth comp alleged conduct that was generically similar. In fact, the three initia plainants had all been sexually victimized by others before the misc they alleged against Dr. Mohan. Each one was fairly portrayed as both cally and psychologically vulnerable.

It was apparent that the prosecution's case presented a significar lenge. Dr. Mohan was a quiet-spoken and scholarly man who enjoy unfailing support of his wife, who had been a barrister in India and wh firmed their deep sense of religion and the decent and moral life that s husband, and their young child lived.

In addition, Dr. Mohan had an enviable reputation in his comr for honesty, integrity, morality, and kindness and as a man who had a g

its dissimilarity and its impact on Dr. Hill's opinion led me to agree that it be tried together. Because of the continuing adverse publicity in North Bay, a change of venue was ordered to Sudbury.

On November 4, 1990, the trial commenced before a jury presided over by the Honourable Mr. Justice Bernstein of the Ontario Court (general division). The pivotal and most critical evidentiary issue to be resolved by Justice Bernstein was the admissibility of Dr. Hill's opinion.

Dr. Hill had arrived at the conclusion that a person who would have committed the improprieties alleged by the first three complainants would be properly characterized as a pedophile. However, owing to the more aggravated features that emerged in the fourth allegation, the person who would have committed that offence could only be characterized as a sexual psychopath. In Dr. Hill's view, one would not find evidence of sexual psychopathy in a pedophile, although it was quite possible that a sexual psychopath would have pedophilic tendencies. Therefore, if the four assaults were committed by the same perpetrator, the offender would be a member of a distinctive aberrant group of sexual psychopaths. Further, Dr. Hill held the unequivocal view that Dr. Mohan was neither a pedophile nor a sexual psychopath, nor did any testing indicate sexual dysfunction or any inclination to deviant sexual behaviour.

During the *voir dire* before Justice Bernstein on the admissibility of Dr. Hill's evidence, I placed considerable reliance on two judgments of the Court of Appeal for Ontario written by the Honourable G. Arthur Martin. As our pre-eminent scholar, Justice Martin is also the lawyer and judge who represents the yardstick by which excellence in criminal law will always be measured. His judgments are both eloquent and persuasive, and I relied on his 1975 judgments in the case of *McMillan* and *Robertson*. In *McMillan*, Justice Martin stated: "Where the offence is of a kind that it is only committed by members of an abnormal group … psychiatric evidence that the accused did or did not possess the distinguishing characteristics of that abnormal group is relevant either to bring him within, or to exclude him from, the special class of which the perpetrator of the crime is a member. In order for psychiatric evidence to be relevant for that purpose, the offence must be one which indicates that it was committed by a person with an abnormal propensity or disposition which stamped him as a member of a special and extraordinary class." In *Robertson*, delivered by Justice Martin four days later, he reiterated the proposition in similar language and stated: "Evidence that the offence had distinctive features which identified the perpetrator as a person possessing unusual personality traits constituting him a member of an unusual and limited class of persons, rendered admissible evidence that the accused did not possess the personality characteristics of the class of persons to which the perpetrator of the crime belonged." Equipped with these authorities, in addition to a variety of pronouncements on which these judgments relied, I argued for the admissibility of Dr. Hill's evidence in Dr. Mohan's trial.

In addition to his conclusion that, if one perpetrator had committed all four offences, he would uniquely categorize that perpetrator as a sexual psychopath, Dr. Hill stated during the *voir dire* that individuals capable of committing both classes of offences would belong to a very small, behaviourally distinct category of persons. He was asked whether a physician who acted in the manner alleged in the indictment would be a member of a distinct group of aberrant persons. Dr. Hill responded that the behaviours outlined could flow only from a significant abnormality of character and would be part of an unusual limited class. In cross-examination, Dr. Hill conceded that, of the many patients he had assessed and treated who had been charged with sexual crimes, only three had been physicians.

Justice Bernstein is widely regarded as a fair and decent judge, one, I agree, who leans on the side of compassion. However, he was not moved by the clarity and persuasiveness of my argument. He ruled that Dr. Hill's evidence was not sufficient to establish that doctors who commit sexual assaults on patients are in a significantly more limited group, in psychiatric terms, than other members of society. He ruled that there was no scientific data available to warrant that conclusion and that the sample of three offenders was an insufficient base for the conclusion. He observed that a large number of men from all walks of life commit sexual offences on young women and, while some may have a type of character disorder, he doubted that expert evidence regarding the normalcy of any accused would be of assistance to a trier of fact in the absence of more distinguishing features within the wide spectrum of sexual assault.

The case went to trial and, on November 6, 1990, Dr. Mohan was convicted. A few days later, I received his instructions to appeal. Although, ultimately, not the exclusive foundation for the appeal, the ruling with respect to the admissibility of the expert evidence was the most compelling ground to be advanced. On January 4, 1991, Dr. Mohan was sentenced to imprisonment for nine months and to probation for a period of two years. On the same day, he was released pending the determination of his appeal. In the interim, his medical practice was suspended by the College of Physicians and Surgeons.

As I indicated earlier, I have acted on a conviction appeal in my own cases on only three occasions. In each one I argued the central appeal issue at trial–the admissibility of critical evidence when that evidence had been excluded. On the two previous occasions, I had ultimately been vindicated by the Court of Appeal. Approximately one year after Dr. Mohan's sentence, I argued the appeal before a panel of our Court of Appeal consisting of Justice Brooke, Justice Finlayson, and Justice Labrosse. The panel reserved judgment.

On April 14, 1992, a new trial was ordered by a unanimous court, which held that the evidence of Dr. Hill was admissible. Justice Finlayson, on behalf of the court, stated that to counter the similar-fact evidence adduced by the Crown, Dr. Hill's evidence was admissible to demonstrate that Dr. Mohan, in this expert's assessment, was not a member of either of the unusual groups of aberrant personalities that could have committed the offences alleged. Justice Finlayson observed that where expert testimony is available from a qualified psychiatrist that pedophiles and sexual psychopaths are members of special and extraordinary classes, the evidence should be admitted. The weight to be attached to that opinion is a matter for the jury. He noted that the Supreme Court of Canada had recently signalled that the court should be more receptive to the use of psychiatric opinion in cases that raised issues beyond the scope of normal human experience. He observed that "our juries are now being forced to wrestle with issues which require more of their reliance upon their God-given common sense." When they are triers of act concerning complex psychological issues, they are entitled to the assistance of those with special knowledge. The jury had been asked to consider and pass judgment on conduct by a pediatrician which, if the complainants were to be believed, was contrary to the standards of any decent person and totally at odds with a pediatrician's training as a healer of children. Consequently, the evidence of persons with professional psychiatric experience in dealing with sexual offences would surely be of assistance. I was relieved–but my vindication was short lived.

I was only moderately surprised by the decision of the Ministry of the Attorney General of Ontario to apply for leave to appeal to the Supreme Court of Canada. Lawyers there seem to recommend an appeal whenever they lose a case. What surprised me was not the application to seek leave–an application now exclusively by way of written memorandum, without any opportunity for oral argument–but the fact that they were successful in leave being granted. I found, and still find, the decision of the Supreme Court of Canada to grant leave in *Mohan* to be inconsistent with other decisions concerning non-traditional and imprecise sciences, particularly those related to human behaviour. Although, historically, triers of fact had decided such issues without the input of experts, the judgment of Madam Justice Wilson in *Lavallée* in 1990 had rejected the Crown's contention that judges and juries were sufficiently knowledgeable about human behaviour that the opinion of an expert on the issue of the battered woman's syndrome was unnecessary. Justice Wilson had stated: "When expert evidence is tendered in such fields as engineering or pathology, the paucity of the lay person's knowledge is uncontentious. The long-standing recognition that psychiatric or psychological testimony also falls within the realm of expert evidence is predicated on the realization that in some circumstances the average person may not have sufficient knowledge of or experience with human behaviour to draw an appropriate inference from the facts before him or her." She stated that this evidence was necessary both to explain the psychological effects of long-standing abuse and to disabuse the trier of fact of incorrect conclusions that their own experiences might otherwise lead them to reach.

Although I was somewhat concerned by the Court's apparent enthusiasm to address the criteria for the admissibility of psychiatric evidence in *Mohan*, I remained cautiously optimistic that the judgment of the Court of Appeal for Ontario could be sustained. The material we filed at the Supreme Court of Canada emphasized that Dr. Hill had based his opinion on experience and scholarship. He had testified that sexual offenders generally demonstrated one of three distinctively abnormal psychosexual profiles, and that the perpetrator of the type of acts alleged by the complainants in Dr. Mohan's case would demonstrate "distinctively deviant abnormal behaviour consistent with one of the abnormal psychosexual profiles." Dr. Hill formulated his opinion through his study and experience in the field, which included dealing with hundreds of sexual offenders over a fifteen-year period. We submitted that the proffered expert evidence fell squarely within the orthodox provisions for the reception of opinion and that the alleged offences were marked by distinctive features identifying its perpetrator as a member of an abnormal psychosexual profile.

On May 5, 1994, in one of its infrequent nine-member unanimous judgments, Justice Sopinka, on behalf of the court, restored Dr. Mohan's convictions. Justice Sopinka articulated a four-component test for the admissibility of expert evidence and identified the criteria on which admission depends. He listed these components as relevance, necessity in assisting the trier of fact, the absence of any exclusionary rule, and a properly qualified expert. Justice Sopinka also restored the distinction between "legal relevance" and "logical relevance" and expressed the view that evidence that is logically relevant can be excluded if its probative worth is outweighed by competing considerations such as prejudice, consumption of time, or the possibility that the evidence might mislead the trier of fact.

The criterion of necessity requires that the evidence provide information that is likely to be outside the experience or knowledge of a judge or jury. The need for the evidence must be assessed in light of its potential to distort the fact-finding process and to turn the trial into a contest of experts. Justice Sopinka specifically indicated that these standards are to be applied to expert evidence that advances a novel scientific theory. The closer the evidence approaches an opinion on an ultimate issue, the stricter the application of the preconditions to admissibility. The court followed the lead of the United States Supreme Court in the case of *Daubert* and now requires that the trial judge ensure that an expert's testimony rests on a reliable foundation. The methodology employed must be scientifically valid and properly applicable to the facts at issue. The judge must consider whether the theory or technique can be and has been tested; whether it has been subjected to peer review and publication; whether standards exist, along with standards controlling its operation; and whether it has attracted widespread acceptance within a relevant scientific community. The court decided that Justice Bernstein was correct to exclude Dr. Hill's opinion: there was nothing to indicate any general acceptance of Dr. Hill's theory, it noted, and no material to support a finding that the profile of a pedophile or psychopath had been sufficiently standardized. Expert evidence must satisfy some minimum threshold of reliability and, in particular, a novel scientific theory or technique must be subjected to special scrutiny to determine whether it meets that basic test.

What, then, is the aftermath of this reversal of fortune? The criminal trial is a human process, and the impact on its participants is profound. Some would argue that the new approach to the admissibility of expert opinion heralded in this case helped to vindicate and ease the pain of the complainants and their families. Others would argue that individuals such as Dr. Mohan ought not to be disadvantaged by jurisprudential change in the law of evidence. Regardless of one's view, the reality of the criminal process in this case is that Dr. Mohan served his sentence of imprisonment, and he is barred from the practice of medicine in every jurisdiction in the world in which he was previously licensed. He now faces deportation, as he had never acquired Canadian citizenship.

As for the impact of the case on future cases, its effect has already been demonstrably significant—and in somewhat unpredictable ways. The *Mohan* principles must apply equally to both sides of the equation—to the Crown and the defence. Recently, and fairly consistently, the defence has successfully advanced the *Mohan* case to exclude previously admissible evidence of the variety of syndromes and characteristics viewed by some as indicative of abuse. The same lack of scientific foundation exists in relation to virtually all the anecdotal hypotheses advanced by Crown behavioural scientists.

Will Rogers noted that we are always saying, "Let the law take its course. What we really mean," he quipped, "is 'Let the law take our course.'" Despite the fact that the law in *Mohan* didn't take *our* course, its ultimate legacy will likely be to the benefit of the trial process.

Taking the Law into Your Own Hands:
Child Abduction and the Defence of Necessity

RAPHAËL H. SCHACHTER, QC

2000

This case was a litigator's nightmare. My client was accused of abducting his children when they were very young and keeping them away from their mother for nearly ten years. He was charged in May 1982, and a warrant was issued for his arrest. He was accused, contrary to the *Criminal Code,* with intent to deprive a parent of lawful custody of a child under the age of fourteen. If found guilty, he was liable to be imprisoned for ten years.

Dura lex, sed lex, one of the oldest clichés in our legal lexicon, translates roughly as "If you can't do the time, don't do the crime." The law, with all its might, and often with all its inflexibility, applies to each one of us. However, being a product of humanity, the law, however imperfect, is also based on principles of compassion and mercy. The defence of necessity is an expression of these values. Its creation by the courts proves that these values are at the core of our legal system. The law recognizes that, in the course of events, human beings are sometimes placed in desperate situations. At these times the Rule of Law does not seem to offer any comfort, but the courts, without condoning illegal behaviour, may excuse it.

The stark facts of the case can be summarized easily. My client and his wife married on May 29, 1971, and subsequently had two children. Ten years later, in 1981, they separated and the wife was given temporary custody of the children. The relationship between the couple became extremely venomous and, in 1982, my client again tried to obtain custody of his children through the courts. His wife was granted custody of the children, however, and my client had visitation rights only.

On April 11, 1982, my client abducted his two children during a visit and left for California. He took them first to Haiti, and finally to Egypt and Yemen. At the time, his daughter was seven years old and his son was three years old. The following month, on May 18, Canadian authorities issued a warrant for his arrest. He was charged under section 250(1) of the *Criminal Code* with abduction. Although my client lived with his two children in various places in the Middle East for the next thirteen years, his wife did locate her daughter in Yemen, where my client was employed, in 1988 and began corresponding with her. By 1990 my client's wife was in regular contact with both children, though infrequently. In 1995 my client moved to the United States with the children, and two years later he returned to Canada with them, to be near his aging parents, who required assistance. On March 18, 1999, my client surrendered to the authorities in Montreal and appeared before the court. He was accused of having deprived his wife, who had legal custody, of possession of their two children.

In my eight years as a Crown counsel, four as a provincial Crown and four as a federal Crown, I knew the value of pleading serious preliminary motions before trial. In this complex case, I investigated whether any preliminary motions were available to me based on the facts of the case. I believed there were grounds supporting a stay of proceedings, based on section 11(b) of the *Charter* and the Supreme Court of Canada's case in *Morin*. I thought we had a clear chance to plead a motion for unreasonable delay and to ask for a stay of proceedings.

The *Canadian Charter of Rights and Freedoms* protects a person's fundamental right to present a full and complete defence. One possible threat to this right stems from an unreasonable delay in criminal proceedings. The Supreme Court of Canada in *Morin* established factors to consider when analyzing the delay: the length of the delay; the reasons for the delay, such as delays inherent to the nature of the case; the accused's actions; the public minister's actions; and the prejudice suffered by the accused. The period that had to be examined in this case ranged from the date of the charges against my client to the date of his appearance before the court.

There were two trials in this case. In the first trial, our motion for unreasonable delay was based on the following facts: seventeen years had passed since the initial charges had been taken against my client and the actual commencement of his trial. During that time, he never tried to hide from Canadian authorities. He never hid his address or telephone number, which were listed in the phone book where he was residing outside Canada. He never stopped travelling, despite being stopped regularly at the border in both Europe and the United States. Since 1995 my client had been living in the United States and he often crossed the Canadian border to visit his parents in Montreal. He was never arrested.

A fascinating development regarding the motion for unreasonable delay occurred which I thought would be crucial to its success, but to my chagrin it was not. On Wednesday, November 17, 1999, the Crown prosecutor had called an officer from Interpol as a witness in order to prove that Canadian authorities had done all that should be done to locate my client. The Crown prosecutor had informed us that the Interpol officer was going to bring a small file of a few pages that Interpol had collected concerning my client's case. However, the file turned out to be four inches thick. The Crown prosecutor asked the court to adjourn until the next day so we could examine those documents. Accordingly, Justice Doyon suspended the trial until the following morning.

I arrived at the prosecutor's office at 3:00 p.m. on the 17th to review the Interpol documents. I was informed I could not photocopy the documents and could consult them only in that office. The Interpol officer explained to us the difference between a red notice, meaning that an arrest had been requested, and a blue notice, meaning that information concerning whereabouts had been requested. In my client's case, only a blue notice had been issued. The Interpol officer confirmed to us that there had been a mistake and that a red notice should have been in the file. He also told me that, on three occasions between 1983 and 1986 and also in 1991, authorities from other countries had advised Canadian authorities that they had detained and released my client. While I was consulting the documents, the Interpol officer received a phone call from his superior in Ottawa ordering him to take the file back immediately. He informed me that I would have to apply to the Commission à l'accès à l'information because the documents were being protected. He informed me that even with an application, I would probably never be able to look at the Interpol documents. I had no choice but to ask the Interpol officer to come to testify the next morning and explain the situation in court.

The next morning I arrived in court, ready to cross-examine the Interpol officer about the Interpol file. However, an additional surprise was waiting for me. The Crown prosecutor and the chief of Crown prosecutors were waiting with new documents. They had just realized that the Montreal police had a full file on my client. The Montreal police documents contained not only precious information, such as communications between the Montreal police, Interpol, and the Crown prosecutor, but also two indications of limited involvement in the file by our presiding trial judge dating from a decade earlier, when he was acting as a Crown prosecutor. The two interventions were minor, however, concerning whether abduction was an extraditable offence in the United States. We decided this new information had to be revealed to Justice Doyon.

The judge let us plead our case regarding whether he should recuse himself. I argued that the documents should have been communicated a long time ago and that this situation had resulted from the sole negligence of the Crown. More important, it added to the unreasonable delay. The interventions of Justice Doyon were so minor that I felt he would not be in a conflictual situation and would be able to carry on objectively. The prosecutor agreed. Nevertheless, Justice Doyon did recuse himself, to assure the principle that justice must not only be done but also appear to be done.

When the second trial began on March 23, 2000, the parties agreed to put into evidence the proof made before the first judge–the testimony of my client and of his wife regarding the motion for unreasonable delay. As well, there was no objection by Crown counsel that defence counsel should be allowed to examine the Interpol and the Montreal police files.

The information contained in these files confirmed our suspicions. On many occasions, Canadian authorities had the opportunity to arrest my client, but they did not act. Two days after the abduction, my client's wife reported it to the police, but the authorities refused to take action. The Montreal police and Interpol Ottawa were working together, and a request to extradite my client should have been made, but it never was. Because of the mistaken blue notice in the file, Interpol never asked for the arrest of my client. They requested only that countries abroad report his travelling and his whereabouts. Several communications occurred between Interpol Ottawa and other countries that had located my client. Each time, Interpol Ottawa affirmed that my client's extradition was not requested. In 1983 my client was located in Israel, and Interpol Ottawa refused Israel's offer to detain and arrest my client. Also, the warrant was only Canada-wide, not international. In 1988 my client's wife got her children's address and started having contact with them. The following year, my client was stopped at the German border. The Germans informed Interpol Ottawa, but Canadian authorities did not request an extradition, even though there was an extradition treaty between the two countries. In 1995 my client moved to the United States. The Crown prosecutor knew my client's whereabouts but did not move to extradite him.

Despite these facts, Judge Sirois dismissed the motion, attributing the delay to my client's actions. The judge insisted on the *Morin* criteria in determining that the accused's actions were responsible for the delay and that he could not invoke his own turpitude and hope to succeed in his motion. I was not amused.

Achieving an acquittal for my client in this case was critical. He was an American citizen working for the State Department in Washington. Anything less than an acquittal, notwithstanding a potential plea bargain suggested by the Crown of a minimum of two years in a penitentiary, would be disastrous for him. It was crucial to explore every possibility based on the facts at our disposal and to hope to win the case.

When I saw the codification of the common law defence of necessity, based on the defence of imminent harm, found in the *Criminal Code* since the amendments made in 1983, together with the relatively recent *Adams* case in the Ontario Court of Appeal, the appropriate defence became clear. It was commensurate with our pattern of fact.

In April 1982 the defence of necessity applying specifically to cases of child abduction was not yet codified, but it applied in respect of common law principles. In 1983 the legislator adopted section 250(4), which became section 285 of the *Criminal Code* in 1993: "No one shall be found guilty of an offense under sections 280 to 283 if the court is satisfied that the taking, enticing away, concealing, detaining, receiving, or harbouring of any young person was necessary to protect the young person from danger of imminent harm." "Imminent harm" is the component of the defence of necessity permitting a violation of the law.

In *Adams* the Ontario Court of Appeal enumerated three conditions in applying the defence of necessity relating to child abduction:

1. An honest belief, even if erroneous, from the accused's part that the child is facing an imminent danger. This belief does not have to be reasonable but is a factor to consider.
2. The abduction was done in order to protect the child from the imminent danger.
3. It was necessary to abduct the child in order to protect him or her. This criteria must be analyzed objectively, but regarding the circumstances as honestly perceived by the accused. Other means that could have been used by the accused should be taken into consideration.

The imminent danger does not have to be of a physical nature and can be psychological. The accused has only to raise a reasonable doubt on each element of the defence.

At trial, the Crown heard only one witness, my client's former wife. Strategically, I felt that the principal thrust had to be portraying her as unstable just before my client's decision to abduct the children.

Unfortunately, the heavy publicity and the unsympathetic nature of the fact pattern relating to my client resulted in our not being able to call certain individuals as defence witnesses. One example was the grade school teacher of my client's daughter. The teacher, we thought, could possibly testify about the laissez-faire attitude of the mother towards the care of her children, and the fact that the daughter's behaviour was worsening as a result of the mother's neglect. When we called the teacher to advise her of our expectations regarding her testimony, her attitude became aggressive and her story changed significantly–to the point where we could not depend on her testimony.

Another witness who would have been crucial to our defence was the doctor who had prescribed Halcion to my client's wife. Halcion is a drug that can produce various nefarious side effects if taken with alcohol, other drugs, or even by itself. It could offer an explanation for the concern my client had with the comportment of his wife at the time he made the decision to leave with the children. When we called the doctor and explained why we were calling, he became furious and clearly told me he would not take part in the "defence of a criminal" such as my client.

Regardless, there was sufficient proof of my client's wife's mental state during the crucial time period. My client testified that because of his wife's drinking and smoking during the pregnancy, their first child was born with fetal alcohol deficiency syndrome. Then, while pregnant with the second child, his wife fell into a depression for which she consulted a doctor for eight or nine sessions. Through an O'Connor motion, we gained access to her medical files. They confirmed that she had consulted a psychiatrist in 1978. Although the file did not contain precise information, it corroborated my client's testimony. My client's wife was consuming Halcion, Valium, and alcohol, she was often out of contact with reality, and she had memory loss. In addition, a report from the older child's teacher indicated that the child needed a stable home. In fact, that child actually called her father and asked him to take her away from her mother. Finally, my client testified that his wife and her family had laid false attempted murder charges against him in March 1982, for which a jury acquitted him after ten minutes of deliberation.

In 1982 my client tried to obtain custody of his children. The whole family was subjected to an evaluation, and the report of the psychologist was clear—the mother was not fit to take care of the children. On January 22, 1982, however, custody of the children was given to the mother. My client was not even given the chance to explain to the family court judge that the criminal charges were still pending against him. He had lost faith in the judicial process and had no alternative left to protect his children other than to leave with them. He wanted to leave until such time that he would be guaranteed that his children would be safe. That was his testimony, his honest belief that the judge would be obliged to deliberate upon.

The rest of the testimony supported my client's position. For example, my client never stopped the children from going back to their mother. The son's testimony confirmed that. As well, my client's sister, who was a notary, was able to observe the comportment of her sister-in-law because she lived close to her brother's residence in Montreal. She stated that the children were left alone most of the time. She also testified that the behaviour of my client's wife's had changed and that she was absent and not in contact with reality. Finally, she stated that my client's daughter had behaviour problems and his son, at four years of age, had reverted to using diapers.

My client's daughter testified that her mother had tried to force her to tell the police that her father had a knife and that he had threatened to kill her. She also testified that, after telling her mother that other children at school had beaten her, her mother told her that she was a liar and that she was the one with the problem. The sister and daughter who had testified on my client's behalf confirmed, in a minor manner, the concept of imminent harm. The fact that the children were now university students and well adjusted in their day-to-day activities, and that the sister was a notary, also assisted with the credibility issue for the defence.

Finally, Dr. Ahmar, a pharmacologist who corroborated the psychological reports, testified to the effects of the drug Halcion. He stated that Halcion has these possible side effects: gross confusion and disorientation, mild agitation; memory loss, amnesia, paranoia, and depression.

On May 23, 2000, Justice Sirois found my client not guilty. He said that a reasonable doubt has been raised on each of the elements of the defence. Applying the criteria elaborated in the *Adams* case, the judge said that my client had an honest belief that his children were in danger and, in his mind, there was no other possible way to protect them.

Part Three: Defence Counsel and the Truth

Reflections on a Half-Century of Criminal Practice

THE HON. G. ARTHUR MARTIN

1992

I first met Bernard Cohn in the fall of 1944 when he dropped into my office, at the suggestion of a mutual friend, to discuss a question of criminal law with me. We met again early in 1945 to discuss the appeal by John Shemko from his conviction in Windsor for murder. Barney, as he was known, had been associate defence counsel at the trial, and I was retained to argue the appeal.

The *Shemko* case depended entirely on circumstantial evidence and was both fascinating and difficult. The body of Frank Scibor, burned beyond recognition, had been found in his automobile in a lane leading from the highway to his home. A second autopsy showed that the deceased had suffered violence to the head and throat.

The theory of the Crown was that John Shemko had waylaid the deceased, struck him on the head, and throttled him, rendering him unconscious, and then had set fire to his automobile. The alleged motive for the murder was that Shemko desired to have Scibor's attractive wife for himself.

An important piece of circumstantial evidence was an automobile emergence brake handle that had been found near the scene of the crime. The Crown cited the evidence of a mechanic, who identified the brake handle as the one that Shemko, not long before the murder, was allowed to take from a scrap heap in a garage, after removing the handle from a ratchet.

I spent a very interesting day with Cohn discussing the evidence and the grounds of appeal. I remember that I was impressed not only by his ability as a defence counsel but by his wisdom and his personality. I also found that I liked him immensely as a person. He was a great humanist, low key, and free from bigotry or prejudice.

Before the appeal was heard, the senior defence counsel at the trial was replaced by James Clark, KC, a renowned jury lawyer who made no claim either to having a profound knowledge of the law or to being an appellate counsel. Cohn ceased to be associated with the case. I continued to act as counsel for the appellant on the appeal. The Court of Appeal for Ontario ordered a new trial on the grounds that inadmissible evidence, prejudicial to the appellant, had been wrongly admitted at his trial.

At the second trial, Shemko was acquitted. Undoubtedly, a successful courtroom demonstration by Mr. Clark played a role in Shemko's acquittal. The demonstration, as described to me by Mr. Clark, was that he asked the investigating officer to fit the brake handle into the ratchet from which it was alleged that Shemko had removed it. The officer, after a number of attempts, was unable to do so. The effect of the demonstration was probably to discredit the Crown's evidence about the identification of the brake handle.

I have always been opposed to courtroom demonstrations, as distinct from out-of-court experiments, because, if unsuccessful, they are devastating. If the defence is based on the accidental discharge of a gun, the failure of the gun to discharge accidentally in a courtroom demonstration unduly magnifies that failure. If the gun sometimes discharged accidentally, although infrequently, as shown by an out-of-court experiment, that might well be sufficient to create a reasonable doubt as to the accused's guilt.

Barney Cohn and I became close friends as the result of our association in the *Shemko* case. We were subsequently associated in many cases and, over the year, we spent a great deal of time together both in Windsor and in Toronto. Cohn had his favourite restaurants, and if you were in Windsor he was sure to take you to one of them. He was also an avid sports fan.

He had been a student in the law firm of Clark, Springsteen and McTague. Charles McTague later became a justice of the Court of Appeal for Ontario. Cohn never hurried, and he was given the nickname of "Speedy" by Mr. Clark.

Bernard Cohn was a wonderful companion. He had a profound knowledge of human nature. He combined worldliness with compassion and understanding. He also had a great sense of humour and a fund of anecdotes, and was a gifted raconteur. Furthermore, he was a very learned, careful, and wise defence counsel. He would carefully study the most recent judgments of the courts in Canada and Great Britain and, of course, the *Journal of Criminal Law*, the *Criminal Law Review*, and the *Criminal Law Quarterly*. He was a professional in the best sense of that word. He enjoyed debating questions of criminal law with such legal giants as Charles Dubin, Thomas Zuber, and John Robinette, all good friends and admirers. Bernard Cohn was a great lawyer, but, even more important, he was a great human being.

Social Change and Its Effect on the Legal Profession

Almost fifty-four years have passed since I was called to the bar of the province of Ontario in June 1938. As I recollect, my call to the bar had an inauspicious beginning. The chairman of the Legal Education Committee, in reading out the names of those to be called to the bar, overlooked my name. However, the omission was rectified and I was duly, if belatedly, called to the bar.

The ensuing half-century has been a period of profound social change, rapidly accelerating in the latter part of that period. This social change is reflected in marked changes in the legal profession. In 1938 Osgoode Hall Law School was the only law school in Ontario. The bar was much smaller then than it is now and comprised some 3,000 lawyers. At the present time, it is composed of almost 24,000 lawyers, of whom some 5,500 are women. In 1938, 106 candidates were called to the bar, only one of whom was a woman. In 1992, women constituted about 43 per cent of the candidates for admission to the bar.

In 1938, the Supreme Court of Canada, the Supreme Court of Ontario, and the county or district courts in Ontario had no women judges. There were no women law teachers. Indeed, women did not become eligible to serve as jurors in this province until many years later. The deplorable situation of women being insufficiently represented in the administration of justice is being corrected with the entry of many more women into the legal profession, their appointment as law teachers, their election to governing bodies of the legal profession, and their appointment to the judiciary.

The organizational complexity of modern society and the *Canadian Charter of Rights and Freedoms* have generally expanded the role of the lawyer in today's society. Courses are given in law schools today in branches of the law that did not even exist when I was called to the bar. Today, the Court of Appeal deals with many important and difficult cases in areas of the law that did not exist when I was appointed to the Ontario Court of Appeal in 1973.

In 1938 few lawyers could survive financially if they devoted a large part of their practice to acting as defence counsel. Most accused were too poor to pay a lawyer. There were, however, a few eminent lawyers who did not confine themselves to acting as defence counsel but were excellent in that role. They usually acted only in the high-profile cases where there was a reasonable prospect of receiving a proper fee, although I have no doubt these lawyers also did some pro bono work.

As a student and a young lawyer, I used to follow these great lawyers, endeavouring to learn the art of the advocate. Counsel acting for the accused in those days tended to be more theatrical and flamboyant than they are today. I will mention only four of the lawyers who frequently or occasionally acted as defence counsel.

Charles W. Bell, KC, was an outstanding defence counsel. He was theatrical in appearance as well as by nature. He was an accomplished playwright who wrote several successful Broadway plays that later became successful motion pictures. He was also the author of *Who Said Murder?* He once said in a newspaper interview that his work in the theatre had been of great advantage to him in his court work. He explained that the theatre has no time for extraneous matters, and it had taught him to go right to the heart of the matter.

Arthur Slaght, KC, frequently appeared for the defence in criminal cases. He was considered to be eloquent, although I think his eloquence would now appear dated and not be effective. He was also a great cross-examiner, and would be so in any era. I have always thought that he would have been very successful on the stage. Mr. Slaght often ended his closing address to the jury with a plea to send the accused back to his little, aged mother, who was waiting with outstretched arms to receive him. Apparently Mr. Slaght had no clients whose mothers were not elderly and frail.

Colonel R.H. Greer, KC, was an outstanding defence counsel. Unlike Bell and Slaght, he was not flamboyant. He was a good judge of the likely reactions of people in the time in which he lived and worked. (The reaction of jurors might be different today and, indeed, some of his cross-examinations, such as those relating to sexual assault, might be excluded under recent decisions of the Supreme Court of Canada.) He was a superb cross-examiner, if, at times, somewhat tedious. He was also powerfully persuasive in his arguments before juries of that day.

The final member of the quartet was I.F. Hellmuth, KC, primarily a civil lawyer, though he sometimes defended difficult criminal cases. He had a wonderful resonant voice and, in his conduct of a case, combined an almost tigerish quality with an elegance of style that made his advocacy outstanding. Not long after I was called to the bar, I decided to practise on my own because of my interest in criminal law. The firm with which I was then associated was involved, for the most part, in real estate and corporate matters. We parted on the best of terms. Not long after I commenced to practise on my own, I received a handwritten note from Mr. Hellmuth in which he said he had noticed I had acted as defence counsel in a number of difficult criminal cases, of which he had many. He said if I ever felt the need of advice, I must feel free to call him—and it would not cost me a cent. I was deeply moved by his letter, and I resolved that if I were ever in a similar position to assist young lawyers, I would.

Legal Aid Fifty Years Ago

No comprehensive legal aid system existed fifty years ago. There was a system of voluntary legal aid in the City of Toronto, and it worked in this way. A young lawyer—they were usually young—who wanted to defend people for nothing, in order to gain experience, left his name with the Crown attorney's secretary. In due course the secretary would call and say, "There is a person at the jail who is coming up for trail on Wednesday" (it was usually about Monday when she would telephone). "Would you defend the accused?" If you said yes you went to the Crown attorney's office, where you were allowed to look at the Crown attorney's transcript of the preliminary hearing (you never had one of your own). You made a few notes and, thus armed, went to the jail to interview your client.

Legal aid in the Court of Appeal was provided on much the same basis. Young lawyers left their name with the registrar of the Court of Appeal. In murder cases, however, the chief justice usually requested a lawyer who had some experience in appellate work to represent the accused. The registrar would simply call you and say there is a murder appeal coming before the court a week from Monday and the chief justice would like you to argue it. You, of course, did not say that you would have to check your diary to see if you were free that day. If you had any other work, you put it aside. You picked up the transcript and got ready to argue the appeal. I do not want to suggest that our motives were entirely noble. The object of the exercise was to get our name in the newspaper, or, if we did good work, a paying client might hear about it and retain our services. Office overhead in those days was extremely low, and we did not have much work to do anyway, so we could do this sort of work.

The first client that I acquired, through a call from the Crown attorney's secretary, was Morris Silverstone, who had made a substantial contribution to the criminal jurisprudence in this country. He is the subject of at least two reported cases. In the cases that found their way into the law reports, Silverstone was represented by experienced counsel. On this occasion he had no funds, and he got me. I had just graduated from law school and had been called to the bar about a month before. Silverstone was my first client.

The case against my client was quite overwhelming. He was arrested at 2:00 a.m. while running in the lane immediately behind a drugstore that had been broken into and entered. Furthermore, the owner of the store testified that he had placed a roll containing 123 coins in the cash register and that the roll of coins was missing. The police testified that they found 123 coins on Silverstone. Not surprisingly, the trial judge refused to accept my theory of a series of extraordinary coincidences, and Silverstone was found guilty. He was sentenced to the penitentiary for five years.

The Mickey MacDonald Murder Case

The first murder case in which I was involved as a defence counsel was a *cause célèbre* in its time. One of the well-known defence counsel in those days was Frank Regan, who was often involved, frequently unsuccessfully, in the defence of unpopular cases. John Robinette recently said of Mr. Regan that "he was very imaginative as to the facts–as to the law, he had but a passing interest." C.W. Bell refers to a lawyer who, when a prospective client present-ed him with any set of facts, invariably replied, "Very tortious, very tortious." Mr. Bell thought there was some similarity between Mr. Regan and the lawyer in question. Mr. Regan saw each client as the victim of a conspiracy. Once in a while, although not very often, he turned out to be right.

On January 7, 1939, not long after I had been called to the bar, a man by the names of James Windsor was murdered. He was seated at his dining-room table celebrating his birthday when three men entered the house. One of the men shot Windsor, and then they left. Not long afterwards, Mickey MacDonald, a man with a lengthy criminal record, and his younger brother Alex were arrested and charged with the murder of Windsor.

Alex was defended by Isidore Levinter, KC, ably assisted by Ben Grossberg, later the Honourable Judge Grossberg. Mr. Regan, whom I had met in an earlier case involving multiple accused, asked me to assist him in MacDonald's defence. It provided an experience that few young lawyers are fortunate enough to have. Mr. Levinter and Mr. Grossberg were outstanding counsel who understood the value of preparation–and, moreover, they were masters of that art. Mr. Regan, notwithstanding some unevenness in performance, was experienced in the trial of criminal cases. He was also an excellent cross-examiner.

The Crown's case was simple. Most of the five eyewitnesses seated around the dining-room table identified Mickey as the killer, and, for good measure, some of them identified Alex as one of his accomplices. The Crown also produced John R. Shea, to whose evidence many frailties attached. I later described Shea as an arch-criminal in the Court of Appeal. Shea said that Mickey MacDonald had stored some revolvers in his apartment. He testified that, on Saturday evening, January 7, 1939, MacDonald came to his apartment and picked up the revolvers, saying he was going out "on a job." Shea said that MacDonald returned later that evening, reporting that he had shot a man.

There was a transcript of the line-up that was held following Mickey MacDonald's arrest, and the defence obtained a copy of it. It was very revealing. Some of the witnesses who so positively identified MacDonald in the prisoner's dock had failed to pick him out of the line-up. One witness who positively identified Mickey at the trial as the killer, saying she "would never forget his face," had asked him to step forward at the line-up and then, after looking at him closely, said he was not the man. I was somewhat sceptical about the validity of the identification evidence.

In those days, there were no private investigators that defence counsel could employ in the investigation of criminal cases, and there were usually no funds with which to pay them, even if they were available. Defence counsel, perforce, acted as their own investigators, a practice that has obvious dangers and that I certainly do not recommend today–not unless great precautions are taken, such as having a reputable person present. An obvious danger is that, if witnesses go back on the statement they gave you or say that you put words in their mouth, you may have to be a witness. Acting as investigators, however, taught us how to assess the credibility of potential witnesses and how to use the laws of probability in unearthing evidence. Sometimes our investigations yielded remarkable results.

Mickey MacDonald kept telling me about seeing a "little girl" called "Madge" in a drugstore at the northeast corner of Dundas and Jarvis streets, and he said he had seen her in the store about 7:30 p.m. on Saturday, January 7, 1939. Windsor was killed about 7:39 p.m., many miles away, and if MacDonald was in the drugstore at 7:30 p.m. or thereabouts, he could not have been the killer. The accused had sent me on many wild-goose chases, and, initially, I was somewhat sceptical about the story. I made a few inquiries, but was not very successful. People did not want to talk to me. However, I persisted in my search and I found out that there was a girl by the name of Madge. Nobody knew where she lived, nobody knew what her last name was, but I did unearth the fact that she liked to roller-skate. So I went down to the nearby Mutual Street Arena, which at one time had been Toronto's premier sports arena but was then a roller-skating rink. I asked ushers and everybody I could contact whether they knew a girl by the name of Madge who was a customer of the Mutual Street Arena. Eventually, I received the information that she, together with a boy, had won some sort of a skating contest not long before. I was able to locate the boy, and I obtained from him her last name and her address. By this time it was 12:30 at night, and the defence was closing the next day. I did not think it was wise to try to contact the witness that night, but I arrived at the door of the apartment where she lived with her family the next morning at 8:00 and, much to my surprise, a pretty young woman, about sixteen or seventeen years of age, came to the door. I said, "I'm Mickey MacDonald's lawyer." She immediately called to her father. I was somewhat apprehensive about the reception I might receive. When the father came to the door, she said, "Father, this is Mickey MacDonald's lawyer." The father immediately said, "She's been telling us for months that Mickey couldn't have been the killer because she saw him over in the drugstore about 7:30 that night, but we thought she had made a mistake." We had found the missing witness at the last moment.

When she emerged from the apartment to go to Mr. Regan's office, she looked somewhat younger. She was wearing running shoes, short socks, and a blazer. She asked me if she could ride her bicycle to Mr. Regan's office, and I walked along beside her. Whatever defects may have attached to Mr. Regan's preparation from time to time, his reaction that morning was in the best tra-dition. He checked out the young woman and her story very efficiently with-in the time at his disposal and subjected her to a searching cross-examination before she was called as a witness. She was an impressive witness and a marked contrast to the Crown witnesses, some of whom were thugs and peo-ple of questionable antecedents.

The first jury, which convicted MacDonald and acquitted his brother Alex, undoubtedly thought she was sincere, though mistaken as to the time or the date. Still, cross-examination failed to shake her on this point.

Mr. Regan was not comfortable in the Court of Appeal and, since the accused was penniless, I was allowed to make the principal argument in that court. In those days, the bulk of appellate advocacy was in the hands of very senior members of the bar. The Court of Appeal appeared quite surprised when I stood up and said I was appearing for the appellant. Two of the mem-bers of the five-judge court, in particular, gave me a very rough time. The court was not gentle, courteous, and patient with young lawyers the way it is today. However, at the conclusion of the case three days later, the court con-gratulated me on my argument. Looking back, I think the judges congratu-lated me on my temerity at being there at all.

The Court of Appeal ordered a new trial, and the second jury acquitted MacDonald. I thought that, as a result of this success, my services would be in demand by accused who could pay a fee, but accused with money continued to retain the established members of the bar.

Some Memorable Witnesses

The late Verne McAree, who for many years wrote a popular column in the *Globe and Mail*, once said that I was fortunate in always having good wit-nesses. He said he knew from experience, because he had been one and I had won my case. It is true that I had called him as an expert witness in the pros-ecution of a publishing company on a charge of publishing an obscene book, and he was an impressive expert witness. I wonder now how anyone could have thought the book in question was obscene, but in 1949 it was a very seri-ous prosecution.

In retrospect, I think the witnesses referred to by Mr. McAree were in cases where I had the good fortune to be on the right side. Even a person who is innocent or a witness who is telling the truth may not make a good impression on the witness stand because of nervousness or for some other reason. I did have some good witnesses, and I cannot tell you about them all. One of the witnesses that I remember was Mr. Butler, an accused in the Aconic case, in whose innocence I came to believe despite the strength of the Crown's case. He was an outstanding witness notwithstanding that he, at times, became quite belligerent. The Crown alleged that Mr. Butler had engaged in "wash trading"–that much of the trading in Aconic shares involved trades between different brokerage accounts owned or controlled by Mr. Butler. The case for the Crown was that these trades were executed for the purpose of creating an appearance of public activity in the shares, or with a view to establishing an artificial price for them. Moreover, one of the Crown witnesses, whom we shall call X, testified that Mr. Butler had instructed him to create activity in the market and, in effect, to engage in "wash trading." Mr. Butler had an explanation for the impugned trades, and his defence, essentially, was that he lacked criminal intent.

A number of Crown witnesses with impeccable backgrounds gave evidence of events in which their testimony differed somewhat from that of Mr. Butler. In response, Mr. Butler stated he would not say these witnesses were lying, but they were mistaken. Crown counsel then came to X and said, "I suppose he is mistaken too?" Mr. Butler replied, "No, not him. He is lying."

One witness, in particular, stands out in my mind. William Bohozuk was charged with the murder of Evelyn Dick's baby, who was found encased in a block of cement in Dick's house. Bohozuk was truly innocent of the charge. One night, his sister brought to my hotel room a little boy aged about nine whom everyone called "Rocky." He was a very engaging little fellow and had a certain charm about him. His evidence went a long way towards proving that Bohozuk was innocent of the murder of Evelyn Dick's baby. My colleague Henry Schrieber and I were completely satisfied that he was telling the truth.

Trial judges at that time used to ask children of tender years who were offered as witnesses questions on a *voir dire* that an adult would have difficulty in answering on the spur of the moment. We had not asked the little boy any questions about his understanding of the nature of an oath. When he was called to the stand, the trial judge asked him what would happen to him if he swore on the Bible to tell the truth and told a lie. The boy, whose head barely showed above the witness box, in a voice that conveyed moral outrage at the mere thought of such wickedness, said, "Why, that's perjury!" The judge seemed somewhat startled at the knowledge of the criminal law displayed by such a small boy. He responded, "And what happens to you if you commit perjury?" The boy said, "Either jail or a fine." The judge asked, "Who told you that?" The boy answered, "Sister Sylvia at school." I relaxed, and the *voir dire* concluded with the judge finding that "Rocky" was well-qualified to take the oath. He was an excellent witness, and the accused was acquitted.

Not all potential witnesses have an appealing personality. I recall on one occasion defending a man on a charge of murdering his wife. He had a very good partial defence of drunkenness. He owned a small business, and his wife had done most of the work because he was usually drunk. I went to the jail to see him. I said, "Did you intend to kill your wife?" He looked at me as though I had taken leave of my senses and replied, "Certainly not, where would I ever find anyone to work the way she did *for nothing?*" There was a certain amount of cold-blooded logic in his answer but I did not think it would endear him to the jury. I decided I would not call him as a witness if I could get along without him. The Crown and the court accepted a plea of guilty of manslaughter part way through the trial, and I think this was the right result.

Generally speaking, however, I thought that if an accused claimed to be innocent, he or she should give evidence.

Expert Witnesses

Defence counsel must develop the knowledge or the antennae to recognize situations in which they may require the assistance of experts in other disciplines. Let me illustrate by reference to a case that occurred many years ago in which the driver of an automobile struck and killed a pedestrian and did not stop. He was charged with dangerous driving and leaving the scene of an accident with intent to evade liability. The case, on a superficial view of the facts, did not appear promising.

The facts were as follows. The accused was driving west on Lawrence Avenue on the evening in question when he struck and killed a pedestrian who got off an eastbound bus on the south side of Lawrence Avenue and then began to cross the street to the north side, which she had almost reached when she was struck. The automobile driven by the accused did not stop after striking the woman. It then mounted the curb, struck a telephone pole, returned to the roadway and continued west. When the automobile came to an intersecting street, it turned and proceeded north.

The attention of a police officer, seated in his cruiser at the intersection, was attracted by the manner in which the automobile was being driven. The officer followed it at high speed. The automobile being pursued stopped, and the driver got out and ran. The police officer pursued the driver on foot and said, "Stop or I'll shoot." The man being pursued immediately stopped and said, "Forgive me, officer, I don't know what I did." There was conflicting police evidence as to whether the accused was impaired.

The accused said he was driving along the street, keeping a proper lookout, and, although he had had something to drink, he was not affected by it. He had felt a bump and did not remember anything more until he heard the police officer say, "Stop or I'll shoot."

The visibility was poor that night because of the wind and the rain—conditions that imposed a higher duty on the accused to drive more slowly and keep his car under control so he could stop if someone loomed out of the darkness. The deceased was wearing dark clothing and carrying an umbrella that she had opened before crossing the road. The open umbrella was likely between her and the westbound automobile driven by the accused, since the wind was from the east that night. Counsel for the accused had obtained a meteorological report.

The deceased, however, was only twenty-five feet in front of a nurse who also got off the bus and walked across the street. She saw the automobile approaching and kept her eyes on it, but she did not see the automobile strike the deceased. She heard the bang and thought that the hood of the automobile had flown up. It was strange that, in the circumstances, she did not see the automobile strike the deceased. She also testified at the preliminary hearing that after she heard the noise, the automobile proceeded at the same speed; it neither speeded up nor slowed down. That also was odd. A driver who knew he had hit someone and was conscious of it would either momentarily slow down until panic overtook him and then speed up or he would instantaneously speed up. The remark that the accused made, "Forgive me, officer, I don't know what I did," struck me as being consistent with a person coming out of a period of clouded consciousness.

Dr. Kenneth Gray, a world figure in the field of forensic psychiatry, examined the accused carefully over a period of time and testified that, from the moment when the accused felt the bump, his consciousness shut off as a result of the traumatic emotional experience and he was in a state of automatism thereafter while driving in a purely mechanical way, without being aware of what he was doing. If the accused was in a state of automatism, it would, of course, negative an intent to evade liability. It would also provide an explanation for the accused's erratic driving after he struck the deceased.

I requested Professor Valtin Henderson of the Department of Optics and Acoustics at the University of Toronto to study the scene. He waited until it was a rainy night. He found that, at the point of impact, old-fashioned lighting created an additional hazard under the conditions prevailing that night, rather than creating greater visibility. A short distance away, more modern lighting had been installed that provided greater visibility. The old-fashioned lighting, casting light and dark shadows on the roadway, created conditions similar to the camouflage used to conceal objects in war.

The expert witness said, in effect, that the deceased was invisible. Thus, a prudent driver keeping a proper lookout, trying to see what was in front, might very well not have seen the deceased. The accused was acquitted.

There was no unfairness in the trial. Counsel for the accused had full disclosure of the Crown's case. The case turned on the recognition by defence counsel of the need for expert evidence and the value of the expert evidence.

Cross-examination

I have always thought that cross-examination is the most difficult art of the advocate to master. Some years ago I read a work of fiction about a lawyer who was on his way to court to address the jury in a criminal case in which he was defence counsel. The lawyer was in a happy frame of mind. The surprises and the tensions inherent in the presentation of evidence by the prosecution or the defence were over. The case was complete, and he was looking forward to the prospect of his jury address. It seemed to me that the author had accurately portrayed the feelings of a defence counsel. Everyone, by hard work and a study of the art of putting together a jury address, should be able to give a satisfactory performance in this aspect of the trial.

Cross-examination is different. Advocates are always concerned with whether they will be able to do justice to the clients' case in exposing bias, error, or falsehood. Many of the great cross-examinations referred to in the literature on advocacy reflect no more than the application of skills and techniques in the use of material gathered by other people. These kinds of skills can be acquired. In addition, of course, the advocate requires the good fortune to possess the necessary material. Moreover, a sense of timing is required to get the maximum benefit from the use of material affecting credibility.

Cross-examination Based on Probability

The most difficult cross-examinations are those in which there are no inconsistent or contradictory previous statements or utterances on material points by the witnesses; where there is nothing in the background of the witnesses affecting their credibility; where the witnesses honestly believe that they are giving a correct account of events; and the cross-examiner must expose the fallacy in the witnesses' testimony by making its improbability apparent to the jury.

In the *Linton* murder case, which took place over forty years ago, the accused had been convicted of murder at the first trial without even a recommendation for clemency. In those days, people convicted of murder without a recommendation for mercy were usually hanged. The Court of Appeal ordered a new trial on the ground of misdirection.

The accused had a valid defence of provocation, which the first jury, however, had rejected. The accused had a housekeeper, Mr. S, who left the accused's employment and reported to her estranged husband, S, and her brother, K, certain alleged misconduct by Linton towards her fourteen-year-old daughter. The brother went to the accused's house late at night and administered a savage beating to the accused. The husband and the brother returned early in the morning, requesting Mrs. S's clothing. The accused, no doubt in fear, remembering what had happened to him earlier, told them not to come in, that he had a gun. He called out to his next-door neighbour to summon the police if they tried to get in. The two men, however, broke down the door. The accused shot S in the stomach, and he staggered out and collapsed on the front lawn. K, the second man, ran. Linton pursued him and shot and killed him in the backyard. A neighbour, whom we will call Mr. Jones, said he was awakened by the sound of shouting and went out and watched the scene from his front porch. He said that he saw S stagger from the doorway and collapse, and, after chasing K, the accused went back into the house, where he remained. About five minutes later, S, who was lying on the front lawn, attempted to get up, whereupon the accused came out of the house and killed the injured man by repeatedly clubbing him over the head with a heavy rifle. The witness gave a very graphic description of the event and said it sounded like a pumpkin being squashed. The heavy rifle was an exhibit, and it was bent into a bow shape. The way the witness told it, the accused, after the first episode, had gone into the house, remained there for an appreciable time, and then, seeing that S was still alive, attempting to get up, went out and deliberately killed him after there had been time for the accused's passion to cool.

The theory of the defence was that no such thing had happened and that the shooting and clubbing were all part of one continuous episode–that they were the actions of a man out of control, crazed by fear and anger. However, if the five-minute interval could not be wiped out, the accused was likely to be convicted of murder again. The witness, however, was very firm in his evidence, and efforts to undermine it at the first trial were unsuccessful. Moreover, he was a very confident and respectable person. The confidence of the witness was somewhat shaken at the second trial when he was confronted with contradictions on some matters between his testimony at the trial and at the preliminary hearing. Counsel then went right to the heart of the matter:

Q. Mr. Jones, the deceased S. was well known to you.

A. Yes.

Q. He was a friend of yours.

A. Yes.

Q. When you saw him stagger out of the house holding him stomach and collapse on the front lawn, you realized he must be seriously hurt.

A. Yes.

Q. Did you phone the police?

A. No.

Q. Did you call your wife to phone the police?

A. No.

Q. Did you phone for an ambulance or a doctor?

A. No.

Q. Did you ask your wife to phone for an ambulance or doctor?

A. No.

Q. When you saw Linton emerge from the house with the gun and hit S., did you yell, "Seth, don't do it" or "Stop it"?

A. No.

Q. Do you mean to say you stood there for five minutes and watched all this happening and you never raised your hand or your voice to try and prevent it and bring assistance?

A. Yes, but ...

By this time there were beads of perspiration on his face and you could almost read his mind. It was as though he was saying to himself, "I guess I don't look very good standing there for five minutes watching what happened and doing nothing about it." So counsel thought this was the appropriate time to provide him with an escape hatch. He asked the final question:

Q. Mr. Jones, the fact is that you were not standing there for five minutes. The interval between the time S. fell to the ground and the striking of S. all happened so quickly that you didn't have the time to do anything, isn't that right?

A. Yes, that is right. [Gratefully]

And, of course, this is exactly what had happened. These events had all happened in one continuing, rapid sequence of events. Linton, crazed with fear and anger and completely out of control, had killed two people. He was convicted in the second trial of manslaughter only, and I think that was the right verdict because, although the killings were savage, the provocation was extreme. But even though I had argued the case in the Court of Appeal and was thoroughly familiar with every line of that evidence, and had talked about it with my associate Walter Tuchtie (later His Honour Judge Tuchtie), who was an extremely shrewd and perceptive lawyer, it really did not dawn on either of us just how improbable that man's story was until very late in the day. It is utterly improbably that a decent person, knowing that a man he knew was lying on the ground, seriously injured, and seeing the accused go back in the house, after chasing another man, would do absolutely nothing but would wait for five minute for the accused to come out and kill the injured man. Common sense suggests that, if there was time, he would go back into his house, telephone the police, and say, "There's an injured man here. Send an ambulance down." In fact, he did not stand there for five minutes waiting for S to be killed. Once counsel could show the witness that it was illogical he could act that way, and make the jury understand how illogical it would be for any person to act that way, they would be prepared to believe he was wrong. Indeed, the witness was prepared to accept it too, once he was shown that it was improbable that he, as a decent person, would act in that way.

Cross-examination is a difficult art, and often you have to discover and expose any improbabilities in the witness's story.

Cross-examination of an Expert Witness Based on Previous Writings of the Witness

An entirely different type of cross-examination happens when highly qualified expert witnesses are confronted with their previous writings. This occurred in the cross-examination of Dr. Keith Simpson in the *Truscott Reference*.

In the *Truscott* case, one of the most important issues was whether the time of death could be estimated with any accuracy from the stomach contents, from the time when the deceased had her last meal. Dr. Pennistan, who performed the autopsy, stated that, in his opinion, considering the amount of food in the stomach in its undigested state, Lynne Harper was killed before 7:45 on the night of June 9, 1959. She had eaten her last meal at 5:45, and he estimated death at within two hours after her last meal. If she had been killed before 7:45, the Crown contended that Steven Truscott had the exclusive opportunity to kill her. Truscott had an alibi from about 8:00 p.m. onward. The defence always strongly contended that it was not possible, on the basis of the stomach contents, to come to an accurate judgment as to time of death. The prosecution called Dr. Keith Simpson, regarded as one of the world's leading pathologists. He had written a book on forensic medicine and was the editor of the twelfth edition of Taylor's two-volume work on medical jurisprudence. He was the author of numerous articles, had performed over 100,000 autopsies, and, without a doubt, was a highly qualified person. We knew what Dr. Simpson's position was going to be because he had written a book review of Mrs. LaBourdais's book on the trial of Steven Truscott. In the review, he said he thought that Dr. Pennistan had come to a very reasonable conclusion.

In preparation for the cross-examination of Dr. Simpson, I researched or caused to be researched every article and every book that had ever been written on estimating the time of death from stomach contents, with particular reference to any that Dr. Simpson had written. Dr. Simpson, having given evidence that, in his opinion, Dr. Pennistan had come to a reasonable conclusion that Miss Harper had come to her death within two hours of the last meal, the object of the cross-examination was twofold. First, to show that the stomach contents, in relation to the time of consuming the last meal, do not afford a reliable guide to the time of death within narrow limits and certainly could not establish that the deceased had died within two hours of her last meal. Second, to show that the presence of *rigor mortis* in hot weather and the lack of an advanced state of decomposition did not confirm that death had occurred before 7:45 p.m. on June 9th but tended to show that death had occurred less than forty-eight hours before the autopsy, which was performed almost forty-eight hours after the estimated time of death. This detail provides explanation, for no cross-examination is meaningful unless you know what the issues are. We read a great deal about the importance of the first question. The first question may be important, though sometimes it is the last one that is the most significant. In this particular case, I knew the first question I was going to ask Dr. Simpson before he got on the plane to come to Canada.

Q. Now, you have written extensively, Dr. Simpson, in the field of forensic medicine?

A. Yes.

Q. Now, I've read a good many of your books and one of the books you have written is entitled Forensic Medicine and, as my learned friend Mr. Scott says, it has gone through five editions now?

A. Yes.

Q. And in the last edition, indeed, you say that this edition has been combed to ensure it is abreast of the times. I notice at page 7 of the book—of course, I realize here that you are dealing with a post-mortem event—you say under the heading of "Cooling," "this is the only real guide to the lapse of time during the first 18 hours after death and an early measurement is often vital to the establishment of an approximate time of death."

A. Yes, sir.

Q. Do you, anywhere in this book, suggest that the stomach contents and the state to which digestion has proceeded following the last meal is a reliable guide to the time of death?

A. No, sir. I think that that is, as may be evident to you, a short book for the student.

Q. It would not have made it much bigger to put in a sentence indicating that the stomach contents were also a reliable guide?

A. No, sir. I appreciate that, but it is not intended to be a comprehensive work, of course, having been only for students.

Q. It should contain the things upon which there is a greater consensus.

A. I think you may expect the next edition, sir, to contain some reference.

Q. You are going to change the next edition?

A. I think it is how one improves one's textbooks, by experience.

Q. When did you decide to change the next edition?

A. Each time I'm writing I'm learning, and each case helps me to improve the next edition.

Q. I will throw this away and buy the next edition. You also deal with this in your 12th edition of Taylor, which you have edited?

A. Yes, sir.

Q. I should say you do deal with stomach contents.

A. There is a reference to the stomach contents there. It is a more comprehensive work.

Q. I think, to be fair, I should read everything that is there so I will not be taking it out of its context. The heading is "Inference as to the Time of Death." It is page 210.

A. I think I know the paragraph you are referring to.

Q. "Inference as to the time of death from the state of food. The site and state of digestion of contents of the stomach and bowels may be used as an additional means for fixing the hour of death in relation to the last meal. Most elaborate tables have been prepared of the time taken by the stomach to digest certain articles of diet but these are wholly unreliable."

A. Could I stop there for a moment if it will not interfere?

Q. No, it will not interfere.

A. I would draw a sharp difference between the state of digestion, which is a chemical process, and the emptying of the stomach. The state of digestion means the chemical process of digestion. I make a sharp distinction between these words.

Q. "The rate of digestion varies in different persons and according to the functional efficiency of the gastric mucosa."

A. Yes.

Q. The stomach cannot empty until the stomach digests the food?

A. No, the stomach can empty even in cases where the gastric juices are absent or almost into the bowels. The rate of emptying does not depend on the state of digestion.

Q. What I am quoting is irrelevant at this state?

A. No, it appears to depend more on the state of stiffening of the food.

Q. I will come to something that is relevant. "Gastric and intestinal activity is much retarded in cases of trauma and insensibility. Even without the paralysis of movement that is common to grave injury or deep insensibility, the process of emptying the stomach may be very much delayed."

A. Yes, sir.

Q. I am talking of something that is germane?

A. Yes, that's very apt.

Q. That's very apt?

A. Yes.

Q. You quote that an examination of the body of a woman strangled at about 11:00 p.m. one February night showed meat fibre, intact peas, fragments of mint leaf and potato together with some apple pips, still present in the stomach. Very little has passed into the duodenum and none into the jejunum. She had had her last major meal of roast lamb, peas, boiled potatoes, mint sauce, apple tart and custard at 2:00 to 2:30 p.m.–no less than nine hours previously.

A. Yes, I remember that case.

Q. The description is remarkably [similar] ... First of all, the cause of death was strangling?

A. Yes.

Q. The cause of death in this case was strangling and the description of the stomach contents is remarkably like the description given by Dr. Pennistan because it is said his examination showed meat fibre, intact peas (and intact peas I think were found here) and fragments of mint leaf, and potato (and in this case Dr. Pennistan felt that he could not identify the material as potatoes because it had passed into a discrete phase, although Dr. Brooks I think in fairness said he could see some pieces of potato). Do you agree that the description is very much like Dr. Pennistan's?

A. Yes.

Q. Very little had passed into the duodenum. Again, this is remarkably like Dr. Pennistan's?

A. Yes.

Q. The process seems to have gone further in the case of the deceased, Lynne Harper, because he used the words, "very little had passed through the duodenum." Is that correct?" The process was farther along than this nine-hour case. Is that correct?

A. Yes.

Q. You have these analogies in the two cases and "she had her last major meal of roast lamb, peas, boiled potatoes, mint sauce, apple tart and custard no less than nine hours previously."

A. Yes.

Here you had in a book, edited by the witness, a case where the stomach contents, similar to those that existed in the case of Lynne Harper, were proved to have existed notwithstanding a lapse of nine hours since the last meal.

Counsel then went on to deal with the post-mortem changes, the rigor, and the state of decomposition, endeavouring to turn Dr. Simpson into a defence witness by showing that these particular things, far from confirming the opinion of Dr. Pennistan about the stomach contents indicating that death took place some forty-eight hours before the autopsy, indicated death had occurred within a shorter period than forty-eight hours.

Q. I think in fairness you say that rigor mortis is the most unreliable of post-mortem events?

A. Yes, sir.

Q. One could not on the basis of the existence or the extent of rigor present either on the afternoon of June 11th or on the evening of June 11th pinpoint the time of death is between 7:00 and 7:45?

A. To start with, pinpoint is not a word one would use to establish the time of death from one observation. It is not a matter of pinpointing. It is always an approximation.

Q. The words of Dr. Pennistan were that he would put the time of death between 7:00 and 7:45. Those are relatively narrow limits.

Putting the time of death, does that not indicate it was determining the time of death?

A. I do not think it was pinpointing, just giving a period of time and putting it in that period.

Q. 7:00 to 7:45?

A. Yes.

Q. Does the existence of rigor and its extent on June 11th enable you to place the time of death within that period?

A. No, sir, these too are variable.

Q. It is much too variable–the onset and duration of rigor mortis. Is the onset of rigor hastened by warm weather?

A. It tends to be, sir.

Q. Is the disappearance of rigor also hastened by warm weather?

A. It tends to be.

Q. And recognizing, as you have indicated, that rigor is an unreliable event nevertheless, you do in your works give what you would expect, is that so, with respect to the passing off of rigor?

A. Yes, sir, I do give the sort of periods that are usual.

Q. I think you have a table in your small book.

A. Yes, sir, this is the student's guide that I first wrote of, yes.

Q. You give a table I think at page 17 on rigor mortis. You say 5 to 7 hours rigor appearing in face, jaw, and neck muscles.

A. That is the start, the likely start, yes.

Q. Seven to 9, spread to arms and trunk and reaching legs; 12 to 18, rigor fully established; 24 to 36, rigor passing away in the same order. Rigor gone in 36 hours. Here we've still got some present?

A. These are the likely periods, yes, sir.

Q. Insofar as there is any value in rigor, the existence of the rigor that was observed by Dr. Pennistan would point to less than a two-day interval.

A. It tends to, sir.

You will note there is very careful use of words by both cross-examining counsel and by Dr. Simpson, who I think was being very fair. The word used by counsel was "expect." If Dr. Simpson had said, "No, I wouldn't expect it," then what was he putting it in the book for, if it was no use at all? But counsel recognized throughout that this was not a mathematical proposition, though there are certain things that normally happen; one is dealing with probabilities, and certainly this is what would be *expected* to occur. It tended to indicate that Lynne Harper was killed after 7:45 p.m. on June 9th. Then, going on to the decomposition:

Q. You have heard the evidence given as to the atmospheric temperature.

A. Yes, sir.

Q. Quoting from memory, I think 88 degrees on the 9th is the high with a low of 65 or thereabouts; on the 10th, high 92, low about 66; 11th, high of 90, low of about 65. Those are very high temperatures.

A. Yes.

Q. And getting very close to the tropical temperatures that you mentioned?

A. Yes.

Q. Between 80 degrees and 100 degrees?

A. Yes, sir, that is certainly fair comment, sir.

Q. Also, again recognizing there may well be some variation in these post-mortem events, you give a table of what you would expect in respect to greenstaining in the flanks?

A. Yes, sir.

Q. You have put this as appearing in two days?

A. I think that is what I was saying there, that one would *expect* it in about two days.

Q. And you say in warm hot months these processes are accelerated.

A. Yes.

Q. Because putrefaction may occur in 24 hours.

A. Yes, sir, I have seen it in Egypt and Cyprus.

Q. And the weather here would be comparable?

A. Yes, it is not very far away from it.

Q. As a matter of fact, if you were to assume that death occurred within two hours after the meal, as Dr. Pennistan did, bringing the time of death to prior to 7:45 on the 9th, and Dr. Pennistan started to perform his autopsy at 7:15 on the 11th, there would be a lapse of 48 hours.

A. Yes.

Q. And he does not mention any greenstaining.

A. No, I don't think there was any described.

Q. Again, if there had been a two-day interval, and I point out it was only half an hour less than two days, you would *expect* it?

A. Yes, sir.

Q. Greenstaining?

A. Yes, sir, I would. You may remember I said earlier in evidence I would expect it, but it does not always appear.

Q. There are variable factors?

A. Yes.

Q. But, nevertheless, it is something you would expect?

A. Yes, sir, I think I would.

Q. The fact that you do not find it, if it means anything, it tends to put the time of death later rather than earlier?

A. Yes, I think you put that very fairly, sir.

On these two points, so far as he is able to go, Dr. Simpson has indicated that the post-mortem description tended to prove less than a two-day interval between the estimated time of death and the performance of the autopsy.

Changes in the Style of Advocacy: The Criminal Bar

In the late 1930s, 1940s, and 1950s a new group of defence counsel appeared on the scene. Styles of advocacy were changing. Eloquence was not lacking in the new advocacy, but it was eloquence of a different kind and more suited to a rapidly changing world in which juries were becoming more worldly and better informed.

I always think of John Robinette as the peerless advocate at home in any court in any kind of case. So was Charles Dubin, brilliant and a great cross-examiner. Arthur Maloney sometimes became quite emotional, but his eloquence, courage, humanity, and generosity of spirit exemplified the best tradition of the advocate. Finally, there was Joseph Sedgwick, whose mastery of language, wonderful voice, ready wit, and knowledge of human nature lent a special quality to his advocacy. His buoyant good humour and courage in the face of adversity made him a wonderful colleague.

The criminal bar remained small, however, because few lawyers could expect to survive economically if their practice was exclusively devoted to criminal law. Legal assistance, when provided to defendants without means in criminal cases, continued to be provided by lawyers on a voluntary basis.

Another tradition of the defence bar was that older lawyers with a wide experience in criminal cases were willing to share their experience with younger lawyers by giving them advice free of charge. That tradition is worth preserving.

Defending capital cases can be lonely and emotionally draining. Most of the small group of lawyers who defended murder cases in Toronto when all murder was capital were, or became, close friends, and we helped each other.

You would receive a telephone call from a member of this group who might say, "I have a murder case and I am worried about a particular aspect of it. Could we have lunch and talk it over?"

The size of the bar now has, no doubt, made this kind of association and help more difficult. However, there are more continuing legal education programs and seminars dealing with criminal law problems. There is more in the way of published material on codes of professional conduct, and there are professional conduct committees to which lawyers can turn for assistance with respect to difficult ethical problems.

Lawyers, as we have noted, acted without fee in many criminal cases, other than murder cases, where the accused lacked the means to pay a lawyer. Obviously, they could not provide assistance for all defendants without funds in criminal cases. Many poor people were undefended. For over a hundred years after the right to counsel was established, the right to counsel merely meant that an accused was entitled to the services of a lawyer if he could retain one.

The concept of the right to counsel as a human right, as distinct from a noble or charitable endeavour on the part of the legal profession to provide assistance for defendants in criminal cases who lacked the means to employ a lawyer, did not evolve until the 1960s. The basic philosophy of the Ontario Legal Aid Plan, which was introduced in March 1967, is that a person requiring legal representation should not be disadvantaged by poverty and, so far as possible, should be placed in the same position as a person who has funds with which to pay a lawyer. This philosophy is unassailable. Like all legal aid plans, it requires ongoing scrutiny to ensure that it is not abused, and ongoing assessment and revision from time to time to ensure that it is abreast of the times. The recognition of the right to counsel as a human right reflected a growing awareness that the ideal of equal justice is not a reality if the defendant in a criminal case is deprived of the choice of counsel by reason of poverty.

At the present time, moreover, an accused who is unable to pay a lawyer, but who wishes to be represented by a lawyer at trial, is entitled under sections 7 and 11(d) of the *Charter* to be provided with a lawyer funded by the state, where representation by a lawyer is essential to the fair trial of the accused. Furthermore, section 10(b) of the *Charter*, which provides that everyone on arrest or detention has the right to retain and instruct counsel without delay and to be informed of that right, imposes on the police the duty of telling the accused of the existence and availability of duty counsel and the existence of legal aid plans.

Before the mid-twentieth century, criminal law, while not entirely over-looked in the law schools, was not considered as important as some other subjects; no doubt, that was so because so few people expected to practise in that field. In the early 1960s, only four students in the first-year class at the Harvard Law School expressed any interest in the practice of criminal law. Happily, that has all changed. Criminal law has now become a major subject at law schools. There was formerly little legal writing in the field of criminal law. Legal works, with the exception of *Kenny's Outlines of Criminal Law*, for the most part consisted of annotated criminal codes and a few works on criminal law primarily designed for the practitioner–works that were excellent in their own way. There were, however, few treatises, such as we now have, examining the principles of criminal liability. Today there is a great deal of literature of very high quality on the criminal law which has been influential in its development.

The three forces that have profoundly altered the practice of criminal law in my lifetime have been the advent of comprehensive legal aid, the *Charter*, and the increased emphasis on the teaching of criminal law in law schools.

The *Charter*

The *Canadian Charter of Rights and Freedoms* has had an impact on our criminal justice system that far exceeded the expectations of many lawyers. I fully support the principles or values protected by the *Charter* and firmly believe that these fundamental rights should be enshrined in a Charter.

The recognition of the importance of the individual is fundamental in a free society, and no society can endure in which the individual has ceased to be important. Recent events in Europe illustrate the truth of this statement. The *Charter* affirms the importance, worth, and dignity of the individual and guarantees that reasonable expectations of privacy shall not be intruded upon by the state except for compelling social reasons. The *Charter*, by its guarantee of the fundamental freedoms of conscience, religion, thought, belief, and expression, is a constant reminder not only to government but to all of us that a true democracy can provide shelter for many different lifestyles, opinions, and beliefs.

Many of the important *Charter* issues have arisen in criminal cases, which is not surprising, since most of the legal rights enshrined in the *Charter* were forged on the anvil of criminal procedure at common law to ensure a fair trial. I do not think that there was any substantial danger in Canada of direct attack upon rights by government or by any significant group in society before the *Charter*. The real danger was one of insidious and subtle erosion by invasions born of expediency, which cumulatively had already significantly impaired such fundamental rights as the right to remain silent, the presumption of innocence, and the right to be secure from unreasonable search or seizure. These erosions are now, since the advent of the *Charter*, being corrected by the courts.

As the courts define and elaborate the guarantees enshrined in the *Charter*, we are realizing more and more that what is considered fair and just in one era, even in highly civilized societies, may not be considered either fair or just in another era. The great Victorian jurists considered that their criminal justice system was superior to any other system in the world. No doubt it was, compared to other legal systems existing at that time. The presumption of innocence applied to a person charged with a crime. The accused had the right to trial by jury. The practice that existed in former times of keeping the accused in the dark until the last moment with respect to the case against him or her had long since disappeared. Since 1836 an accused charged with a felony has had the right to be represented by counsel–but, as I have pointed out, that merely meant the accused were entitled to be represented by counsel if they could retain one. Sir James Stephen, in the late nineteenth century, was able to say that the situation of the accused who were not represented by counsel was often pitiable, even if they had a good case. Today, we would not tolerate the unfairness of the accused, charged with serious offences, being deprived of counsel because they lacked the means to pay one.

The Effect of the *Charter* on the Spy Trials–If the *Charter* Had Existed

During the last half of the 1940s a number of cases, known as the "spy trials," attracted wide public attention. They had their origin in the defection of Igor Gouzenko, whose story reads much like a novel.

Gouzenko was a young Russian employed in the Soviet Embassy in Ottawa as a cipher clerk. In later statements, he said that he was impressed by the freedom possessed by the individual in Canada and was concerned about Russia maintaining a spy ring in the country. Canada had assisted Russia in the war.

Gouzenko left the Soviet Embassy on September 5, 1945, taking with him certain documents he had selected that disclosed the existence of a spy ring operated at the embassy. That day and the following day he made a number of calls to public offices and newspapers, but no one took him seriously. On returning to his apartment that evening, disillusioned and weary, he saw two men keeping the apartment under surveillance. Shortly afterwards, someone knocked on the door and called his name. Gouzenko kept silent, but his presence was revealed by his child running across the floor. He went through his back door to the apartment of a neighbour, a non-commissioned officer of the Royal Canadian Air Force (RCAF), who agreed to take in Gouzenko and his family. The RCAF officer set off on his bicycle to summon the police. Two police officers arrived in a cruiser, and Gouzenko told them his story and requested protection. Shortly after midnight, four men from the Soviet Embassy broke into Gouzenko's apartment. The two constables found them ransacking the apartment.

The following day Gouzenko was taken to the Royal Canadian Mounted Police (RCMP), where he told his story and turned over his documents. This time, people listened to him.

After Gouzenko's disclosure, Order-in-Council PC 6444 was enacted on October 6, 1945, by the Governor General-in-Council under the *War Measures Act*. It authorized the acting prime minister or the minister of justice to order that a person be interrogated or detained if either minister was satisfied that the person might communicate confidential and secret information to a foreign power or otherwise act in a manner prejudicial to the state. The order-in-council now appears draconian. People were detained and interrogated without being informed of the reason for their detention and without being advised of their right to counsel. And that was legal at the time.

Subsequently, on February 5, 1946, a royal commission consisting of Mr. Justice Taschereau and Mr. Justice Kellock of the Supreme Court of Canada was established under the *Inquiries Act*. The commission had power to summon witnesses and compel them to give evidence under oath and to inquire into whether public officials or other persons in a position of trust had communicated secret and confidential information to a foreign power.

A substantial number of persons were detained by the RCMP and interrogated. They were then brought before the commission of inquiry as witnesses under subpoena and examined under oath. Some of the people brought before the commission, although they were witnesses in form, were in fact suspects. There was no obligation on the commission at that time to advise the persons called as witnesses of their right to counsel or of their right to object to answer under section 5 of the *Canada Evidence Act*. If invoked, this section would have prevented their evidence from being used to incriminate them in subsequent criminal proceedings.

Interesting questions arise as to the effect of the *Charter* if a similar situation were to arise again. Perhaps there would have been no violation of the *Charter*, section 9, which provides that "Everyone has the right not to be *arbitrarily* detained or imprisoned." Clearly, there would have been a violation of section 10 (if it had then existed), which provides that everyone has the right on arrest or detention:

(a) to be informed promptly of the reasons therefor;

(b) to retain and instruct counsel without delay and to be informed of that right.

Could the order-in-council authorizing the detention and interrogation of suspected persons, which, by implication, authorized their detention and interrogation without informing them of the reason for their detention and their right to retain and instruct counsel without delay, be considered a justified reasonable limit on section 10, under section 1 of the *Charter*, because of an emergency situation involving the safety of Canada?

The Crown did not seek to have admitted in evidence at their trials the answers obtained by the police interrogation of those detained, but evidence before the royal commission given by the detainees was admitted against them at their subsequent trials. Would the evidence of the detainees before the royal commission have been so infected by their unconstitutional detention and interrogation under the *Charter* that this evidence would, since the advent of the *Charter*, be excluded?

The law at the time was clear that evidence compulsorily given under oath before a body legally authorized to take the evidence was admissible, without proof that the evidence was given voluntarily. There is, however, a serious question in my mind as to whether the compulsory examination of the detainees by the royal commission in the circumstances would have withstood scrutiny under sections 11(c) and 7 of the *Charter*. Charges were subsequently laid against a number of people for conspiracy and for offences under the *Official Secrets Act*. Some people were convicted largely on the basis of their evidence given before the royal commission.

The *Official Secrets Act* contained a number of presumptions. Under section 3(4) of the *Official Secrets Act*, if a person had the name and address of someone who was a foreign agent, that person was presumed to have been in contact with the foreign agent unless proof was established to the contrary. Section 3(3) of the Act provided that, in any proceedings against a person for an offence against that section, the fact that a person had been in communication with a foreign agent was evidence that the person had, for a purpose prejudicial to the safety or interests of the state, obtained or attempted to obtain information that might be directly or indirectly useful to a foreign power.

The presumptions created by section 3 of the *Official Secrets Act* are artificial and, in my opinion, would not survive *R. v. Oakes*. Certainly, section 13 of the *Charter* would have precluded the use of the evidence given by a number of people before the royal commission to incriminate them at their subsequent trial. Section 13 provides:

> Self-incrimination.
>
> 13. A witness who testifies in any proceedings has the right not to have any incriminating evidence so given used to incriminate that witness in any other proceedings, except in a prosecution for perjury or for the giving of contradictory evidence.

I was involved as defence counsel in five of these spy cases, four in the Court of Appeal and one at the trial level. In retrospect, the case at the trial level was rather easy. One of the documents that Gouzenko had taken away with him said that a Royal Canadian Air Force officer, called Poland, had supplied a valuable map, so the police went around and detained Squadron Leader Fred Poland. Then they ransacked his office. On several occasions he had written in his diary the name Pavlov, who was the head of the Russian Secret Police. The presumption arose that Poland was in communication with Pavlov, followed by another presumption that he had obtained or attempted to obtain information prejudicial to the safety of Canada. Then, of course, there was the document that said a Royal Canadian Air Force officer named Poland had supplied a valuable map. The document was, of course, hearsay. Gouzenko had never met Poland. Gouzenko had to admit in cross-examination that every person in the spy ring had what he called a "cover name." The name in the document was an alias and was not the real name of anyone.

Poland was a very feisty type of man. When the police came to his door at about midnight and took him into custody without informing him of the reason, he called out to his wife, "Well, if you don't hear from me, dear, I'll be in the salt mines of Siberia." The police thought, "Ah, very suspicious." They had not mentioned anything about Russia, and here he was talking about the salt mines of Siberia. Poland later explained this remark. He said the way in which he was taken into custody, without being informed of the reason, reminded him of the way the Russian czars dispatched people to Siberia.

Poland had a very good explanation for why the name Pavlov was in his diary. He had met Pavlov at a cocktail party given by the Free French Legation and he liked him. He was a very charming man. The Pavlovs had a new baby, and Poland and his wife went over to the Pavlovs' home to visit them. Pavlov and Poland agreed to have lunch together, so Poland diarized the name Pavlov. Imagine a person involved in a Russian spy ring putting the name of the head of the Russian secret police in his diary! Poland's story could only be true. He telephoned Pavlov to invite him to lunch, and Pavlov said, "Well, Poland, I am very busy today. Call me in ten days or so." He made a note in his diary to call Pavlov in ten days. He telephoned Pavlov again in ten days, but received the same answer. After a few more telephone calls he got the idea that Pavlov did not want to see him, and he stopped calling him. That was really the case against Poland.

The judge, in acquitting Poland, said, "Mr. Poland I am acquitting you not because I have a reasonable doubt about your guilt, but because I am completely satisfied that you are innocent."

Some Further Reflections

As I have indicated, I am one of those who view the advent of the *Charter* with favour. I am not suggesting that we should not be sensitive to *Charter* defences, but *excessive* or *undue* reliance on *Charter* remedies can, in my view, lead to a decline in the overall skills of the advocate. In most criminal cases, the facts are controlling. The facts are not always what they appear to be. Frequently, of course, investigation shows they are what they appear to be. Most of those criminal cases that are won will continue to be won by exhaustive and intelligent investigation of the facts, and by the application to the facts of the skills of the advocate in presenting the case, in cross-examination, and in persuasive argument on the facts before the judge or jury.

In modern times, both the Crown and the defence have available to them much greater resources in the way of investigative aids and scientific evidence. The defence has the benefit of the principle of disclosure of the Crown's case. Criminal investigations are more complex and trials are becoming longer. Some increase in the length of trials is, of course, to be expected. However, the increase in their resources places a great responsibility on both Crown and defence counsel to use them wisely and to avoid prolonging trials unnecessarily. In the biography of Sir Bernard Spilsbury there is a reference to the trial in 1912 of Seddon for murder by poisoning. Counsel for the prosecution was Sir Rufus Isaacs, the attorney general of Great Britain. The defence counsel was Sir Edward Marshall Hall, the greatest British defence counsel of his time. The author says that this was the longest murder trial that had taken place up to that time. The trial lasted ten days. It seems to me that at the present time a murder case of any complexity is just getting underway in ten days.

In 1966 the American Bar Association appointed a committee to examine the role of the defence counsel—among other things. A few American lawyers, during the turbulent 1960s, thought it was necessary to espouse the ideology of the client and to use the trial of the accused as a political platform. The chairman of the committee was the Honourable Mr. Justice Burger, later chief justice of the Supreme Court of the United States, who became a good friend. In May of that year I was invited to come to Washington to express the Canadian view of the proper role of the defence counsel. There were present that day, among others, Frank Hogan, the district attorney of Manhattan County, the senior district attorney in the United States, and Edward Bennett Williams, an outstanding American defence counsel. Williams had successfully defended such different clients as James Hoffa, on a charge of perjury, and Senator Connolly, on a charge of taking "kickbacks." He thought that the image of the defence counsel in the United States at that time was not good, and he examined the reasons for it. In expressing the Canadian point of view I said, in part:

> In Canada, those who act for the defence in major criminal cases are in the very forefront of the Bar. The body which regulates the conduct of lawyers in Ontario is the Law Society of Upper Canada. ... The titular head of the Law Society is known as the Treasurer. Two of the last three Treasurers have been lawyers who have outstanding reputations as defence counsel. [I was, of course, thinking of Joseph Sedgwick and John Robinette.]
>
> Actually, to be a defence lawyer where I come from is a sort of a status symbol. When a man dies, you will often read in his obituary that he was a noted criminal lawyer. He really wasn't, but obviously his family and friends think that enhances his prestige. There is no reason why the defence lawyer should not be an outstanding figure at the Bar.

The role of the defence counsel is to provide professional advice and assistance to the client in accordance with the strict ethical standards that govern the role of defence counsel. The defence counsel is not a messenger, an *alter ego* merely to carry out the wishes of the client irrespective of whether they comport with professional standards. The role of defence counsel is to be the champion of the client's cause and to see that his or her rights are not wrongly invaded from any quarter. Sometimes, of course, the best advice you can give an accused after a thorough investigation of the facts is to plead guilty and endeavour to obtain a favourable disposition. The choice whether to plead guilty or not guilty is, of course, the client's.

The vital and necessary role of the advocate has never been more eloquently described than by Lord Birkett when he said in his book *Six Great Advocates:*

> I am quite sure that when men and women are brought into the civil or criminal courts, for whatever reason, they should be able to turn for assistance at what may be the critical moments of their lives to a trained body of advocates, independent and fearless, who are

pledged to see that they are protected against injustice and that their rights are not wrongly invaded from any quarter. The vocation of the advocate calls for the nicest sense of honour and for a complete devotion to the ideals of justice, and I believe it to be a lofty and necessary calling which is vital for the maintenance of that way of life in which we have come to believe.

I firmly believe that with the extension of legal services and the increasing complexity of modern society, the vital role of the advocate, as stated so eloquently by Lord Birkett, is more widely recognized and understood by the public at the present time than in any previous period in our history. Historically, the advocate has been an essential figure in the administration of justice. The great advocates of the past have passed on a tradition of courage, independence, and excellence, and the modern lawyer is the better for it.

A strong, independent, and courageous bar is, in my opinion, essential to the existence of a free society.

This chapter was first published in *G. Arthur Martin: Essays on Aspects of Criminal Practice*, by G. Arthur Martin and Joseph W. Irving, and is reprinted here by permission of Carswell, a division of Thomson Canada Limited.

The Art of the Advocate: *R. v. Thatcher*

MR. JUSTICE GERALD N. ALLBRIGHT

1991

Advocacy is the art of the advocate–and every advocate is different. It's the same with artists. If you ask twenty-five legitimate artists how they approach a painting, you'll get twenty-five different answers. In law, there is no area where the abilities of a lawyer make as much difference as in criminal defence advocacy. When you get the criminal defence, you don't have a lot to work with. You have some facts and you have your creative skills. There are some confines on advocates, but we can make all the difference, strongly for or strongly against our cause, depending on what we do. It's a highly personal matter, so I'm not going to be pretentious and tell everyone how to run a case or how to approach being an advocate. Based on my twenty-one years of experience, I'll simply set out my unique view of advocacy.

I've always had a strong aversion to telling war stories about trials because of my fundamental philosophy and survival tactic: Don't celebrate the wins, and don't commiserate the losses. Treat them all the same. Whatever the outcome for the accused, the world keeps right on going for the advocate. In a similar vein, the most important case in your career is whatever case you're working on today. To the person who I am defending, the most important case I will ever do is this case.

In my view of advocacy, defence counsel have many tools. They are not meant to be Machiavellian or manipulative, and they must be displayed within the bounds of propriety and ethics. Let's begin with the judge. Your best friend in the court is whoever is sitting at the front of the room. I don't want any favours from the bench, but I do want the judge to give me an even break. I expect judges to do their job and to tell me when I'm wrong. However, I also expect a degree of respect that allows me to perform my function as counsel. Judges are a friend in the courtroom because they wear a blindfold and remain impartial. It's the same with the Crown counsel. Some of my best colleagues are Crown attorneys. In the courtroom, they're an advocate for their view, and I'm an advocate for mine. I've often found that my client and I are better off if there's a strong Crown counsel on the other side because I know I'm going to be dealt with fairly. I know I'm not going to get surprises, and I'm prepared to deal with anybody's abilities no matter how good they may be.

The most important element in my world as defence counsel is control. I believe it's important that I control the courtroom from the moment I walk into it until the moment I leave. I accomplish this in many different ways. Sometimes it's obvious and sometimes it's not. Sometimes I'm successful and sometimes I'm not. It's important to have a presence when you walk into a courtroom. You must be comfortable, and you must let everyone in the courtroom know that you know what you're doing. In jury cases it's vital, and it starts from the moment the jury panel is called and the way you participate in their selection. It's crucial that jury members know you have an input into their selection, whether you're registering a challenge to a juror or indicating that you're content. There is a limit to what you can say and do in the jury selection process, but by expressing your opinion in a voice that says you have some authority, the jury begins to think you have a reason to be there. It may not make any difference to their selection, but the jury starts with the proposition that counsel has some idea of what he is doing.

It's also important that jury members like you because they will equate you with your client. Whether it's appropriate or not is another matter, but they will. It's hard for a jury to convict an accused when they like counsel. I've had jurors come up to me after a trial and say the hardest thing about convicting the accused was that they felt bad for me. In fact, they made the right decision. I have a strong theory that juries are usually right. The collective wisdom of twelve men and women is impressive. Also, whether you like it or not, juries expect to be entertained a bit–a feat you can accomplish without being offensive. One of the best ways is through humour. There is nothing inappropriate about a humorous remark in a courtroom when it is not ill timed or at anyone's expense, except perhaps your own. It doesn't belittle the process in any way, but it shows that you are a part of the process and that you are approachable. If the jury likes you, they will listen to you and give you a chance to persuade them. I don't ask them to let me pull the wool over their eyes, but I know that if they like my approach, they will be less offended by the way I deal with a witness and will be less likely to convict. Overall, you can very effectively put yourself between a jury and an accused without offending the integrity of the process or being unfair or improper.

How you control a process varies from time to time. Part of control is knowing what to fight about and what not to fight about. There are usually only one or two issues that are germane to a trial. If you restrict your focus to those issues and make it obvious that the other things are not issues of concern, the court appreciates it. Then, when it is important to talk about an issue, the court will listen to you, regardless of whether it's a judge or a jury. That's all part of control. I know that some of you may be offended by the concept of a lawyer wanting to control the court, but I believe that it's very real and very important. Even if your control in a particular case is that you never appear to be angry or to take much issue with anything, but at the end you make a simple statement that you agree with everything except one issue, that's still an element of control and it will work for you.

Advocacy is a highly individualized and personalized skill. Some people have strength in law, where the logic of their argument flows from law. Others have strength in their ability to articulate, to be eloquent. Some people have a physical presence, while others have a voice. Everyone has unique skills and abilities, and advocacy skills are built around them. That's why every effective advocate is different. They know that the atmosphere they create in the courtroom is extremely important. Even the way they ask a question has ramifications. We could all ask the same question, and it would have different degrees of impact–some effective, others neutral, and a few devastating. That's simply how it is.

Trials have a life of their own. There are ups and downs in a trial, but it all works out in the end. However, advocates must have a clear idea of where they are going with their side of the case. If they don't, they cannot be convincing.

We all learn from our mistakes. I remember learning a lesson many years ago on a first-degree murder trial with a young accused who vehemently denied committing the murder. It was a brutal murder, involving a number of stab wounds on an elderly victim. I spent hours in the back room doing a tougher cross-examination on my client than the Crown did, yet his position remained, "I did not do it." It was obvious to me that the statement he gave to the police, which he claimed was made under duress, was in effect a confession to manslaughter, but not murder. In my address to the jury I said: "Ladies and gentleman of the jury, this is a very simple case. My client says he did not do what he is charged with doing. He didn't do it." Normally, I leave it at that, but that's not what the rest of the evidence said, so I added, "He didn't do it, ladies and gentleman—but if he did do it, surely it wasn't murder." I knew that this theory was going to be hard to fly, and it was. The jury came back and I could see it on their faces. They had wrestled with tough questions: "Did he do it or didn't he do it?" "Was it murder or manslaughter?" But they were not clear on the basic issue. So they came back and convicted him of first-degree murder. Sometimes, in cases like this, you get stuck with the instructions. In any event, the Court of Appeal salvaged me and saved the young man a number of years of his life by clarifying that it was manslaughter. From this case I learned the valuable lesson that there are only one or two really important issues, no matter what my client says to me.

Beyond control, the other essential tool in the courtroom is the right to cross-examine and to ask leading questions. If you took everything else away from us advocates, even the presumption of innocence, and left us the right to cross-examine and use leading questions properly, we could still survive. There is absolutely nothing that is deadlier in the hands of good counsel than cross-examination. I have seen good counsel take a case that was overwhelming at the outset, use nothing but cross-examination, destroy a Crown's case, and have a jury come back and acquit an accused. Recently, I defended a young woman on a charge of first-degree murder. The Crown had a tape of a conversation between the accused and a friend in which they discussed the murder. She talked about a jungle-style killing in which nobody heard or knew anything. She even gave details of the matter. The Crown called the friend, who testified where they were when they met, when it happened, what was said, what the stabbing motions looked like, and so on. As the trial wore on, I found that every time I cross-examined a witness, including the key witness, I got something out of that witness. By the end of the Crown's case, I had absolutely no need to call my client. The jury came back and, against all odds, acquitted her completely.

This example brings up another aspect of exercising control: explaining to the jury why my client is not going to testify. Jury members like to hear from the accused because they want to hear the accused say she didn't have anything to do with it. There is a perception that if accused persons didn't do it, then why aren't they going to testify about it? What do they have to hide by not taking the witness stand? To solve this problem of control, I make it very clear to juries in my closing address that I make the decisions. I say, "In this trial, ladies and gentleman, I decide what we're doing by way of defence. I make the decision what witnesses will be challenged. I make the decision what witnesses will come to that box to be sworn. If you don't agree with my decision not to call this accused, don't visit that on her. That's my responsibility." Some juries, like the one in this case, will accept my explanation and understand that there may be many reasons why I did not call my client to testify. Other juries may be sceptical, but I hope they will at least take a moment to decide.

You don't have to explain to judges, however. They know there are myriad reasons why you don't call an accused. For example, the accused may have a four-page criminal record, and although he would deny being involved in this particular offence, he would also have to answer to his long criminal record. You may also have an accused who would be a bad witness. Some accused cannot articulate their own innocence, even when they are innocent. Moreover, what I, as counsel, believe about my client's guilt or innocence is completely irrelevant. If counsel start becoming the jury or the judge, the client needs another lawyer. Somebody has to act as defence counsel and not judge the accused.

Other things are also important in a trial. Preparation is important, in every facet of the case. I did a preliminary inquiry in a case where a young fellow was charged with injecting ground-up antihistamine pills from a dirty ashtray into an unclean syringe and into his and others' arms. A young girl died as a result of that process, and the young man was charged in Saskatchewan with manslaughter—with criminal negligence causing an unlawful death. At the preliminary inquiry, I was kicked around in court by the Crown's expert witness from the crime laboratory. This expert did everything but put the noose around my client, and I knew I was in trouble. He used technical terms and talked about pharmaceutical matters that I didn't have a clue about. I realized the only way I could control the situation was to know more about this limited area of concern than he did. So I went to the dean of the College of Pharmacy on campus. I also went to two medical practitioners and sat down with them. I got the expert to identify all the other experts in the area, the texts that were germane, and where to go for references. Then I went to these other experts and came to the point where I knew more than the crime lab expert knew about this area. As a result, the trial was an entirely different matter from the preliminary inquiry. At the trial, the expert got kicked around because the evidence showed that no one could reasonably have anticipated that the dirty antihistamine would be lethal. That was the fundamental premise, the one simple issue. The courtroom drama was an exercise in control, but also an exercise in preparation.

Cross-examination, as I've said, is my main tool in court, and there are two vital aspects that I never lose sight of. First, every witness has an Achilles heel, an area that's vulnerable. It may not always be obvious, but it's there. Second, I have to get something out of every witness. I may not get the Perry Mason revelation, but I can't let a witness go without getting a fact or a clue.

Sometimes the most devastating cross-examination is the statement, "Your Honour, I choose to ask no questions of this witness." The impact lies in what it tells the jury members. First of all, it says I am not going to waste their time. It also informs the jury that I don't find anything contentious with that witness, but the next time I get up and ask a question, they should listen. Moreover, because I've said "I *choose* to ask no questions," it leaves the impression that I considered it and made a decision. I–not the judge, the Crown counsel, or the accused–made the decision that the evidence was completely irrelevant.

I recall a trial where the jury came back with a verdict of not guilty of murder but guilty of manslaughter–a decision I thought was right. For the first five witnesses in the seven-witness trial, I rose and said, "My Lord, I have no questions for this witness" or "I have no need for the witness to remain and he may be excused." I'm sure that the jury was wondering, "Is that all this guy does? Is this what high-priced counsel from the big city looks like and does? I have no questions?" When I finally rose and asked the second-last witness some questions about the state of the accused and how much alcohol was consumed, the jury hung on every word. I asked half-a-dozen questions, and I have no doubt that every answer they got was imprinted in their mind. I asked the last witness about a hundred questions, with a similar result. There was no doubt that the jury, by the end of it, concluded I knew what I was doing, whether they agreed with me or not, and we went to the real issues.

I'll turn now to my most notorious case, *R. v. Thatcher*–the one I lost. I don't want this brief discussion to sound like an appeal because I respect the jury's verdict, the Court of Appeal's decision, and the Supreme Court of Canada's determination. This analysis is simply my view of the case. Mr. Thatcher was charged with killing his wife. The Crown had a dual theory: either he had done it himself or he had hired someone else to do it. I was dismayed from the outset because that sounded like two charges, and I was always told you couldn't join a count with murder. There's a world of difference between defending against whether he had actually committed the act himself and whether he had hired somebody to do it, so I tried to narrow it to one or the other. The concept of facing both of them together was overwhelming. Unfortunately, the Supreme Court of Canada ruled it was acceptable to say that the accused either did it himself or hired somebody to do it. I found the decision unusual because, theoretically, there could be six jurors with a reasonable doubt that he did it himself but believed that he hired somebody, and six jurors with the opposite doubt. Therefore, there could be twelve jurors who entertain major reasonable doubt about the Crown's theory, which sounds to me like a not guilty verdict. However, our courts determined that you could come to a conclusion of guilt on that basis.

During the case, the Crown called some interesting witnesses who I'll discuss in the context of cross-examination. When I'm cross-examining, I'm in control. I don't care what a witness said for the Crown, I don't care how incriminating he was in the examination-in-chief. When I'm cross-examining, I decide where we're going. I know what I need to get out of each witness, and I control the process. The converse happens when I call evidence. When I call an accused, I try to present an individual who is loving, kind, generous, and a pillar of the community–one whose four-page record is just an abbreviation. After my best efforts, I sit down. Those are the toughest courtroom moments, aside from waiting for the jury to deliver the verdict, that I live through because I've seen the best witnesses absolutely destroyed by a good Crown counsel. So, when I'm calling evidence, I'm not in control. But when I'm cross-examining, I'm very much in control. That is probably the exact opposite of what many people believe, but it's true.

In *R. v. Thatcher* in 1984, one of the first witnesses the Crown called was the pathologist, Dr. Vetters, for this particularly brutal crime. The pictures, some of which didn't go in, were horrible. I found no joy in being in a courtroom defending somebody for such a major tragedy. The doctor described the scene in great detail, as he was entitled to. It was the longest examination-in-chief of a pathologist I've ever seen, but it was effective. The jury sat there and was offended by the death of that poor woman. I felt I had to do something to counter it, so I drew on my theory about every witness having an Achilles heel and my need to get something out of every witness. I had one question only for the pathologist: "Dr. Vetters, I appreciate your being here. I understand very clearly what you said and, as I understand it, what you told us very graphically sets out how Mrs. Wilson died. But I take it, Dr. Vetters, that although you can tell me how she died, that doesn't in any way help us know who killed her." That was the most obvious question in the world, but in the atmosphere of the courtroom at that moment I needed something to show that nothing in his evidence indicated that my client had anything to do with the murder. Although it was a small step, it was step number one because it reminded the jury of the purpose of the trial.

Another key witness was Mr. Dodson. He had known Mr. Thatcher for years and had worked in the legislature with him. He described the man he saw leaving the garage, the one who was obviously the killer. The graphic description he gave to the police at the time of the killing was turned into a sketch and published in the newspaper. I was afraid of Mr. Dodson's evidence, even though I knew it was his first time in court and he was trying his best to be a helpful witness. At the preliminary inquiry, it was important to me to make sure in my cross-examination that I got as much out of him as I could. Usually I don't want to press some witnesses at a preliminary because I want the element of surprise at trial to be very real. With Mr. Dobson, however, I was afraid that his confidence in his assertions might lessen during the several months' delay before the trial. I therefore pinned him down on the fact that the individual coming out of the garage didn't look like Colin Thatcher—and that he had experienced a good opportunity to see him. It turned out I was right. At the trial, I was able to use the testimony from the preliminary inquiry to get the evidence I don't think I would otherwise have gotten. Reluctantly, by the end of his testimony, Mr. Dobson was no longer confident in what he had seen, but he still agreed with what he had said at the preliminary inquiry about the assailant not looking like my client. His Achilles heel was that he had given me that evidence at the preliminary, and there was no way he could back down from it. I had to get something out of him, and I did.

Another witness was Mr. Anderson, who had a wire on him while he talked to Mr. Thatcher. He had been asked to participate in the killing, had produced cars and the gun, had put a silencer on the gun, and had, ostensibly, helped my client. He also had the interview where they purportedly talked about the death of the victim. He, too, had an Achilles heel: he had been involved. Surely, a jury had to be sceptical about the credibility of somebody who was involved. As well, I cross-examined Mr. Anderson for hours and we went laboriously through the tape. I used one recurring theme in my cross-examination: "Witness, you had a golden opportunity at this stage. If you're talking the death of Joanne Wilson, to put the nail in the coffin, all you had to do is ask Mr. Thatcher how it felt to pull the trigger." That was Anderson's Achilles heel from an evidence point of view. In my view, he couldn't ask that question because he knew what the answer would be–and it wouldn't have incriminated Mr. Thatcher. Throughout my cross-examination, not once was there any direct reference to a murder. As well, I chose a theme for the opening of my cross-examination that I have been both applauded and booed for. I walked up to Mr. Anderson, stood as close as I could, and said: "Witness, 'Thou shalt not kill'–you've heard of that, haven't you? Does it mean anything to you?" That question set the tone about this witness. If he participated in the murder, what kind of a man was he? His character was blemished from the start. Some people have said it was a great opening, and others have said I simply should have sat down and said "No questions."

Lynne Mandel was Mr. Thatcher's girlfriend from California. She testified that he told her he had killed his wife, and they actually sat down in Palm Springs and talked about what had happened. My opening question to her tested my credibility. I was quite frankly annoyed with her as a witness and I said, "Witness, if what you tell us is true, what kind of woman sleeps with a man that she knows has just killed his wife?" I don't know how effective it was, but I saw one of the jurors look over at her as if to say, "Yeah, what kind of a woman? Answer the question!" I didn't expect that she would, and some people might say that it's not a proper question because, if you don't expect an answer, you shouldn't ask. In any event, she didn't have an answer to my question. Her Achilles heel was this major character blemish. If what she said was true, then she was not credible as a witness. Notice I said "Witness, *if* what you say is true." It was important to me that the jury not conclude that I believed what she said. I wanted to leave a question that would suggest I didn't accept it.

Mr. Culver, who used to be the Conservative Party leader in Saskatchewan, certainly didn't help my case, so I tried to discredit him in a similar fashion. He testified that Mr. Thatcher talked to him about getting a hit man. The best Achilles heel I could come up with was to say: "Look, if you knew that, and she'd been shot at once before, and you believed that he was responsible for it, what kind of a man, knowing that possibility, doesn't say anything? What kind of a human being knows that and doesn't say anything?" I suspect the jury members shared my displeasure with Mr. Culver, but they obviously didn't disbelieve his evidence.

Then Charlie Wild, who literally had the proverbial three-foot-long record, testified. He claimed that he had been hired by Mr. Thatcher to take part in the killing of his wife, but that he was a con man and never really intended to get involved. I suggested to Mr. Wild that his Achilles heel was his long criminal record and that he was facing another break-and-enter charge for being found after hours at a drugstore in Brandon, Manitoba. He had gotten seven years the last time he found himself in a drugstore after hours. It wasn't unreasonable to assume he was going to get a few more than seven this time round. Wild was a good witness. I think I usually win most exchanges with witnesses, but Wild was good, and the jury rather liked him because he was a likeable rogue. Still, he was comfortable with my suggestion that his great reward was about to come. The jury certainly wouldn't have taken him out for dinner or trusted him with the keys to their Toyotas, but they accepted what he said. At least, he had an Achilles heel that I got out of him.

The one witness the Crown called who struck me as odd was a policeman who testified as part of the theory that Mr. Thatcher killed his wife, then drove to Moosejaw. This witness got on the stand and stated, "I'm a police officer. I drove from downtown Regina to downtown Moosejaw in twenty minutes." Of course, his Achilles heel was that every other individual in Saskatchewan knew you couldn't do that. It's a forty-five mile drive. That didn't deter him, however, and I think the jury and I were simply puzzled by him. I asked a few questions, but he wasn't overly credible. Overall, it was a process of one witness at a time, trying to get something from all of them.

Mr. Kieve, the Crown attorney, got something from Mr. Thatcher during the cross-examination. The first part of Mr. Kieve's cross-examination, in my view, was brilliant and heart hitting. However, it was a long cross-examination, and, in all fairness to my friend and to the process, I didn't think the rest of it really did much. One short segment in particular didn't have anything to do with the shooting, with the tape, or anything else, all of which was equivocal. It had to do with Mr. Thatcher's view of himself as one of the best husbands you'd ever seen before the break-up of the marriage. It was an innocuous point, and it should not have made a difference. Yet Mr. Kieve scored very heavily on that part of the cross-examination and, in the end, he had gotten all he needed out of Mr. Thatcher.

The last tool I hope I can use in court is the strength of the final jury address. Jury addresses are powerful. Advocates who are articulate, eloquent, logical, and committed to the truth of what they're saying can sway jurors. I've sat through jury trials and watched my colleagues. First, the Crown counsel gets up and speaks to the jury, and I'm on his side. Then defence counsel gets up and speaks to the jury, and I'm on his side. Clearly, it's a situation where counsel can make a difference. I've seen a criminal trial won on a jury address. It was a very serious criminal trial, and defence counsel came out with a performance that would have made an actor proud. This guy was good. He was almost in tears, and the most important thing was that he meant every word he was saying, at the time he said it. If a jury address is that powerful, the last jury address is even more powerful. It is, effectively, the last thing that is heard about the case, because the judge is meant to be neutral, which most of them are. Because of that, a powerful closing address from counsel is an invaluable tool.

In *R. v. Thatcher* I didn't get the last address because I called evidence. In my address I tried to solve part of the case for the jury, since I've always felt that, if I were a juror, I'd want part of the case solved for me. I'd like counsel to say, for instance, "Ladies and gentlemen, the key issue is very simple, it's this document." In *R. v. Thatcher* it was a credit-card receipt found at the scene, with Mr. Thatcher's signature on it, which I though disproved the theory of a hit man completely. I was already satisfied that there wasn't enough evidence to prove he had done it himself, so my focus was on the hit man theory. My theory followed this simple logic: If I'm a hit man and I'm working for you, am I going to drop your credit-card receipt at the scene of the crime? If I drop your credit card at the scene of the crime, you are going to go to the police and make a deal: you'll become a witness, get an accessory charge, and point the crime right back to me. It was my theory that the credit-card receipt disproved the concept of a hit man completely because no hit man is going to drop his client's credit card at the scene of the crime. It struck me as being a beautiful piece of logic. Unfortunately, judges can be strong in a courtroom, and the judge told the jury they should completely ignore that little piece of logic.

I will very quickly mention the appeals. I took the appeals reluctantly because I love trial advocacy. Things happen at trials: you deal with real, living, breathing witnesses, and you can make a difference. I applaud people who are comfortable in appellate settings, but I've never had the feeling that my presence was making a whole lot of difference one way or the other. That is partly a reflection of what an appeal is: an appeal on the legal record. I took the appeals primarily because Mr. Thatcher wanted me to. One positive aspect of my career is that, in twenty-one years of practising in courtrooms, I've never been fired by a client. I've declined to do some appeals, but I've always been asked. It's a product of having a good relationship with my clients, because the easiest person to blame for a conviction is the lawyer. So I took the *Thatcher* appeals. At the Saskatchewan Court of Appeal, the minority judgment said that the fairness issue was there and that the principle about weighing evidence should be looked at as possible grounds for appeal, so urged that the appeal be allowed a new trial. The majority, however, didn't view it that way, and the matter went to the Supreme Court. The top court ruled that all the grounds were without merit and dismissed the appeal. Clearly, I've got to respect that judgment, and I do.

Other advocates would have handled the *Thatcher* case differently, depending on their strengths, approach, and view. I did what I thought would work for me. Unfortunately, the jury didn't agree with me. However, of all the juries I've been in front of, I've never seen jury members so wrought with emotion. They clearly were troubled by their verdict. Some reporters stood on ladders to see into the jury room, putting the jurors under a great deal of pressure. They found the verdict hard to reach. Five days into their deliberation, they concluded that Mr. Thatcher was guilty on one or both of the theories, and they convicted him. It was a trial in which, at the outset, I had no idea of the difficulties that would arise, pressures I've not experienced before or since. However, in keeping with my theory of celebrating the wins and not commiserating the losses, the Monday after the trial I showed up for my next trial in the courtroom down the hall. It was a theft trial and, at that time, it was the most important case I'd ever do.

You Can't Judge a Crown Brief by Its Cover: How Preliminary Inquiries Can Avoid Unnecessary Trials

DAVID M. COHN

2001

Victor Branco was a musician with a rock-and-roll band called Naked Planet and a part owner of a recording studio in Toronto. He had no criminal record. He came to my office after he had been charged with trafficking cocaine and possession for the purpose of trafficking cocaine. He vigorously and repeatedly protested his innocence while telling me his version of the events.

I knew it was critical to obtain full disclosure of the prosecution's case. In any criminal case, an accused person has a constitutional right to full and complete disclosure. This document is prepared by the police who have investigated and arrested the accused. The police provide the disclosure to the Crown prosecutor, and the Crown prosecutor in turn supplies it to the defence.

The leading case on the constitutional right to disclosure from the Supreme Court of Canada is *Stinchcombe v. The Queen*. This case held as follows, which I set out here from portions of the case:

> The fruits of a police investigation which are in the possession of counsel for the Crown are not the property of the Crown for use in securing a conviction, but the property of the public to be used to ensure that justice is done ... There is a general duty on the part of the Crown to disclose all material it proposes to use at trial on a charge of an indictable offence, and especially all evidence which

may assist the accused, even if the Crown does not propose to adduce it. The general principle is that information ought not to be withheld if there is a reasonable possibility that the withholding of information will impair the right of the accused to make full answer and defence. The obligation to disclose will be triggered by a request by or on behalf of the accused and may be made at any time after the charge. Where there is no statement but simply notes taken by an investigator, then those notes should be produced. If notes do not exist, then a statement summarizing the anticipated evidence should be produced.

After speaking with Branco at my office, I requested and ultimately received disclosure from the Crown prosecutor. This document is variously referred to as "the disclosure package," "the Crown brief," or "the anticipated evidence of the witnesses." It ought to contain all the relevant material in the possession of the Crown and the police–including the notes of each of the police officers, along with any reports made out by the police officers involved, the property reports that dealt with objects and items seized on the evening in question, any photographs taken, and any other materials produced or collected by the police either during the course of the investigation or afterwards.

I requested and received a large volume of disclosure material. According to the disclosure, on June 14, 1996, eight members of a Toronto District Drug Squad, under the direction of an officer in charge, conducted surveillance on a house located at 33 Sheridan Avenue in Toronto. The drug squad had reason to believe that Mr. Alan Sutcliffe was involved in large-scale drug trafficking because of previous information they had received. The following summary sets out the investigation as depicted in each of the eight officers' notes.

At approximately 10:00 a.m. on Friday, June 14, 1996, the eight officers set up surveillance in the area of Dundas Street and Sheridan Avenue looking for Mr. Sutcliffe. At approximately 12:00 noon, the officers spotted Mr. Sutcliffe with a Mr. Giurasco in a 1987 Oldsmobile. That vehicle, driven by Mr. Sutcliffe, arrived at 33 Sheridan Avenue at about 12:00 noon. Sutcliffe and Giurasco joined a number of males at a picnic table in front of the house. According to the police, included among the males at the picnic table was Victor Branco.

The police claimed, according to their notes, that Mr. Branco was then observed going to a nearby charcoal grey Jetta at approximately 1:05 p.m. At this point, the police alleged in their notes, according to two observation officers, Mr. Sutcliffe handed a black purse or bag to Mr. Branco. Mr. Branco opened the trunk of the Jetta and placed the bag or purse in the trunk, and then he left the area in the Jetta.

At approximately 1:30 p.m. Mr. Sutcliffe and Mr. Giurasco got into the Oldsmobile and drove around the neighbourhood. They were eventually lost by surveillance officers. About an hour and a half later, at 3:00 in the afternoon, the Oldsmobile returned to 33 Sheridan. Then, at 3:45 p.m., the Jetta driven by Mr. Branco returned. According to the notes, Mr. Branco parked his Jetta in the driveway and exited to speak to Mr. Sutcliffe. Branco and Sutcliffe were then seen going to the trunk of the Oldsmobile. Mr. Sutcliffe removed a green knapsack and handed it to Mr. Branco. It was then alleged in the notes that Mr. Branco went to the trunk of his vehicle, the Jetta, with the knapsack, looking as though it was empty. After placing the knapsack in his open trunk and dealing with it in some way, Mr. Branco returned the knapsack to Mr. Sutcliffe. The police claimed that the knapsack now looked very full and heavy. Mr. Sutcliffe placed the knapsack over his shoulder, walked to the trunk of his Oldsmobile, and put it into the trunk. Sutcliffe closed the trunk and climbed into the driver's seat. Mr. Giurasco got into the passenger seat, and the Oldsmobile left the residence. The notes further indicated that the police followed Mr. Sutcliffe's vehicle and arrested Mr. Sutcliffe a short distance away. Mr. Giurasco disappeared into the crowd during the course of the arrest, but, unfortunately for Mr. Giurasco, he forgot his identification in the car. He surrendered himself to the police a few days later.

According to the notes of each of the officers, the police found approximately seven kilograms of cocaine in the knapsack in the trunk of the Oldsmobile. Mr. Branco's vehicle was then boxed in by other officers at 33 Sheridan Avenue, and Mr. Branco was arrested for possession for the purpose of trafficking. The police claimed they seized, approximately, a further kilogram of cocaine in Branco's trunk. Sutcliffe, Branco, both of their vehicles, and the seized cocaine were transferred to a police division in Toronto.

It appeared from a reading of the synopsis that the police had a solid case against my client. The police saw the delivery of the cocaine, maintained observations on both the purchaser and the vendor of the cocaine, and arrested both ends of the transaction within minutes of its completion. Both vehicles were found containing cocaine, seven kilos in the Sutclifffe vehicle, and one in the Branco vehicle.

The function of criminal defence counsel is to challenge and contest the allegations of the prosecution. Generally, defence counsel strive to have a certain set of facts accepted at the end of the day, or at least to contest the Crown's allegations to the extent that they give rise to reasonable doubt. What a criminal defence counsel generally cannot do is to leave the Crown allegations intact and then have the accused testify at trial that those allegations are false. In that scenario, the matter is a credibility contest, usually between a number of police officers and your client. It is not a good strategy to have such a credibility contest.

Getting full and complete disclosure is important, but of greater importance is the review, investigation, and analysis of the disclosure. As I will discuss later, a preliminary inquiry provides an excellent vehicle for challenging the evidence put forward by the prosecution. If anyone were to take the disclosure in this case at face value, guilt would appear to be overwhelming. How could the prosecution's case be unravelled to support Victor Branco's claim of innocence?

The first step was to obtain all the disclosure documents. In this case the bulk of the disclosure consisted of the photocopies of the notebooks of all the officers on the scene that day. And, to understand this disclosure better, I needed to discuss it with my client and get his perspective on it.

In all my meetings with my client in this case, he clearly protested his innocence. He wanted to defend the case vigorously, and he adamantly denied trafficking and being in possession. In one of these meetings, Branco said he was shocked to discover that his arrest had been broadcast on the 11:00 p.m. news. I had not known about this broadcast, so I decided to obtain the videotape of it. This videotape turned out to be one of the first breaks in the case, but I will deal with that later.

I also went with Branco to the scene of the alleged transaction in order to understand exactly where the police claimed they were when they made their observations. In this particular case, the allegations took place in June. By the time I had full disclosure in the fall, the leaves had fallen from the trees. The police claimed to have viewed the purported handing over of the narcotics from Branco to Sutcliffe from a considerable distance. The police notes alleged that they viewed the transaction from the other side of a park, through the trees and a screened fence. To replicate the ability of the police to observe this, I had to wait until the leaves were back on the trees in the spring of the next year and to retain a professional photographer to photograph the scene. The ability of the police to make this observation became a critical issue. After my first visit to the scene, I was convinced that there would have been no way for the police to see through all the foliage and the fences in their way. I believed they could not have observed what they said they observed.

It is only at this stage, understanding both the allegations and the defence, that counsel is in a position to advise the accused on his choices in the trial. Following my advice, Branco elected to be tried by a court composed of judge and jury, which meant that he was exercising his right to have a preliminary inquiry.

The purpose of a preliminary inquiry from the defence perspective is twofold. First, it is useful to determine if there is enough evidence to put the accused on trial. Second, the preliminary inquiry has become a forum where the accused is provided with an opportunity to discover and appreciate the case to be made against him at trial. A preliminary inquiry affords the defence the chance to cross-examine prosecution witnesses and it highlights the weaknesses in the prosecution's case.

To prepare for the preliminary inquiry, I needed to examine the Crown brief meticulously. The major portion of disclosure in the Crown brief consisted of photocopies of the memo books of the eight officers conducting surveillance on the date in question. Each officer was required to keep a memo book of the day's events and to sign off, and to have the officer in charge sign off when he or she reported off duty for the shift. It is important to understand that there are regulations to ensure that the police have done what they were supposed to have done.

The legal requirement of each officer to take notes comes from the *Police Services Act* and the Regulations thereunder. The rules and regulations are actually set out in the back of standard issue notebooks received by Metropolitan Toronto police officers. Included in these rules is the duty of an officer in charge to "perform the following when a member reports off duty: Check that the memorandum book is properly completed. If the memorandum book is correct, affix signature on the line following the last entry."

The reason this rule is in place is to promote note-taking while the events are fresh in the mind of the officer, and to avoid any suggestion of later additions to the notes by an officer or collaboration with other officers. When an officer reports off duty from a shift, the memo book must be complete and the officer in charge must sign off.

In the disclosure, the police notes looked as though they had been done properly. All the officers wrote in their own notebook that they reported off duty at 11:00, or thereabouts, on the evening of June 14. The officers had all the things in their notes that they said they had seen before they reported off duty. To an impartial observer they looked perfect. It looked as though each officer wrote the notes up and reported off duty, all on June 14th.

The first serious indication that all was not right was during the evidence of the second witness at the preliminary hearing. He was one of the officers involved in the surveillance. When asked by the Crown prosecutor when he made his notes in relation to June 14th, he stated, "The following Monday, June 17th."

Fortunately, I was listening carefully, and this delay took me by complete surprise. On cross-examination, the officer acknowledged that it was the practice of the Toronto Police Services to have notes completed on the day of duty and to have them signed off by the officer in charge at the bottom of the notes, where it says ROD, (report off duty). When questioned as to why the notes weren't done on Friday the 14th, he said the day had been too long already. On cross-examination, this witness also indicated that when his notes were done up on Monday, June 17th, other officers were in the room at the same time. He further testified that the detective who was the officer in charge did not sign off on his notes, although he should have, according to the rules and regulations. This admission persuaded me that there were serious flaws in the case for the prosecution. At this point I knew that at least one officer, and maybe more than one, did not write the notes up when required by the rules and regulations. I even thought that the officers might not have done up the notes independently of each other. Given Branco's protestations of innocence, the defence position was that the notes were not an accurate depiction of what had occurred and that all of the officers' notes were identical as a result of collaboration.

The same line of questioning about the notes continued with the following police witnesses. Each one conceded that he did not write up his notes on June 14th, but rather on the 17th, though they all provided different reasons why. The defence took the position that the notes were done up on the 17th, three days after the event, but that they were made deliberately to look as though they were written on June 14th.

These officers, as well as the officer in charge, testified during the trial. Armed with the evidence of the previous witnesses about the way in which the division had made the notes, the cross-examination of the officer in charge was fruitful for the defence. Here is a portion of that cross-examination:

Q: You take responsibility for ensuring that their notes were done on each day?

A: Yes.

Q: In compliance with the Rules and Regulations of the Metropolitan Toronto Police Force?

A: Yes, sir.

Q: The rule clearly reads that when an officer reports off duty, that the officer in charge shall check that the memorandum book is properly completed and, if the memorandum book is correct, affix his signature on the line following the last entry.

A: Yes.

Q: You didn't perform that duty?

A: No.

Q: You do acknowledge that you were the officer that was to perform that duty?

A: Yes.

...

Q: As an officer in charge, are you not to ensure that the Regulation of the Metropolitan Toronto Police Services are complied with?

A: Yes.

Q: You didn't do that?

A: I didn't, at the end of every tour of duty, for these officers, sit down and sign their books, no, sir.

Q: You didn't do that which you were required to do. You have agreed with that?

A: Yes, sir.

...

Q: Do you know why the Police Regulations are such that an officer is to do up his notes on the day that the events are fresh in his memory and that you are to sign them on that day?

A: Yes, sir.

Q: Why is it?

A: So there is an accurate recollection by the officer of the events that he investigated or underwent.

...

Q: So you were just trying to say that the officers were dependent on each other and they did their notes up all at the same time together?

A: Yes.

...

Q: You felt the regulation was just not worthy of following, or what?

A: No, the Regulation ... yes. The Regulation is more important within the uniform field, where the supervisors and officer-in-charge do not have a chance to see the members on a daily basis. They just report to him on duty and off duty.

Q: But you made your own rule, really, didn't you?

A: No, no, I agree with you, sir. Because I was with these fellows every day ...

Q: You made your own rule?

A: No.

Q: You didn't follow this rule and you made your own rule.

A: I didn't follow this rule, yes, you are right. Yes, sir, I agree.

Q: And you made your own rule. You will get these weekly or something like that?

A: Yes, I agree, yes, I did.

Q: That unit was following its own rules, which were different than those of the Metropolitan Toronto Police Force?

A: Yes, sir.

The defence had made considerable progress from the time when witness number two testified that the notes weren't actually done on June 14th, as they appeared to be made. We now had the officer in charge of the unit acknowledging that the rules were not complied with, there was some collaboration, and the notes were all done three days later on the 17th but appeared to have been made on the 14th. When officers consult one another in preparing their notes, they raise serious questions concerning the independence and reliability of their testimony.

During the cross-examination of one of the officers, he mentioned that he and the exhibits officer went by the scene of the crime on Monday, June 17th, before writing their notes on Monday afternoon. He indicated that he was asked to go there by the officer in charge and to take some photographs. No such photographs had been disclosed to the defence. There would have been no way to learn of the visit of these officers at the scene on Monday the 17th or to have known of the photographs except for this mention from the witness in his testimony.

I requested to see these photos in court, and the prosecutor provided them. They assisted in pinpointing the exact location of the crucial surveillance officers. These undisclosed photos further supported our contention that it was impossible for the police to make the alleged observations from that location. As well, very serious unanswered questions were raised as a result of this undisclosed June 17th visit: Why return to the scene before completing their notes? Why not mention, in their notes, the fact that they returned? Why not disclose the photos? More problems for the prosecution case would soon emerge.

For Branco to successfully defend this case, the officers would have to be disbelieved on two essential matters: first, their observations of Branco's allegedly handing over a number of kilos of cocaine to Sutcliffe, and, second, the issue of finding approximately a kilo of cocaine in Branco's trunk. It was very important, therefore, to track precisely the continuity of what the police claimed they seized from Branco's trunk. Branco's position, obviously, was that he did not have drugs in his trunk.

A police photographer who was not related to the Drug Squad was on duty on June 14th. She was a SOCO–a "Scene of Crime Officer." She came from an entirely different police division. This officer testified that she took photos at 5:30 p.m. of the drug exhibits seized that day. She said she took these photos at the Drug Squad after the seizure was returned to the station. As well, sometime after 7:30 that night, CityPulse Television News was invited to the Drug Squad. The Drug Squad had spread all the cocaine in its various packaging on a table and invited the media to film it.

The video Mr. Branco and I viewed provided a major break in the case. While preparing for the preliminary hearing, I realized that one of the bags that was photographed by the SOCO officer (a small sandwich-size plastic bag) and allegedly seized from Branco's trunk was not in the videotape. Therefore, even before the preliminary inquiry commenced, I thought there were major continuity problems for the police. It seemed that the SOCO photos taken at 5:30 showed the drugs in a somewhat different form from when CityPulse videoed them sometime after 7:30. If something had been seized from the Branco vehicle, surely it would have been consistent in shape and size from start to finish.

A further problem for the Crown arose with the exhibits. The prosecution has the onus of proving the nature and the continuity of the drug exhibits. In preparing the case, I was troubled by the property and the drug reports. If I was reading the reports correctly, it appeared that the exhibits officer had randomly taken samples from each exhibit to submit for analysis–a perfectly normal practice–but left the gross weight of the remaining block of cocaine at exactly one thousand grams per exhibit (for most of the exhibits). She maintained this precise weight to be true during her evidence at the preliminary hearing.

Under cross-examination, the exhibits officer was left in the awkward position of trying to maintain that these random chipped-off samples left exactly one kilo. In one example she said she randomly chipped off what turned out to be 2.36 grams to be sent for analysis, yet she stated that left exactly one thousand grams in that exhibit. Again, with another exhibit, she said she randomly chipped off 3.73 grams to be sent for analysis–and that left exactly one thousand grams in that exhibit. She said she took the samples without the intention of leaving exactly one thousand grams, but that just happened with almost all the drugs seized. I submit that such evidence goes beyond any mathematical possibility of veracity.

The exhibits officer went on to testify that she kept a set of exhibit notes, as she was required to do. She said these notes would have been put inside the main file for the case. When she was asked to pull them out of the file, she found that the notes were missing.

Then a further problem with the Crown's case developed. The exhibits officer testified that the Sutcliffe cocaine had been wrapped in Handi-Wrap lined with Bounce sheets. She stated under oath that, on hearing this description at the station that night, one of the other officers, Detective F, went to Branco's car and retrieved a box of Handi-Wrap from the trunk.

The problem with this evidence was not possible to spot in the disclosure but came to light only during the preliminary hearing. The photograph taken by the SOCO officer of Branco's trunk at 5:30 p.m. showed one box of Handi-Wrap that had clearly been opened and used. However, the actual exhibit presented in court was sealed and had never been opened. It looked as though it was store-bought and unopened. The defence asked to solidify this contradiction under oath, and the following exchange was recorded in the cross-examination of the exhibits officer, Officer H:

Q: The box of Handi-Wrap that I'm going to make the next exhibit that we have been referring to does not appear to be open?

A: That's correct.

Q: It's fair to say that you wouldn't think that these were the same boxes. (Comparing SOCO photograph to the exhibit)

A: No.

Q: Am I correct?

A: That is correct.

Q: How was it that you received the Handi-Wrap box that we just put in as an exhibit?

A: I received it from Det. Constable F.

Q: Was that the only Handi-Wrap box that you received?

A: That I recall, yes.

Q: Would you have a note of anything else? We went through all of it Wednesday and it wasn't there.

A: That's all I have a notation of in my book.

Q: Certainly that was the only box that you received from Constable F?

A: That is correct, yes.

...

Q: So he came back with the Handi-Wrap and the Bounce. My question to you is this, if you can direct your mind to it, please. Were you given to understand where the Handi-Wrap that we just put in as the last exhibit came from?

A: From the trunk of the car. Detective Constable F went down to the trunk of the car and brought it back.

Q: But you have agreed that the Handi-Wrap package doesn't appear to be the package in the photograph.

A: They don't appear to be the same package. That's correct.

I was now in a position to cross-examine Detective F, who purportedly seized the Handi-Wrap from the Jetta. The following exchange is an excerpt from my cross-examination:

Q: I am going to show you a photograph which is numbered Exhibit three in these proceedings. It purports to be a photograph and has been identified as a photograph of the trunk of the Jetta. Is this what the trunk looked like?

A: From what I remember, yes.

Q: And it has some Handi-Wrap in there, right?

A: Yes.

Q: That Handi-Wrap, I think it's obvious that it's been opened, that the seal on it has been broken.

A: Yes. The box looks pretty mangled.

Q: I will leave that in front of you. You gave the Handi-Wrap to Constable H?

A: I believe I did, yes.

Q: What time did you do that? Do your notes help you?

A: I believe it was 9:15.

Q: Does that help you in this regard?

A: Yes. It says turn over Exhibits to Detective Constable H.

Q: Did you turn over what's in that photograph to Detective Constable H?

A: What? Everything in the trunk?

Q: No. The Handi-Wrap that I referred to.

A: Yes.

Q: I'm going to show you what has been marked as Exhibit twenty-six in these proceedings. This would ... I think you will agree with me that this is a sealed and unopened box of Handi-Wrap. Would you agree?

A: Yes.

Q: That's different than this particular item in the exhibit. Constable H has said that as well. Do you agree?

A: Yes.

This exhibit was perhaps the simplest yet most telling piece of evidence in the whole case. How could this discrepancy possibly be explained by the prosecution? There were, in fact, many more problematic pieces of evidence from the Crown's perspective, but no more detail is necessary.

The issue to be determined at the conclusion of a preliminary hearing is whether there should be a committal for trial. The test used is whether there is any admissible evidence on which a reasonable jury, properly instructed, could convict an accused. To be quite candid, even with all the defects, discrepancies, inconsistencies, illogic, and serious problems with the Crown's case, the likelihood was that there would be a committal for trial because of the very low threshold and because, in this proceeding, there is no weighing of evidence. The provincial court judge at a preliminary inquiry must take the Crown's case very seriously and, despite all the difficulties with the evidence, there was some evidence, if believed by the ultimate trier of fact, that my client trafficked and possessed cocaine for the purposes of trafficking.

However, before final submissions in this case, the provincial court judge asked if the prosecutor and I would have an "exit pre-trial" with him. An exit pre-trial allows the judge to express his or her opinion off the record to both prosecution and defence counsel. I agreed, and the judge expressed his opinion.

Subsequent to the exit pre-trial and before making submissions on the issue of committal for trial, I wrote a letter to a senior Crown attorney in the Department of Justice outlining the problematic issues in the case. The case was remanded for a few months before scheduling and making submissions on committal. A few days before the case was scheduled to return to court for submissions, I received a call from the Department of Justice indicating that it intended to stay the charges. A stay freezes the charges for one year, and, after that time, the charges disappear for all intents and purposes.

On December 11, 1997, Mr. Branco and I attended court, and the prosecutor entered a stay of the charges. The year passed and no further action was taken. This case is an illustration of the importance of the preliminary inquiry and of using it, together with full disclosure, to avoid unnecessary and expensive trials. I hope it is also an illustration of not taking a Crown brief at face value.

I'll let G. Arthur Martin have the last word because he stated the role of defence counsel most eloquently:

The role of defence counsel is to provide professional advice and assistance to the client in accordance with the strict ethical standards that govern the role of defence counsel. The defence counsel is not a messenger, an alter ego merely to carry out the wishes of the client irrespective of whether they comport with professional standards. The role of defence counsel is to be the champion of the client's cause and to see that his or her rights are not wrongly invaded from any quarter. Sometimes, of course, the best advice that you can give an accused *after a thorough investigation* of the facts is to plead guilty and endeavour to obtain a favourable disposition for him or her. The choice whether to plead guilty or not guilty is, of course, the client's.

* * *

In conclusion, I would like to tell a few anecdotes about my father, Bernard Cohn. Much of what I know about him came from others. He was always very modest when he spoke about himself, so most often, his friends and relatives told me stories about him.

My father's father died of diabetes a few months before the development of insulin for public use. My father was seventeen at the time. He became responsible for looking after his younger brother, among other things.

Gambling was in my father's blood from a young age. Growing up in Windsor, there was ample opportunity to gamble both legally, at racetracks in Windsor or Detroit, or in an "underground" manner. On one such occasion when my father and his brother were in Detroit, during their teens, gambling at an unlicensed venue, there was a raid by the Detroit city police. As the police were emptying the place, they instructed the people inside to walk out to a waiting paddy wagon. My father, while being marched out, stepped sideways into the gathering crowd. He watched his brother walk into the wagon, unable to assist him. That created a potentially difficult problem, in two respects: my father would have to explain to his mother where his younger brother was; and, perhaps more important, he had to raise bail money to secure his brother's release. He dealt with the former issue by arranging pillows in his brother's bed so it would appear that the boy was not in custody. And he covered the latter issue by way of a pool-shooting competition that he won. Apparently no one at home was the wiser during the thirty-six hours it took him to raise the bail money.

Family came first. Next in priority were my father's duties and obligations to the court and to his clients. However, once those duties had been fulfilled, there was often the ability to catch what he referred to as a "double header"–the afternoon at one racetrack and the evening at another. I was fortunate from an early age after school to be able to tag along hundreds of times to an evening at the racetrack.

On one of those occasions, my father and I were headed to Hazel Park Racetrack in Detroit. When I was a child in the 1960s, border security was certainly not the same as it is today. Because of our frequent trips to Detroit and back to Windsor, we often knew the customs authorities by face on both sides of the border. On most occasions, we did not even have to show identification to the customs officers. On this particular evening, my father seemed to recognize the customs officer, slowed, waved, and the customs officer said, "Pull over to secondary, please." "Primary" is the customs officer in the booth. "Secondary" is the location where a vehicle is parked and there is inspection of some nature both to the vehicle and to the occupants. Unfortunately, there was no time to stop for any protracted period because my father had a significant tip on the horses running in the daily double. A stop of more than five minutes would be fatal to his ability to place his wager. At secondary we were asked to exit the vehicle, and my father approached the customs officer. He explained very succinctly that he needed to get to the racetrack–and quickly–as he believed he had a horse that could not lose in the first race, and a horse that had even less chance of losing in the second. He explained that if he was kept for more than four minutes further, he would be forced to sue the American government for the damages that would be created by not allowing him to bet in a timely manner. The customs officer, my father, and I all laughed until we almost fell down, and the customs officer urged my father to hurry back into the vehicle and take off.

As far as I was aware, my father did not mix his professional life with his personal life. Having said that, one old Kentucky gentleman named Ed Curd became a client of my father in the 1950s. Curd was the definitive bookie. He was the man who was credited with developing point-spread betting. Among his friends were tough guy actor George Raft, odds maker and television sports commentator Jimmy "The Greek" Schneider, famed basketball coach Adolph Rupp, and a popular Kentucky governor named Abe "Happy" Chandler. In 1950 and 1951 Mr. Curd featured in a US Senate committee investigating crime. Gangster Frank Costello (who inspired Marlon Brando's performance in *The Godfather*) admitted in a televised committee session that he gambled. When asked with whom, he said, "With my little friend Ed Curd in Lexington, Kentucky."

Curd commented once that "the next witness ... testified that day about basketball betting. He named me and, within a week, the income tax people were after me." By the time Curd was indicted in the United States for tax evasion, two years had passed and he had conveniently taken up residence in Canada. I believe that my father met Ed Curd at that time. Fire and gasoline! Ed Curd lived in Windsor, and the world's best handicapper fell into the lap of a person who liked to bet. As I am told the story, my father struck a deal with the US government. In 1956, apparently, Curd returned to Lexington to forfeit his farm and mansion, plus pay the government US $275,000, which, as he was heard to say, "is more than 2 million dollars in today's money." In addition, Curd was fined $10,000 and given a seven-month prison sentence, which he served at a military base in South Carolina.

My father, after representing Ed Curd, became extremely friendly with him and, afterwards, Curd frequently came to Canada to visit my father and our family. He often stayed at the Prince Edward Hotel, since demolished, at the corner of Park and Ouellette in Windsor. On one occasion, Curd and my father were partners on an extremely large bet on a basketball game. With the score jockeying back and forth, and both men watching the game in Curd's hotel room, my father could not take the pressure anymore. With a minute left in the game, he went out into the hallway and began to pace. After five or ten minutes, when Curd had still not emerged, my father went back into the room. Curd was lying on his back with his eyes closed, holding his heart. The television set was off. My father feared the worst for Curd and for his bet. When my father went to attend to the ailing old Kentucky gentleman, Curd smiled, opened his eyes, and, with a strong Southern drawl, said, "Pards, we won by ten. I just wanted to keep you interested."

The Murder of Bruce Lorenz:
The Role of Defence Counsel

EDWARD L. GREENSPAN, QC

1987

Gordon Allen was born and raised in Orillia, Ontario, and had a number of jobs in his rather uneventful life before he met and took up residence with Lauralee Lorenz in Toronto. She was a nurse who, after meeting Allen, eventually separated from her husband, Bruce Lorenz, a real estate lawyer with a large downtown Toronto law firm. Within days of leaving Bruce, Lauralee took her two young boys, one of whom had been adopted, with her to set up home with Gordon Allen. Allen had never been married before. From all reports the relationship between Gordon Allen and Lauralee Lorenz was, initially at least, a good one. She brought money into that relationship from her separation, they operated a business together, and Allen came to care deeply for her children. Because of their ages, the children called him "Dad," and Allen came to look upon the younger boy as his own son.

Eventually, however, their business began to decline. Lauralee continued to have contact with Bruce Lorenz and he with his older son. After his separation from Lauralee, Bruce had been considered for a partnership in the prestigious law firm of Borden and Elliot, but was rejected. Lauralee and Bruce often spoke about this rebuff, and Bruce voiced the opinion that it was related to their marital difficulties.

For this reason, as well as the failure of Gordon Allen and Lauralee's business, Bruce and Lauralee decided to resume living together. When Allen became aware of their decision, he apparently accepted it, though he did not agree with it. It seemed to be primarily a business decision, or at least that entered into it. The Lorenzes hoped that, by Lauralee returning to Bruce, he would obtain the much desired partnership. Lauralee, in turn, could benefit directly from Bruce if the partnership was obtained. Their clear intent did not seem to involve a renewed love affair, and Lauralee's relationship with Gordon Allen did not end. During the late fall of 1977, Lauralee visited Gordon in Orillia on several weekends and Gordon continued to see the children.

To the outside world, Bruce and Lauralee appeared to be a reconciled couple. Bruce Lorenz's parents had this impression, as did his law firm. Lorenz renewed his application for a partnership, and the decision was scheduled for the spring. In March 1978 Bruce and Lauralee travelled with their children to Florida, returning on a Saturday at the end of the spring break. The result of the decision about Bruce's partnership was to be released on the Monday following his return from Florida.

When Bruce Lorenz went to work that day, he was informed, yet again, that he would not be made a partner. It appears that he spoke to Lauralee about it in the morning. According to her, he was quite disappointed and said he would go out alone for a while that evening. As a result, she made arrangements to have dinner at her home with a close friend. Lauralee called her friend during the day and, according to the friend, insisted on having dinner together that very night. The friend later reported that she found that demand peculiar.

After work, Bruce Lorenz went to the Osgoode Hall subway station near his office and was seen there meeting a man and talking to him. The two men boarded the subway together and travelled north to Bloor. Bruce Lorenz was later observed with a man at Bloor station getting on the Bloor-Danforth line going east to Warden. At Warden the subway parking lot is a good hundred yards from the station itself. Lorenz and the other man would have arrived at that subway station sometime between 6:00 and 6:10 on that Monday night. At approximately 6:25 p.m., two couples on their way to the Sportsman's Show at the Canadian National Exhibition grounds drove past a car in the Warden parking lot and noticed a man's legs protruding from the window of the car. They thought the man was drunk and drove on. A parking lot attendant also drove by at around that time and concluded the man in the car had probably passed out. He contacted the police at around 6:35 p.m.

On their arrival, the police found the body of Bruce Lorenz in the car with his legs protruding out the front-seat window, where the driver's window had been rolled down. Initially, the police, seeing blood outside the driver's door and on the side of the car, believed that Lorenz had fallen on the ice but had managed to make his way into the car. Lorenz had matted blood behind his ear, and the police concluded he had fallen, struck his head, and made his way to the car, where he died.

The police arrived at the Lorenz home around 11:00 p.m. They told her there had been an accident and her husband had died. At the time the police were unaware of what the coroner subsequently discovered when he went to the Warden Avenue parking lot: when he turned Lorenz's head to the other side, he saw an exit wound of what was later determined to be a .22-calibre bullet. A bullet had entered Lorenz's head and exited the other side. Had the coroner not come upon the scene, Bruce Lorenz's death might have been attributed to an accidental fall. Because of this disclosure, I am eternally grateful to all coroners.

After the police informed Lauralee Lorenz that her husband had died as a result of an accident, she called Bruce Lorenz's brother, an Ontario provincial police officer who lived in Kitchener. He later claimed that, during the conversation, Lauralee said Bruce had been shot—although it is interesting to note that he said nothing about this alleged telephone conversation until part way through the preliminary hearing. By that time he was the executor of Bruce Lorenz's estate and a potential beneficiary, although he would not have known that at the time of the alleged call.

The timing of this call is important. The coroner was fortunately slow enough in getting to the scene of the crime to allow enough time for this call to happen. Had he got there earlier, had Lauralee Lorenz been informed earlier that her husband had been shot to death, then this call would not have become such a problem. After the coroner's discovery, the police went again to the Lorenz home later that night and told her that her husband had been murdered. That same Monday night, one of Lauralee's neighbors told the police that she had a boyfriend named Gordon Allen before she moved back with Bruce Lorenz and that he had red hair.

When the police visited the law firm of Borden and Elliot the next day, they interviewed Bruce Lorenz's secretary. She told them she had walked down into the subway station that Monday evening with Bruce Lorenz and that the man Lorenz met in the subway had red hair.

Lauralee Lorenze related the fact of her husband's murder to Gordon Allen in a telephone call. As well, on Tuesday morning, she called Bruce's secretary and asked whether he had signed his new will the previous day. Before leaving for Florida, Bruce had prepared a new will, which had been dictated and typed while he was in Florida. The new will would have made Lauralee Lorenz the major beneficiary, yet, under the old will, Bruce had removed her from ever benefiting from his death when she left him for Gordon Allen. According to Bruce's secretary, Lauralee expressed shock and incredible surprise when she heard that the new will had not been signed. When the police learned of Lauralee's call, as well as the fact that the man Bruce Lorenz met at the subway had red hair, they went to Orillia, took pictures of Gordon Allen –black and white pictures– then returned and showed them to the secretary. Although she could not identify Gordon Allen as the man she had seen Bruce Lorenz meet at the subway station, she said that it "might well have been the same man."

The police began a wiretap on both Allen and Lauralee on that Thursday, the very day of Bruce Lorenz's funeral. The wiretap disclosed regular telephone contacts between Lauralee's home and Gordon Allen's home, just as the earlier phone bills showed very frequent calls between the Lorenz home and the Allen home before the death. One of the first phone calls intercepted contained a discussion where Lauralee and Gordon agreed, for the sake of appearance, that he would not attend the funeral. The police investigation over the ensuing weeks included monitoring phone calls as well as interviewing both Lauralee Lorenz, Gordon Allen, and people close to them. The telephone conversations showed that Lauralee became aware of the fact that she was a suspect and, as a result, she was angry and suspicious of the police and their activities. The police told Gordon Allen that he was a suspect, but not her. They told Lauralee Lorenz only that Gordon Allen was a suspect. The police interceptions contain many instances of Lauralee protesting Gordon Allen's innocence.

On one lengthy call–after the police had taken into their possession a brown corduroy winter coat owned by Gordon Allen which the Crown alleged Allen had worn at the murder–Lauralee told Gordon Allen in a singsong-like whisper, "Be careful." This call included a discussion about whether their phones were tapped. Also of some significance was the fact that Bruce Lorenz's father told the police that he had lent a .22-calibre rifle to Bruce several months before his death, but a search of the house after his death revealed that the gun had gone missing and simply could not be located.

Three weeks later, Gordon Allen and Lauralee Lorenz were arrested and charged with the first-degree murder of Bruce Lorenz. When the police arrived at Allen's home to arrest him, they showed him an affidavit purporting to be that of Lauralee Lorenz, which alleged that Gordon Allen had made threats against Bruce Lorenz and that he was insanely jealous of Bruce. Gordon Allen replied that he did not now why Lauralee Lorenz would make such a statement to them. In fact, this affidavit was the sole creation of the two investigating officers—Lauralee had told the police no such thing. At the time of Allen's arrest, the police searched his home and took some gas receipts that were lying in plain view in his bedroom. Gordon Allen told the police once again, as he had told them earlier, that he had been in Orillia the entire day that Bruce Lorenz was killed and that he had an alibi. However, one of these gas receipts proved to be a windfall for the police because it placed him in Toronto, purchasing gas at Keele Street and the 401 on the very day of Bruce Lorenz's murder. In fact, analysis of the numbered gas receipts issued both before and after the receipt that Allen had received showed that this particular gas receipt was issued some time between 5:30 and 6:30 p.m.

Not all the evidence relied on by the Crown arose before Gordon Allen's arrest, nor did all of it come from police investigations. Allen did his part to assist the Crown, too. In an affidavit filed at his bail hearing, Allen stated that he held an undergraduate bachelor's degree as well as an MBA. One of the many unpleasant surprises I got during this trial was to wake up one morning to hear on the news that Gordon Allen, the man whose credibility would be so important in his own murder trial, had just been arrested and charged with swearing a false affidavit. He had no university degrees—he had just made the story up years before and had lived the lie ever since. The charge involving the false affidavit did not proceed until after the murder trial was completed, but the Crown attorney was permitted to cross-examine Allen during his evidence on the fact that he was prepared to swear falsely in an affidavit to the Court—no small weapon considering the issues in the murder trial.

We proceeded through the preliminary hearing on the basis of a joint defence on behalf of both Gordon Allen and Lauralee Lorenz. At the conclusion of the hearing, we argued that the case was entirely circumstantial against both accused and that both should be freed. Nevertheless, they were committed to stand trial and a date for their trial was fixed. Preparation of the joint defence that neither Gordon Allen nor Lauralee Lorenz had been involved in the murder continued as the months went by. Trial was scheduled to commence on a Monday morning in January 1979.

On that day, Gordon Allen, Chris Buhr, our firm's articling student, and I appeared for trial. Mr. Justice Allan Goodman of the Supreme Court was there as well. But the Crown attorney was not present in the courtroom, nor were the police. Lauralee was not there either, and neither were her lawyer or her lawyer's articling student. After several hours, the judge convened the court and directed that inquiries be made, as none of the missing persons had yet been located. I told the judge that I was more than happy to start right then because I liked the odds.

Eventually, later in the day, Lauralee Lorenz's lawyer and the Crown attorney appeared to ask for the case be put over one day. Then they left. No explanation was offered. Nonetheless, I got a migraine headache that remained with me for the entire three months of the trial. The migraine replaced the joint defence we had been preparing for so long because, on Tuesday morning, when the court opened, everyone was there. This time the Crown announced that the prosecution was going to accept Lauralee's guilty plea to accessory after the fact to murder. I immediately argued that *The Queen v. Vinette* in the Supreme Court of Canada precluded such a plea, let alone any conviction, in the absence of the conviction of the alleged principal. The trial judge agreed and remanded her potential plea until after the trial of Gordon Allen. The murder charge was, however, stayed against her.

We were then provided with her "will say" statement. There she claimed that, around 8:30 on the evening of Bruce Lorenz's death, she received a phone call at home from Gordon Allen, who, according to Lauralee Lorenz, said: "Guess what, I just shot your husband. Oh my God, all that blood." According to the statement, Lauralee screamed in response to those words and was put in a state of shock–a shock so great that all her mind could do to deal with those words was to shove the thought deep into her subconscious mind. She claimed that, from the instant she heard the words, she blanked out what she had been told. According to Lauralee, it was only one and a half years later, on the Saturday morning before the commencement of her trial, that her recollection of those words was revived and then only through the assistance of sodium amytol (truth serum) administered by the head of the Clarke Institute, Dr. Robert Coulthard, in the presence of her lawyer and at his request. According to the evidence of her lawyer, who testified at Gordon Allen's trial, he arranged for the sodium amytol because he was concerned that something was bothering her as she prepared for her first-degree murder trial, and he wanted to get to the bottom of it!

We were so staggered by the change of events caused by the withdrawal of the charge against Lauralee Lorenz that we could not immediately begin to consider the implications of what that meant to our defence of Gordon Allen. Nor, for that matter, I suspect, could the Crown attorney, who was so eager to take the deal. In fact, it was only after we left the court that day that we had a chance to think about its far-reaching implications on the evidence in the case. On one hand, the Crown attorney had acquired Lauralee Lorenz as a Crown witness, ready to give direct evidence against Gordon Allen. But, on the other, the Crown lost some vital pieces of evidence. For example, as evidentiary rulings eventually determined, the Crown lost the .22-calibre rifle alleged to have gone missing from Bruce Lorenz's home shortly before his murder. The gun was admissible on a trial involving Lauralee Lorenz and Gordon Allen, but was not admissible, as Justice Goodman ultimately ruled, on a trial involving Gordon Allen alone. Similarly, the intriguing, if not controversial, evidence to be given by Bruce Lorenz's brother about the phone call from Lauralee Lorenz on the night of the murder was not admissible on a trial involving Gordon Allen alone. In other words, whatever Lauralee Lorenz may have told her brother-in-law about how Bruce Lorenz died was no longer admissible as evidence against Gordon Allen. No one, least of all the Crown attorney, who even opened to the jury about the missing rifle, had ever considered any of these implications when Lauralee's deal was struck.

The trial lasted some ten weeks. Lauralee Lorenz testified and claimed that, although she knew nothing of her husband's death before it occurred, she had received a call on that same night of his death in which Gordon Allen admitted he had just done it. When the friend who had dined at the Lorenz home that night gave her testimony, she recalled that Lauralee had indeed received a call between 8:30 and 9:30 p.m., but she had a different recollection of the call from Lauralee. According to the friend, Lauralee spoke softly and at some length on the phone. She laughed chatted amicably, then hung up the phone and told her friend it was Gordon. No screams, no hysterics, "just a very friendly phone call," she said.

Lauralee Lorenz testified that her recollection had been refreshed by a dose of sodium amytol. Not to be outdone, I arranged for Gordon Allen not only to be administered sodium amytol but also to be hypnotized while under the influence of sodium amytol. A double whammy! Again, not to be outdone, we made sure that Allen was given considerbly more truth serum than Lauralee Lorenz had ever received. And the results? Gordon Allen hadn't killed Bruce Lorenz after all–or at least he didn't recall that he had. So much for truth serum.

The sodium amytol/hypnosis encounter with Gordon Allen was fascinating for me as a medical layman. While Allen was under hypnosis, his finger was cut deliberately by the physician involved. Allen was told while under hypnosis that his finger was being cut but that he should not bleed. Like magic, upon the command, Allen did not bleed. When the physician then told Allen he should bleed, almost a minute later the finger virtually spurted blood. Needless to say, I was impressed. The physician told me that sodium amytol normally causes nausea. and people who have been administered it do not want to eat afterwards. Nevertheless, while under hypnosis, Allen was told by the physician that he would wake up feeling good and with a voracious hunger. On the way home from the hospital, Allen asked that we stop for something to eat, and I then watched him wolf down several hamburgers. Again, I was impressed.

There were some other interesting aspects to the case as well. As I have said, on the evening that Bruce Lorenz was killed, he went to the Osgoode Hall subway station after leaving work and met a man there with red hair. When Lorenz met that man, the man was overheard to comment on Lorenz's tan and to ask him if he had been away. Lorenz responded that he had been to Florida with his family. According to Lorenz's secretary and another lawyer at Borden and Elliot, both of whom overheard that conversation, it appeared not only that the man did not know Lorenz had been in Florida but that Lorenz knew that the man did not know that. This was of some significance because a number of the phone calls between Gordon Allen and Lauralee Lorenz before the death had occurred when Lauralee was in Florida. Furthermore, on some of these phone calls, Lorenz had spoken with Allen. In short, not only did Gordon Allen know that Bruce Lorenz was in Florida but

Bruce Lorenz knew that Gordon Allen knew that. This fact became of some importance as later events unfolded.

Again, as I have said, right up until the day of his arrest, Gordon Allen had insisted–to the police and anyone else who would listen–that he had not been in Toronto on the day that Bruce Lorenz was murdered. Faced with the incontrovertible evidence of his signature on a gas credit card dated that very day, Allen's position changed. At his trial, Allen testified that he had met a woman in Orillia several weeks before the murder and had made arrangements to go out for dinner with her on the Monday in question. The woman lived in Toronto, and Allen testified that he had travelled from Orillia to the hotel next to the gas station at Keele and 401 in Toronto, where he telephoned the woman in anticipation of their date. The woman had originally agreed to the date at a time when she and her boyfriend were having some difficulties, but in the intervening weeks they had reconciled. She told Allen that she was having dinner with her parents that night, apologized for forgetting the intended date and suggested that Allen call her some other time. In fact, as the woman subsequently testified at the trial, she really did not want to hear from Allen again.

Allen testified that given that news from the woman, he went next door to the gas station, purchased some gas, turned around, and drove back to Orillia, where he went to a bar some time after 7:00. He saw a few friends there and then returned home, where eventually he called Lauralee Lorenz. The woman Allen said he had spoken with about the dinner date recalled their telephone call. It had occurred at almost precisely 6:05 p.m., and she recalled that Allen sounded friendly and relaxed as they spoke. She said that she was embarrassed at having forgotten the date but that Allen did not seem upset at all. At that time she had been taking a word-processing course. She knew exactly when she finished the course and how long it took her to drive home, and she remembered that she hadn't had time to take her coat off before Allen called. The timing of all these events became important at the trial–the timing of this phone call as well as the timing of Allen's return to Orillia–because Allen did go to the bar on his return to Orillia, whether fresh from a murder or returning from a cancelled date. Witnesses at the bar in Orillia put Allen there shortly after 7:00 p.m., creating a significant issue as to whether Gordon Allen, had he murdered Bruce Lorenz, could have had the time to drive from the Warden subway station at about 6:20 and return to Orillia forty minutes later.

Also, of significance was whether Gordon Allen had been the man that Bruce Lorenz had met in the Osgoode Hall subway station. If that were the case, he was travelling with Lorenz on the subway system right up until Warden station; and, if that was so, when was the phone call to the woman ever made? On the Crown's theory, the phone call, if it happened, had to have been made with Bruce Lorenz standing right beside Gordon Allen at the Warden subway station, just moments before Allen would shoot him in the head.

As I said, the Crown alleged that Gordon Allen had been wearing a light brown corduroy coat when he killed Bruce Lorenz. The prosecution persisted in this allegation despite the evidence of Bruce Lorenz's secretary, who had seen Lorenz speaking with a man in the subway on the day of Lorenz's death. She said that the man speaking with Lorenz had been wearing a coat made of some expensive material—in any event, not corduroy. The heart of the police claim was forensic evidence which they claimed showed blood on the coat. A forensic examination of that brown corduroy coat and Gordon Allen's car showed traces of a substance that the Crown alleged were traces of blood. As a result of testing those substances with what is known as the phenolphthalein test, a senior member of the Centre of Forensic Sciences was prepared to testify that, in his opinion, the positive reaction to the phenolphthalein test demonstrated by these articles confirmed the presence of blood. The phenolphthalein test had long been accepted by Ontario courts as a determinative means of ascertaining whether blood was present on some object. I was disturbed by this evidence and convinced that it would pose a real problem for Gordon Allen at his trial.

In my research to prepare for the trial, I turned to the 12th edition of Taylor's *Principles and Practice of Medical Jurisprudence*, edited by the eminent pathologist Keith Simpson. Much to my surprise, I read that the phenolphthalein test was only a preliminary test for determining whether blood existed on a given object, and that further tests were necessary before a definitive pronouncement could be made. Taylor was adamant that the phenolphthalein test was "a test for [the substance] peroxidase, and not a test for blood." It turns out that although peroxidase is present in blood, it is also present in millions of other substances. At the trial, I got the forensic expert for the Crown to admit that this test could result in a positive reaction—to show that so-called blood was present—from testing for ketchup, mustard, or relish. I told the jury that if my jacket had been tested with the phenolphthalein test after eating a Big Mac, I'd have ended up in the same prisoner's dock as Gordon Allen!

Part of the reason that the trial lasted for ten weeks was that the Crown threw in every scrap it could find. In particular, it threw in a bomb. At the time that Gordon Allen was arrested, in addition to the credit card receipts, police found a radio control device, the kind of device that is used to open garage doors while inside your car or to operate model airplanes or boats. Allen testified that he bought that device to operate a toy boat he was build-ing for the Lorenz children. But the Crown's theory was that Allen had pur-chased the radio control device to build a bomb for Bruce Lorenz's car, so he could blow up the car from afar, presumably with Bruce in it. In support of this crazy theory, the Crown called the head of the Montreal Bomb Squad, who was prepared to testify that, in his lengthy experience in Montreal, such devices had occasionally been used by members of organized crime to deto-nate explosives. Presumably they might have been used to operate one or two garage doors as well. All the police had seized from Gordon Allen was the radio control device. There were no explosives, no wires, just the radio con-trol device. As I cross-examined this bomb expert at the trial, I got him to concede that what the police had of this so-called bomb was everything you would need to blow up a car, except the bomb! And what made it even worse for the beleaguered bomb squad chief was that a planned demonstration of such a device did not come off exactly as planned. He had lugged from Montreal what he claimed was a working model of a radio control bomb for a car, although without the actual explosives, of course. With great drama and flair, he produced the radio control device to detonate the bomb and pushed the button. Nothing happened! Blushing like a beet, he rechecked his wiring, examined the radio device, pushed the button again, and still nothing hap-pened. Eventually, he gave up on the stupid thing, and so did the Crown on his evidence!

Gordon Allen was cross-examined for four days by the Crown attorney prosecuting the case. One of the things he cross-examined Allen about was the color of his hair. As I have indicated, shortly after the murder, the police had taken black and white photographs of Allen. In addition, there was eye-witness evidence that the man Bruce Lorenz had met in the subway station had red hair. The fact that the police believed Allen also had red hair was important to the Crown's case. Imagine their surprise when the trial commenced and Allen showed up with hair that was singularly brown, not red at all. The Crown went so far as to allege that Allen had dyed his hair, and that dying his hair was evidence of consciousness of guilt. But Allen testified that during the winter, his normal hair color was brown, and it bleached red only as a result of the summer sun. During the trial, and in front of the jury, I offered the Crown a lock of Allen's hair to test, to confirm that it had never been dyed. The Crown attorney didn't even take me up on the offer. Not only did he not have color photographs from the police but the record of arrest by the police described Allen's hair as being dark brown.

Eventually, the evidence finally finished, the jury addresses were given, and the trial judge charged the jury on the only possible verdicts: guilty of first-degree murder or not guilty at all. All or nothing. The jury retired on a Friday to deliberate. Any trial counsel will tell you that the worst time spent during any trial occurs once those deliberations start. Guessing and second-guessing what the jury is doing is rampant, and the longer the jury is out, the worse it gets. In this case we wearily dragged ourselves in on the Saturday morning again to await the decision. No lawyer, no matter how confident, ever really knows what a jury will do. Sometimes the only hint you get of where the jury is headed is from a question that the jury may return to ask of the trial judge. And on that particular morning, we got a hint. We were told by the sheriff's staff who supervised the jury that there was a birthday party that morning for one of the jury members. That was the best news I'd received the entire trial. What jury of honest, decent people would hold a birthday party on a Saturday morning if they were about to convict a man of first-degree murder? Even my migraine perked up at that. And so, in fact, once the jury members finished the birthday cake, they announced that they had reached a verdict: not guilty of the first-degree murder of Bruce Lorenz. So much for Laurel's rediscovered recollection.

The postscript to this fascinating case concerns Lauralee Lorenz. As I said earlier, she had attempted to plead guilty to the charge of accessory after the fact to murder, but her case had been postponed pending the potential conviction of the alleged principal, Gordon Allen. Given Allen's acquittal, Lauralee Lorenz has never been committed. As a result, even though she tried to plead to that charge earlier and had testified under oath at Allen's trial that she was guilty of that offence, the charge of being an accessory after the fact was withdrawn against her.

As a further irony, the comments in *Regina v. Vinette* in the Supreme Court of Canada were ultimately reviewed by the Ontario Court of Appeal in *Regina v. McAvoy*, and it concluded that, in fact, an accessory after the fact may be successfully prosecuted regardless of whether the principal has already been convicted. Had that decision been in effect at the time of the trial, Lauralee Lorenz could have gotten what she wanted–a conviction for accessory after the fact to an offence that the jury ultimately concluded had never occurred!

Gordon Allen eventually pleaded guilty to a charge of swearing a false affidavit involving his phantom MBA and received an absolute discharge. The two homicide officers who had created the false affidavit of Lauralee Lorenz and shown it to Gordon Allen on the day of his arrest in an attempt to extract a confession from him pleaded not guilty to charges relating to that document and were convicted after a trial by a jury. Ironically, that was the only conviction a jury ever made in this entire case. The officers received discharges, but their careers took turns for the worse because of those offences. The punishment they ultimately received was considerably more than any sentence imposed by the Court.

To this date, the murder of Bruce Lorenz remains unsolved.

Do We Care about the Truth?
Real Truth v. Legal Truth

THE HON. MICHEL PROULX, QC

1988

Throughout the centuries, the merits and weaknesses of the adversarial system have been debated. Though it has been said that the purpose of the trial is the pursuit of truth, one of the central elements of the debate is whether the trial–the adversarial arena–is the best way to reveal the truth. As Mr. Justice Haines of the Ontario Supreme Court once said, "Truth may be only incidental to a point. The trial is not a faithful reconstruction of the evidence as if recorded on a giant television screen." For this reason, we often distinguish the legal truth from the real truth.

The adversarial system may not get to the truth for a variety of reasons. Among them are the rules of exclusion of evidence, the imperfections of the witnesses, the skill (or lack of it) of the lawyers involved, and the judge's mistakes. Any or all of these elements can impede the legal system's pursuit of truth. Although the role played by the defence lawyer in the pursuit of truth is viewed with much scepticism by the public, the issue is rarely discussed within the profession itself. Therefore, I decided to address this question here: Does the defence lawyer care about the truth? We have already had a convincing argument from Eddie Greenspan that it is wrong for counsel to pass moral judgment on a client, and that the client's legal guilt should be determined by the court. While Greenspan's point is well taken and remains a basic rule of ethics, it can also be argued that a defence lawyer has no obligation to remain passive and silent or to be, as Mr. Justice Martin said, "a mere mouth-piece for the client."

As the United States Supreme Court observed recently in the *Nicks v. Woodside* case, "the suggestion sometimes made that the lawyer must believe his client, not judge him, in no sense means a lawyer can honorably be a party to or in any way give aid to presenting known perjury." Beginning with his first interview with his client, the attorney gets a version of the facts that may be the truth, or part of it, or none of it at all. How does he deal with this inevitable reality? The story he gets is never as clear and certain as a piece of crystal. As Mr. Justice Stephens of the United States Supreme Court said in that same *Nicks* case, "A trial lawyer … must often deal with mixtures of sand and clay. Even a pebble that seems clear enough at first glance may take on a different hue in a handful of gravel." To demonstrate the problems the defence lawyer confronts in the issue of truth at all stages of the criminal process, I will describe four typical situations, using my own cases as examples.

The first story, which I entitle "The Biggest Obstacle to the Defence Is when Clients Lie," goes back to the month of July 1964, one year after I was admitted to the bar. My mentor had decided to take off for a holiday and thought I could look after the office in his absence. Soon after he left, I took a call from a man who had just been arrested on a coroner's warrant. The first interview with the client, a forty-year-old lab technician, was disappointing for me. The man was in such a state of shock and despair that he could bare-ly speak about anything. Because I was not aware of the circumstances lead-ing to his arrest, I remained passive during the entire interview. With time, my involvement in the file revealed more detailed facts. The suspect was employed in a manufacturing plant in Montreal. The year earlier, in 1963, he had under-gone major lung surgery that left him with the use of only 50 percent of the total volume of his lungs. He also suffered other serious medical problems and was hospitalized for several months. Finally, he was sent home, but he needed someone to take care of him during the day for a period of four months. His wife could not stay home from her job to care for him, so she asked a divorced woman in her late twenties who lived next door with her parents to take care of her husband while she was away. The drama started there.

For many months the man was nursed by the attractive young woman. He went back to work in the early part of 1964, though he was seriously phys-ically handicapped. Nothing was ever revealed about what happened between the man and the caregiver from the fall of 1963 to the day when she disappeared in mid-May 1964. However, on June 7, 1964, her weighted body was discovered floating in the Richelieu River, thirty minutes' drive from Montreal. Her head was bent back by a rope, which surrounded her neck and connected first to her hands, tied behind her, and then to her feet. A second rope around her neck was attached to a few bricks. Also, there were three stab wounds, one inch deep, in her abdomen. According to her parents, the last time they had seen her and talked to her was in the early morning of May 16, when she left the house in sport clothes.

My client was asked when he had seen her for the last time, and he answered that, in the very early morning of May 16, he had driven her to downtown Montreal near Eaton's department store and left her there. Between her disappearance and the discovery of her body three weeks later, the police did not have a clue what had happened to her. After June 7, however, one very incriminating fact brought the police to my client. For the previous five years he had regularly gone fishing at the Richelieu River, and each time he had rented a rowboat from a couple who operated a small rental company. The couple got to know him, his wife, and his children quite well. According to the couple, the man rented a boat on May 9 and May 16, and they were positive that, on both occasions, he was accompanied by a younger woman. At the end of the day, to the couple's surprise, they noticed that our man came back from his fishing trip alone. They later identified the woman as the victim. That evidence alone, coupled with my client's lie relating to where he left the victim on the morning of May 16, was sufficient to provide grounds for his arrest.

When I met my client in the cells that first day, he was not communicative and wanted only to talk about his emotional reaction to the arrest. After a few days of incarceration, he insisted, despite my advice, on telling the police a long story. He had gone on a fishing trip with this woman, they stopped for lunch, and, later, he went back fishing by himself. When he returned, he saw her lying on the ground. He thought she was dead and, in a state of panic, he threw her in the river. I knew at the time it was unwise for my client to spin this tale to the police, and I wish I had known the famous lines that may have made him realize he was not helping his case. The words are from the play *Glengary Glen Ross:* "Always tell the truth–it's the easiest thing to remember." Mark Twain also said: "When in doubt, tell the truth." Henry Roblatt, a famous American criminal lawyer, indicates in his book *That Damn Lawyer,* published in 1983, that he frequently asked his clients to take a lie detector test to check if they were telling the truth. I'm still not sure whether we should go that far with the client, but I believe we need to know what is a lie and what is the truth. It's probably more productive to use psychology, get to know the client, and wait for the right moment to show our hesitation to go on with an untrue story. We may inspire ourselves from what Schopenhauer said in 1851: "If we suspect a man is lying, we should pretend to believe him, for then he becomes bold and assured, he lies more vigorously, and is unmasked."

In the case I am describing to you, everyone involved had a theory about what really happened on May 16 on the island. It was even more open to speculation when, at the coroner's inquest, my client was called as a witness and publicly repeated what he had said previously to the police. He even added that he had seen three intruders around who had threatened him. He further tried to suggest that these intruders could have had something to do with the woman's death. What my client didn't know, however, was that at the time he testified at the coroner's inquest, the pathologist who had performed the autopsy on the victim's corpse was still uncertain about the cause of death. First, he could not conclude that the three stab wounds were deadly, since the quantity of blood in the lungs was not sufficient. This condition suggested that the stabs were administered at the moment of death or even after death. In addition, he noted a fracture of the cartilage of the larynx and, what was most important, the presence of blood in the soft tissues surrounding the cartilages. Though he could not eliminate the possibility that this fracture happened after death as a result of the pressure of the rope around the neck, the medical legal expert was more inclined to believe that the most reasonable explanation was that the victim died by manual strangulation. In short, he could not indicate with absolute certainty the cause of death, nor could he say whether the victim was dead or alive when her weighted body was put into the river. For these reasons, he was not able to exclude the possibility of natural death, even though it was a very remote possibility.

To complete this puzzle, composed of fragments of evidence that the police had gathered, I should add two more elements. Following an investigation of a few small islands in the vicinity, the police discovered an old, dismantled brick oven. They were eventually able to show that the bricks found attached to the corpse came from that oven and that it was accessible to a rowboat landing place. However, what really linked my client to the body was when he indicated to the detectives where he had thrown the victim's clothes into the water. Two frogmen eventually found the clothes, tied in a bundle with a small rope and kept at the bottom of the river by a few bricks. The rope proved to have been cut from a cord that belonged to the hood of the accused's raincoat. The raincoat was found with the rest of the cord in his garage.

My client was eventually charged in early 1965 with non-capital murder, or second-degree murder as we call it now. He did not testify at his trial but took a chance on his explanation–that he had left his companion while he went fishing, found her dead on his return, and, panic-stricken, disposed of the body. He took a chance that this explanation would be supported by other witnesses, and, considering the loopholes in the medical legal expertise as to the cause of death, he could hope for an acquittal or a verdict of manslaughter. Caught in his lies and his disturbing story to explain why he disposed of the body, my client probably felt that his silence would keep him away from more difficult problems.

I was disappointed but not surprised when the jury returned the verdict of murder. I realized then that people can die with their secrets. The story does not end there, however. I appealed the conviction to the Court of Appeal, which eventually ordered a new trial. The five judges, each writing a separate opinion, concluded that the trial judge had totally misled the jury about the testimony of the medical expert. The odds were then presented to my client, who decided he could not afford to risk a conviction for murder again and confessed the crime of passion. The Crown accepted the plea of manslaughter. What a long road to come to the truth! Maybe Nietche was right when he said, "All truths that are kept silent become poisonous."

This case seems to me to be a clear demonstration of how the lawyer, though not the judge of the facts, can still play an aggressive role in the valuation of his client's version. There are situations where counsel has to challenge his client, warning him that his story seems odd and will likely not be believed. Of course, the message should not be that the client should play with the truth, but, rather, that the truth could help him. This advice has to be presented to the client in a constructive or therapeutic way–as coming from the counsel, who wishes only to help and to advise to the best of his knowledge and experience. Once defence counsel has issued the warning, he must live with the frustration of knowing that his client's choices are out of his hands.

My second scenario I'll entitle "You Never Do Know the Truth, Even after the Trial is Over." A man and his wife were charged jointly in the same trial with the crime of arson–for deliberately setting a fire at the premises they rented to run a flower shop. The wife was operating the business with the help of her daughter, while the husband worked full time as a union representative and had nothing to do with the store. In the months before the incident, it appeared that the business was not doing well, and the husband had to donate some of his income to keep it going. The couple did not own the building, but they were fully insured for all their belongings on the site in the case of fire.

One Friday night in June 1983, at 9:23, a fireman noticed dense smoke coming through the roof of the flower shop. A few minutes later the whole crew of firemen were on the scene of the fire. By that time, the fire had already caused serious damage to the premises and to the property next to it. The business was a complete loss. Suspecting something odd, the officer in charge of the fire squad called for the special team of arson investigators. The next day a chemist from the forensic laboratory concluded from his observations that the fire had been set at three different locations in the flower shop and that, in his opinion, once the first was lit, it was impossible that anyone could have ignited either of the other two locations. Since nothing on the premises could explain the source of the fire in any of the three cases, the probability that they were all accidental was so remote that he drew the obvious conclusion of arson. Our own expert carefully verified this assessment.

This situation became more intense for the two accused and their counsel when it was established that their neighbour, who had known them for years, had seen the husband inside the flower shop through the glass door at 9:05 p.m., eighteen minutes before the fireman detected the smoke. In addition, the Crown had a statement given by the wife to the police in which, though she denied any responsibility for the fire, she admitted being on the premises from 6:00 p.m. until closing time, when her husband came to pick her up. According to her, they both left a few minutes after nine, which was compatible with her neighbour's declaration. Finally, and to make it tighter for my two clients, it was shown that the only access to the business was from the front door, which was locked when the fireman arrived on the premises.

Faced with this circumstantial evidence, it did not take me long to spin a cobweb around my clients. In response, they hotly denied any allegations of participation in the arson. They realized how close they were to the moment of ignition of the fire–that the eighteen minutes between their departure at 9:05 and the observation made by the fireman at 9:23 were likely too few to raise the possibility of an act done by an intruder, and that the short space of time in itself constituted what is called in law an exclusive opportunity to have commit the crime. But despite all this circumstantial evidence, my clients continued to protest their innocence. "How can I win this case?" I asked them. "Once the trial judge has all these facts before him, would it be enough to come forward and deny it, to try to impress the judge with your good character record? How can he get a reasonable doubt?" All these questions had to be raised, mostly to prepare my clients for what seemed likely to be a verdict of guilty and a very harsh sentence.

Before the trial, having spent many hours of preparation and discussion with my clients, the real question that hounded me above all legal and ethical considerations was straightforward: Did they do it or not? Or did she or did he, but without the help of the other? They sounded like honest people, and I was inclined to think that they must have told me the truth. In other words, I had a doubt. As the date of the trial approached, I distanced myself from the case for a few days to try to solve my conflicts, and soon enough I found a solution. I had the right way to argue this case. Going back to the basics, to the fundamental principles of law relating to parties, to an offence, and to the assured complicity, I was able to apply a principle well established in both English and Canadian jurisprudence to this case. It reads as follows: "Where two persons are joined in one indictment and charged on separate counts with the same offence and there is no evidence against one accused that he committed the offence either alone or in consort with the other, then on the accused admitting there is no case against him to go to the jury, it is his right that his case should not be left to the jury and the same applies for the other and both are to be acquitted." This quotation comes from the case of *Shell and Packett* in the Court of Appeal of Ontario. With that defence in hand, I went to the trial with confidence. At the end of the formidable case for the Crown, I calmly rose and presented to the court a motion of non-suit on the grounds I outlined above. The motion was eventually granted, and the two accused were both acquitted without having to proclaim their innocence under oath.

That verdict, however, never answered my question, and I still don't know what the truth is today, though, strictly speaking, the final judgement should have decided the issue. Had the couple been faced with separate trials rather than jointly indicted, my anxiety would not have been so easily resolved. The motion of non-suit would not have been presented, and it could well have been a different story at the end. Probably one or both of my clients would have been convicted. This case illustrates how a defence lawyer can sometimes best serve his client and the administration of justice by disregarding the issue of truth and focusing on purely legal issues. In this story, it is reasonable to conclude that the system may have helped one or even two guilty persons escape a conviction. But, by the same token, the system may have helped an innocent person escape a conviction, which remains one of the fundamental goals of our justice system.

My third story relates to the Sherbrooke trial, which I'll entitle "*Being Alone with Your Truth through a Long Dark Night.*" It is no secret that, after years of practising criminal law, you begin to attract the most sensational and controversial issues. Occasionally, these cases fill the headlines every day, are discussed in heated voices at the best dinner parties, and result in the public scorning you, your client, and the entire justice system when your client is acquitted. I spent ten months in 1985 working on a case that so inflamed public opinion that complete strangers felt it was their moral duty to come up to me and question my personal value system. The case involved Sherbrooke police officers who were charged with manslaughter after they shot two innocent carpet layers in a motel in Rock Forrest. In the public mind, the accused were killer cops. At the very least, they were criminally negligent and, in all probability, bloodthirsty murders. This "truth" screamed from newspaper headlines, television commentators, radio broadcasts, and editorials.

Many of the facts were incontestable. The victims, who had been pursued as armed robbers who had murdered a Brinks guard, were, in fact, innocent citizens. They had been in bed, probably sleeping, when the early morning surprise raid began. When it was over, one of them was dead and the other seriously wounded. Clearly, the police had made a tragic error, but the public never understood that the error was not the point of the trial. The issue was simple: Had the two officers on trial committed the crime of manslaughter?

As background to the case, the police had been searching for two murderers of an armored truck driver who had been coldly assassinated in the course of an armed robbery. Less than twenty-four hours after the robbery, the police received information that the murderers were in a motel in the vicinity of the robbery. We all know now that this information was wrong, but, at the time, the police had reasonable and probable grounds to believe that it was right. Evidence given at the trial established that a chain of unfortunate coincidences and eyewitness errors could explain why the police believed the men in the motel were the murderers.

To arrest these dangerous suspects, the officers assigned to the case decided to raid the room and catch the criminals by surprise. The first police officer, who had to enter the room, opened the door and shouted "Police." He was stopped in his tracks by the end of the bed, which was directly in front of him. At this very moment, he saw a man getting up from a reclining position in the bed while, at the same time, the door he had opened was pushed in a closing movement towards him by someone on the inside. The police officer, thinking his life was in danger, responded immediately by firing one shot through the closing door, which by then separated him from the man in the bed. As he fired, he jumped back out of the room, calling "Attention" to his back-up officer. By this time the door had completed its movement and closed. The back-up officer thought the shot had been fired by someone inside, so he fired his machine-gun into the closed door. Although the first shot through the moving door did not hurt anyone, the subsequent shots that were fired through the closed door killed one man and wounded the other. That, of course, was the version of the two police officers.

The defence rested mainly on the first shot. Because the back-up officer fired the machine-gun when the door was closed, based on belief that his partner had been shot or at least that a shot had come from inside, it became crucial to the case to establish that the first shot, which triggered everything, had not been fired when the door was closed. Our theory held that the police officer who fired through the door with his machine-gun did so in self-defence because he believed that the first shot came from inside the room. He had no time to move away from what he thought was the line of fire in front of the door, which had been closed by someone on the inside right after the first shot. He thought he had no other choice than to protect himself and the other officer by firing on the person inside who had fired the first shot. The ballistics expert confirmed that the first shot was fired through the door at an angle of 45 degrees. He also established that someone at a short distance could easily assume that the shot had been fired from inside the room. This evidence became a key factor in the case.

The medical expert also helped our case when he testified about the position of the victim when the bullets hit him. He suggested that the victim had probably been in a sitting position in his bed and was bending towards the foot of the bed when he got hit. The first police officer had reported seeing someone in bed making a movement before the door began closing in his direction. Our strategy in the trial focused on the truth, particularly the sequencing of events, and we hoped that the jury would discard the rumours and consider the facts as they were. Although I faced extremely adverse public opinion in the months leading up to the trial, I was optimistic about the outcome of the case. All the expert evidence backed up my client's original story.

The trial ended with the acquittal of the two police officers. The day after, many editorials blasted the jury's verdict. Even today, two years later, people recall the trial and express their dissatisfaction with the outcome. In their minds, the truth continues to be that the murderous Sherbrooke police officers fired a machine-gun at two sleeping men through a closed door.

My fourth story I'll entitle "When, after a Long Journey, the Truth Abruptly Ends the Matter." The defence counsel's greatest nightmare is to see an innocent client found guilty–to know what the truth is but not be able to prove it. One of the most memorable legal and human battles I fought followed this scenario.

The first contact I had with my client came right after his conviction by a jury in Montreal on a charge of arson, for which he was sentenced to thirty months in jail. A man in his later forties, he had owned a car body shop for several years and had been very successful. Despite having almost no education, he had created the security he needed. His business was his whole life. One Saturday night in March 1979 an explosion destroyed the entire building where he operated the garage. My client was insured for a large sum of money, but the insurance company, after investigating, refused to pay. None of the experts who examined the scene were able to determine if the fire was accidental or deliberately set. After eliminating most causes, the experts all concluded that the explosion had been caused by gas. They thought it unlikely to have been natural gas, because no natural gas leak was detected. This incident in itself raised suspicion, but it was not enough evidence to allow the insurance company to refuse to pay for the damages or the police to lay a charge of arson.

A greater suspicion arose from the fact that, a few days before the fire, my client had cleaned his garage and moved some materials and tires to his father's barn. In his first statement to the insurance adjuster, he did not report this fact, and he added this merchandise to his claim of loss. Subsequently, in the course of the investigation, he corrected his first statement.

The most damaging evidence came from an old woman, Mrs. Anderson, who had lived across the street from the garage for many years and had known my client since he began to upgrade his business. She swore that a short time before the explosion, she had seen my client through her kitchen window, which faced the garage, leaving his garage in a hurry and rushing into his car. She added that she looked at her clock, and it was precisely 8:05 p.m. The fire alarm was given at 8:20 p.m. This evidence in itself was very incriminating, unless my client could provide a convincing explanation. He strongly denied that he had run away from the garage a short time before the explosion and insisted that he had been home sick at the time. Through this denial, my client confined the issue to a simple proposition: If you believe the old lady, he was guilty of arson because his unexplained presence and his running from the garage a few minutes before the explosion could only lead to the inevitable conclusion that he himself set the fire. My client was eventually charged with arson, based on the neighbour's evidence.

At his trial before a jury, the defence lawyer made great efforts to destroy the Crown's case. First, more than one independent witness stated that the neighbour's testimony should be taken with some restraint: she had a bad reputation as a neighbour, both her husband and she had a serious drinking problem, and she seemed seriously impaired by alcohol. Second, my client had the defence of an alibi, who established that he was at home for many hours before the explosion. Third, several witnesses proved that my client was financially in a good position. Finally, some witnesses testified about his good character. One additional factor was very favourable to the accused: even though the insurance company had refused him the indemnity payment, my client, while on bail pending his trial and under difficult financial conditions, had rebuilt the garage on the same premises. Despite all this supporting evidence, the jury found my client guilty. The verdict was rendered on May 24, 1980.

My client immediately appealed his conviction and sentence and was given bail during the appeal. At this point, he retained me. From the first time I met him, despite the verdict, he professed his innocence with what seemed to me to be great sincerity. Devastated by the verdict, he simply could not understand why he had lost his case. He wondered what had not been done that should have been done. My client was a very religious man, and he kept saying that God would help him, that one day he would be cleared of the mess he was in. Though he expressed great confidence in my young associate and me, and in the success of the appeal, we advised him that he should not expect the Court of Appeal to proclaim his innocence and acquit him. We told him that he might get a new trial.

On November 18, 1982, the Court of Appeal dismissed both appeals against his conviction and his sentence. My client was in a state of shock. What had seemed a nightmare for him with the loss of his business and a prison term at his age became a dreadful reality. I still remember him crying and looking at me, begging me to find a solution—at least to give him some delay. A few days later we served a Notice of Motion for Leave to Appeal to the Supreme Court of Canada, and, on that account, we were able to get bail pending the appeal. The presentation of the Motion for Leave was set for the end of the month of February 1983. We made it clear to my client that he should get himself ready to face the inevitable, but his determination and his claim to innocence made him risk everything. My client informed us that he would challenge the most vital part of the case against him: the testimony of the neighbour. He asked a female friend to pretend to be a saleswoman and to visit the neighbour—to try to make her talk about him and the fire—which by this time had occurred three years before. His plan worked. The "saleswoman" reported to us that during the conversation, Mrs. Anderson indicated that there were witnesses who had heard her say about my client, "I fixed him up." With this information, we asked the same woman to go back again with an electronic device to tape the entire conversation. The miracle happened. A few days later we possessed a tape on which we could hear the following exchange:

Q. Your husband is not here today?

A. No, dear, I lost my poor husband almost three years ago.

Q. Sorry, Mrs. Anderson. Is it in connection with the explosion of the garage?

A. Oh, that Phil [my client], I fixed him up.

Q. How come, Mrs. Anderson?

A. Before the explosion, me and my husband called Phil many times to come to grease my washing machine, and the last time he said "Don't bother me." But I fixed him up.

Q. What do you mean by "I fixed him up"?

A. I went to court and said I saw Phil running out of the garage before the explosion.

Q. It's true.

A. No, dear, it was not true. I was so mad at him, that's why I said that.

We could not believe what we heard. It was frightening but also exciting not only for my client and his family but also for us who had gone through this appeal. This fresh evidence went to the crux of the whole case against my client. We had to move everything around with great urgency. The motion before the Supreme Court of Canada was scheduled for the following week. We decided to divulge this new evidence immediately to the Crown attorney, with the expectation that he would consent to the adjournment of the Motion for Leave. The Crown listened to the tape, could hardly hide his astonishment, and replied that he would inform us in the next twenty-four hours of his decision. Meanwhile, the Crown attorney asked two detectives to verify the authenticity of the tape by paying a visit to the now notorious neighbour.

When the detectives arrived at Mrs. Anderson's apartment, they asked her if she had received visits from the saleswoman and if she could recall the discussion about her testimony at my client's trial. She flatly denied the discussion, so the detectives made her listen to the tape. She remained stubborn, and they asked her to listen to the tape again. At one point they could hear the twittering of a bird, and the detective asked: "How could that tape have been made up when we can hear on it that same twittering as we hear now in your kitchen?"

The detectives made a full report to the Crown attorney. They described the neighbour as a most unreliable witness, one who had probably caused the most serious injustice a person can suffer: to be found guilty of a crime he did not commit. From that point on, we obtained full cooperation from the Crown attorney. Through his support, we made a very unusual motion to the minister of justice by virtue of section 617 of the *Criminal Code*, which gives the minister the right to direct a new trial or a new hearing before the Court of Appeal. After a careful review of the case and the new evidence presented, the minister of justice decided to grant our client a new hearing before the Court of Appeal based on the previous record and, obviously, on the new evidence.

A few months later, the Court of Appeal heard the case and, on February 7, 1984, ordered a new trial, though we had argued for an acquittal. The Crown didn't want to proceed with a new trial under the circumstances and opted for *Anuli Prosequi*. That finally ended the terrifying and disturbing experience for my client, after almost five years of waiting to see his fate decided. A satisfactory settlement was made with the insurance company, and my client got enough money to ensure him some stability and happiness.

In describing these four cases, I do not pretend to have discussed the pursuit of truth from all points of view. Issues related to the truth and to the criminal justice system abound, such as the distinction between the legal truth and the factual truth, or the matter of conscience for a lawyer who catches himself playing with the truth. Other questions are raised when a client confesses his guilt to his counsel, or in the way a lawyer controls the truth in presenting his client's case. Whatever the issues, I have tried to show that, contrary to what many people think, defence counsel do care about the truth.

Part Four: From Law to Politics

From Defence to Offence:
The Case for New Brunswick

FRANK J. MCKENNA, PC, QC

1994

You might wonder how being a criminal lawyer prepares you to be a provincial premier. In fact, the two go hand in hand much more than you might think. It seems that almost everything I do, almost every skill I need as a politician, is enhanced in some way by the discipline and experience I had in the practice of law. I can think of a hundred times when my legal training or my courtroom experience has been invaluable to me in politics. For example, to practise criminal law, you must have an indomitable will to win. You have to want to win so badly that it makes your teeth chatter when you go into the courtroom. You have to want to win so much you'll do almost anything within legal bounds. If you don't do that, you'll lose a lot, especially in a criminal court. You must be prepared to do everything you can to win.

I've become quite refined as I have become older. When I was younger, I was so competitive in court that every time the prosecutor started making progress on cross-examination or making a significant point, I got upset and spilled the water pitcher all over the table. While the jury was watching me run around, trying to mop up the water and clean everything up, the prosecutor usually hit his best points. I remember doing a bootlegging case. An Indian woman from one of the nearby reserves was charged with bootlegging, and I couldn't think of any way to win. Finally, I went out to see her at the reserve and, while visiting her, I realized that every woman I met looked exactly the same to me, so I brought them all into the courthouse and defied the policeman to pick out the person he had bought the liquor from. Obviously, he couldn't. He said it could have been any one of the twenty people. We won the case. One thing I found out in criminal court is that everything is fair game. You can help your clients by using almost any stratagem, as long as it is within the law.

When I was first practising as a criminal lawyer, my firm used to do breathalyzer cases by the score. The breathalyzer law was relatively new, and there were a number of discrepancies in the certification of the machines that were used. Out of the first hundred breathalyzer cases I did, I think I won ninety. We won on every technicality imaginable because there were so many loopholes. I remember one breathalyzer case in which my client was most certainly guilty. We didn't have a hope, but we used to take these cases on contingency fees because they were so easy to win. We'd get three or four hundred dollars if we won, nothing if we lost. In this particular case we walked into court and simply let the prosecutor go through all the evidence they had. And they had plenty, including proper identification of the accused. The situation was desperate. The final thing they needed was that the "demand" had been made legally. Police officers are obliged to tell an accused person: " I demand that you come with me. I have reasonable and probable grounds to believe that you've committed an offence under section 236 of the *Criminal Code*, so come with me for the purpose of giving a breath sample, etc." Unless their demand is a legal demand, the accused can't be found guilty. Every police officer knew what had to be done. It's the one thing they learn and never forget. In this trial, we had reached the final element of the prosecution's case, and the counsel asked the police witness:

Crown: Did you in fact give the accused the legal demand?

Officer: Yes, I did.

Crown: Could you have forgotten to give the legal demand?

Officer: No, I never forget.

Crown: Could you have forgotten the words?

Officer: No, I could never forget the words.

Crown: And why could you never forget the words?

Officer: Because I have it on a card.

Crown: And could you ever forget the card?

Officer: No, I carry it with me at all times.

Crown: And where do you carry it with you at all times?

Officer: I carry it with me in my hat.

Crown: Would you read from it?

Officer: Oh, my God! I forgot my hat!

There he was in court with no breathalyzer card and he couldn't remember the words. My client was found not guilty.

In another case, we were much less fortunate. Initially everything looked good and I thought we were actually going to win the case. It was an arson case, and I couldn't figure out why the prosecutor was always smirking at me as if he had an ace up his sleeve. He got to his last few witnesses, and he started calling neighbours in the immediate vicinity of the house that had burned down. He asked these neighbours what they saw and heard, and they said they saw three children running out of the burning house, screaming in unison at the top of their lungs "One, two, three – Fire! Fire!" As soon as they said this, a look of horror came over my client's face–followed immediately by a look of horror over mine. I finally realized what he'd done. He had set the house on fire and told the kids to run outside, count to three, and yell "Fire!" Needless to say, my client spent a few years in jail.

The second thing I learned as a criminal lawyer that I've used as a politician is always to expect, and be prepared for, the unexpected. You are never going to have a situation that is completely under control. The Yvon Durelle case is a perfect example. Durelle was charged with murder, and the defence was self-defence. My client killed a fisherman who had antagonized him after an argument. The fisherman had also been menacing other people in the Bay St. Anne community, where he lived. It was a tough case because the accused had indicated publicly that he had some animosity towards the deceased. As well, he had killed the deceased with five bullets, and it was difficult to prove why he needed to shoot the man five times in self-defence.

We spent considerable time interviewing Yvon Durelle, who had participated in so many boxing matches around the world that they were certainly having an impact on his memory. We wanted to make sure that the version he gave on the witness stand would be the one most in line with the truth and also consistent with his innocence. We didn't coach him, but we talked to him a lot until he gave us the right answers. When we asked him, "Why did you shoot the guy five times?" he answered, "Look, I was scared, scared to death. The guy was coming at me in a car and he reached down, and I was sure he was going for a gun. I shot, but didn't think I hit him, so I kept shooting." We presented experts from Alberta and Ontario and all kinds of other people to prove this theory. Then, when Durelle got on the witness stand, I asked him about the key element in our case, which we had gone over so many times:

McKenna: Mr. Durelle, were you in fear of your life?

Durelle: Yes, I was.

McKenna: Why did you shoot him five times?

Durelle: Because that's all the bullets I had.

Always expect the unexpected on the witness stand. Later on in the case, we had a similar situation involving Durelle's testimony. We had to prove that he had a reasonable apprehension for his own safety. We wanted to demonstrate that several people in the community had been threatened by the deceased and had related the threats to others, including Yvon Durelle. We asked him some key names to help him remember. For example, "Do you remember somebody named Nelson Durelle?" He said that Nelson Durelle was also threatened by the deceased, who showed him his gun and told him he would use it on him if he had to. I also asked if he remembered Albert Porier: my client indicated that Porier had been in a knife fight with the deceased and that the deceased fought him viciously. Finally, I asked him if he knew Bodgie Martin, who was a well-known local in Bay St. Anne. He was supposed to say yes, because Martin had apparently had an altercation with the deceased. Instead Durelle burst out laughing uncontrollably. I asked him again, "Do you know Bodgie Martin or not?" He replied: "I know Bodgie Martin. His wife is screwing around with everybody in Bay St. Anne and he doesn't even know about it." At that moment, Bodgie Martin's wife ran out of the courtroom and Bodgie followed right behind her.

The third thing I learned while practising criminal law that has proved useful in the business of politics is that you must be fearless when it comes to experimentation. You must literally try anything and everything to get a client off. I reached the outer limits of this skill during a case of assault causing bodily harm to a policeman. What was particularly interesting about this case was that the attacker was a trained guard dog–a German Shepherd trained by a dog master. The police alleged that the accused got into an altercation with the officer. He set his dog on the officer, who was then mauled quite severely. My client was charged with assault causing bodily harm, using the dog as the instrument. At the time, as a young defence lawyer, I was perplexed about how to get this guy off. It sounded like a good case for the prosecution, and things looked pretty desperate for my client. I asked the accused if the dog really was safe. He said, "Look at that dog. He's a perfect little angel. That dog would never hurt anybody." So I put the dog on the witness stand, though I didn't have to swear him in. We proceeded to give the dog various commands to find out whether he would obey them or not. Bravely I asked the accused, "What were the words that you're alleged to have used?" He said "Sick 'em, boy." The dog just looked at me, his ears went up a little bit, and then he rolled over on his back, as happy as could be. I was sitting there fearing for my life, and the dog was having a ball. The judge looked down at the dog and said, "This is a joke. This dog isn't trained to attack. This is crazy. Case dismissed." Then, as I was walking back to my office, a policeman walked in front of the dog, and the dog snarled at him. I turned around to my client and said, "What in the name of God is going on?" He said, "He's only trained to attack uniforms." I said "Case closed." That was a close call.

The practice of law has enhanced what I've done in politics in a number of ways. There are a lot of jokes about lawyers and politics. Clarence Darrow started it all when he said, "The trouble with law and government is lawyers." I don't agree. Some of the political situations I've been in have been much easier to handle because of the extraordinary experiences I had in the courtroom. I spent weeks during the Meech Lake negotiations, locked in a room while hundreds of thousands of Canadians awaited our decision and hundreds of journalists swarmed outside, as I fought over some of the most important constitutional issues in Canada in 125 years. The pressure was extraordinary. I saw premiers, people I respect, break down and cry. I saw others become so stressed out they were incomprehensible. I saw emotion beyond anything I've ever seen before as the negotiators were exposed to this horrible, gut-wrenching pressure, trying to do what was right for Canada and trying to be true to their own beliefs. I saw people trying to find a way to reconcile what was, perhaps, the unreconcilable. I found it extraordinarily and excruciatingly hard, but I didn't find it as hard as the many occasions I have waited for a jury to come back with a verdict in a murder case. There is nothing in life that equals the pressure, the excitement, and the suspense of doing a jury trial, of waiting for the moment a jury returns, opens the envelope, and reads the verdict. There is nothing like seeing the accused collapse beside you, or members of the family shrieking with joy or crying in anguish, as the case may be. The sheer drama of that has never been duplicated for me in political life.

I also found this pressure in law to be exhilarating–and addictive. An old, experienced lawyer told me after my first murder case that life would never be the same again. He told me that once you've experienced this high, you'll always have to seek it out. He warned me I would find the depths to be much lower as a result of it, which is so very true. I found that after every murder case I ever did, after weeks of intense drama and pressure, my spirits would soar for a day or so, then crash into the depths of despair, looking for the same adrenaline rush I had experienced during the case. If you are going to do courtroom law at that level, you must prepare yourself mentally and physically, almost as if you are in training for a marathon.

It's important to maintain your dignity under that pressure, because, ultimately, that is really what separates the practice of law from people who settle their disputes on corner lots. Dignity under pressure: it's a difficult thing to achieve, but it's a wonderful thing to see. In a kind of humorous way, I saw the most dignified performance of my life in the Supreme Court of Canada. I was there for a murder case. Three judges were present at the court, including Mr. Justice Ritchie. We had finished the case, and the justices were all walking to the top of the raised platform, above their chairs. Suddenly Mr. Justice Ritchie, who must have been eighty years old at the time, tumbled all the way down the stairs and fell flat on his face on the floor. The two other judges walked down very casually and formally, side by side, and stood next to him. Each one grabbed him by an arm and lifted him up. They all bowed to the courtroom and walked out as if they did this routine every day of their lives.

The practice of law has given me a chance to let my mind run wild and be innovative. And that is exactly what we've been trying to do in the province of New Brunswick.

Contributors

The Hon. Gerald N. Allbright was called to the Saskatchewan Bar in 1971. Before his appointment to the judiciary, Justice Allbright practised primarily in the areas of criminal and civil litigation, as well as serving as chairperson of extensive labour arbitrations. He has been president of the Saskatchewan Trial Lawyers' Association and the Law Society, 1981–82. Justice Allbright sits on the Court of Queen's Bench for Saskatchewan in Saskatoon.

G. Greg Brodsky, QC, was born in Melville, Saskatchewan, on April 15, 1940. He graduated from the University of Manitoba Law School in 1963 and received his LL.M. from the University of Manitoba in 1965. He was admitted to the Bar in Ontario in 1971 and in Saskatchewan in 1977. Specializing in criminal law, he was appointed Queen's Counsel in 1976 and is currently the "Brodsky" in Brodsky & Company, Winnipeg, Manitoba. He was the first president of the Manitoba Trial Lawyers' Association in 1976, now called the Criminal Defence Lawyers' Association, and held that position for twelve years. He is a Life Bencher of the Law Society of Manitoba and past national chairperson of the Criminal Justice section of the Canadian Bar Association.

David M. Cohn is a sole practitioner in a private criminal defence practice in Toronto. He completed his B.A. in economics at the University of Western Ontario in 1976 and his LL.B. at the University of Windsor in 1979. He articled with Aiken, Capp, Barristers & Solicitors in Toronto and was called to the Bar in Ontario in 1981. Over the past twenty-four years, he has defended approximately three thousand criminal cases, at all levels of court, and has conducted well over 125 jury trials. His cases cover a broad spectrum, including homicide, drug offences, proceeds of crime, sexual assault, fraud, firearms and weapons charges, gaming offences, highway traffic offences, offences against persons and property, parole and probation, and cases involving young offenders. He is a loyal member of the Criminal Lawyers' Association and has written legal articles for the organization.

Austin Cooper, QC, has been a defence counsel in the field of criminal law since 1953. He has extensive experience as both a trial and an appellate counsel. He has also written and lectured widely in the areas of advocacy, evidence, and substantive criminal law. A Fellow of the American College of Trial Lawyers, he was, 1992 recipient of the prestigious Douglas K. Laidlaw Medal for Excellence in Advocacy. He is a founding member and former director of the Advocates Society in Ontario, and former chair of the Civil Liberties subsection of the Canadian Bar Association. He served as a Bencher of the Law Society of Upper Canada from 1971 to 1987, after which he was made an ex-officio Bencher for life. Between 1996 and 1997, Mr. Cooper was lead counsel for the Commission on Proceedings Involving Guy Paul Morin.

He has been involved in many well-known cases, including the 1978 trial of rock musician Keith Richards of the Rolling Stones, who was caught bringing heroin into Canada during a concert tour. In 1982 he successfully defended Susan Nelles, who was accused of murdering twenty-four babies in Toronto's Hospital for Sick Children. More recently, Mr. Cooper defended lawyer Ken Murray, who was charged with obstructing justice by holding onto the videotapes he had retrieved on behalf of his client Paul Bernardo.

Marlys Edwardh, a graduate of Osgoode Hall Law School, received a Master's degree in law from Boalt Hall, University of California at Berkeley. She is a partner with Ruby & Edwardh in Toronto. Since being called to the Bar in 1976, Ms. Edwardh has practised in the fields of criminal, constitutional, and administrative law. She has served as counsel to a number of royal commissions, including the Krever Commission concerning the blood system in Canada.

Ms. Edwardh received an honorary doctorate from the Law Society of Upper Canada in February 2002 and was awarded the G. Arthur Martin Criminal Justice Award by the Criminal Lawyers' Association in October of the same year. She is currently one of the senior counsels representing Maher Arar at the Commission of Inquiry into the Actions of Canadian Officials in Relation to Maher Arar.

Brian H. Greenspan is a partner in the Toronto firm Greenspan, Humphrey, Lavine. He received his B.A. from the University of Toronto in 1968 and his LL.B. from

Osgoode Hall Law School in 1971. He was awarded the Laidlaw Foundation Fellow-ship, and in 1972 he received his LL.M. from the London School of Economics. In 1974 he was called to the Ontario Bar. He taught the administration of criminal jus-tice at Osgoode Hall Law School for seven years, and he was a special lecturer in crim-inal law at the University of Toronto Law School for fourteen years. He was also a member of the faculty of the Federation of Law Societies Criminal Law Program for nineteen years.

Mr. Greenspan served as president of the Ontario Criminal Lawyers' Association from 1989 to 2003. He was the founding chair of the Canadian Council of Criminal Defence Lawyers/Conseil Canadien des Avocats de la Defense, and from 2000 to 2003 he was a director of the Ontario Advocates' Society. He is a director of the Association in Defence of the Wrongly Convicted, and a member of the Society for the Reform of the Criminal Law, the Canadian Bar Association, the National Association of Criminal Defense Lawyers, and the American Bar Association. A Fellow of both the American College of Trial Lawyers and the International Society of Barristers, in 2002 he was awarded the Douglas K. Laidlaw Medal for excellence in oral advocacy.

Edward L. Greenspan, QC, is the senior partner of the Toronto law firm Greenspan, White. He has practised in Toronto for thirty-five years, receiving his Queen's Counsel in 1982. Mr. Greenspan taught criminal law at the University of Toronto Law School for twenty-eight years, and criminal procedure and evidence at Osgoode Hall Law School for fourteen years. He has received honorary doctorates from the Law Society of Upper Canada (1999), the University of Windsor (2002), and Assumption University (2004). He is the author of *Greenspan: The Case for the Defence* (with George Jonas), and co-author of *Martin's Annual Criminal Code*, the most widely read annotated code in Canada. He has been the editor-in-chief of *Canadian Criminal Cases* since 1975.

Mr. Greenspan has been involved in some of the most high-profile cases in Canada. His practice includes defending persons charged with criminal offences, act-ing in *Securities Act* and income tax investigations, prosecuting coroners' inquests, defending persons charged under the *Occupational Health and Safety Act* and the *Environmental Protection Act*, and defending professional discipline complaints before administrative tribunals.

The Hon. G. Arthur Martin (1913–2001) was the pre-eminent Canadian criminal defence lawyer of his time and a reformer of the Canadian justice system. He gradu-ated from the University of Toronto Faculty of Law in 1935 and from Osgoode Hall Law School in 1938, winning both the Gold Medal and the Chancellor Van Koughnet Scholarship. He was called to the Bar of Ontario in 1938, and to the Bar of British

Columbia in 1950. He was appointed King's Counsel in 1945. For thirty-three years he practised criminal law exclusively, representing accused persons in more than seventy murder trials and appeals. He was a lecturer in criminal law at Osgoode Hall Law School for twenty-five years and wrote numerous articles on criminal law and procedure. In 1973, after a term as treasurer of the Law Society of Upper Canada, he was appointed judge of the Ontario Supreme Court. He served fifteen years on the bench, until his retirement in 1988.

Justice Martin acted as vice-chairman of the Ouimet Committee on Criminal Justice and Corrections, and as chair of the Martin Committee on Crown Disclosure and Plea Discussions. He was a member of the 1965 Joint Committee on legal aid reform and chair of the Ontario Legal Aid Programme Committee. He received an honorary doctorate of laws from Queen's University and was awarded the Robinette Medal by the Osgoode Hall Law School Alumni Association. Justice Martin was the first recipient of the G. Arthur Martin Criminal Justice Medal, an annual award presented by the Criminal Lawyers' Association. He became an Officer of the Order of Canada in 1991.

Frank J. McKenna, PC, QC, was appointed Canadian Ambassador to the United States in January 2005. Prior to his appointment he was counsel with McInnes Cooper in Moncton. Mr. McKenna practised criminal law in Chatham, New Brunswick, from 1974 until 1982, when he was elected to the provincial legislature. He became premier of New Brunswick in 1985 and served in that capacity for ten years, winning three consecutive elections.

He received the Vanier Award for Outstanding Young Canadians in 1988. In 1993 the Economic Developers' Association of Canada named him Economic Developer of the Year. He was presented the Canadian Advanced Technology Association (CATA) award of distinction for public sector leadership in the development and application of advanced technology in 1994, and was named the inaugural member of the Public Service Wing of the Canadian Information Productivity Awards Hall of Fame in 1996. He currently serves on the board of directors of numerous corporations and is also active as a volunteer with organizations such as the National Adult Literacy Database, the Investors Learning Centre, the Canadian Landmine Foundation, the C.D. Howe Institute, and the Canadian Paralympic Committee.

The Hon. Mr. Justice Saul Nosanchuk received his B.A. from the University of Windsor in 1954 and his LL.B. from Osgoode Hall Law School in 1959. He specialized as a criminal defence trial lawyer in private practice from 1959 to 1976, when he was appointed to the Ontario Court of Justice. Justice Nosanchuk has taught criminal law, criminal procedure, and criminal sanctions at the University of Windsor Faculty of

Law since 1973 and is an adjunct professor of law. He has been a guest lecturer on such topics as the criminal trial process, psychology and the law, sentencing, restorative justice, and criminology at various institutions, including Osgoode Hall Law School, the University of Windsor, the University of Guelph, St. Clair College, and the Ontario Police College.

He is a past member of the executive and current member of the Essex County Law Association and the Ontario Judges' Association. He is also a past member of the National Association of Criminal Defence Lawyers (US) and the Criminal Defence Lawyers' Association of Windsor and of Ontario. He is currently a member of the Canadian Mental Health Association (Windsor-Essex) Mental Health Justice Systems Task Force reporting to the Ministry of Health. Justice Nosanchuk has been active in many community organizations, including the John Howard Society of Windsor (of which he is a former president), St. Leonard's House-Windsor (of which he is a past member of the Advisory Board), the pilot project introducing the Community Service Order Programme into the Essex County criminal justice system (of which he is a former chair), and the Essex County Area Committee for Legal Aid.

Noel C. O'Brien, QC, is a partner in the Calgary law firm O'Brien, Devlin, Markey and MacLeod. Mr. O'Brien graduated as the Gold Medalist from the University of Windsor Law School in 1976. He has lectured on advanced criminal law for more than ten years at the University of Calgary Faculty of Law. Mr. O'Brien has appeared before all levels of court in Alberta and British Columbia as well as the Supreme Court of Canada. He has substantial experience in jury cases and has acted as defence counsel in numerous high-profile cases, including over sixty-five murder cases, many of which resulted in total acquittal.

Joel E. Pink, QC, has practised law in Nova Scotia since 1969, and exclusively in the area of criminal law since 1973. He appears regularly in all levels of court with jurisdiction in the province. He has represented accused persons in the provinces of New Brunswick, Prince Edward Island, and Newfoundland, and often has a matter pending before the Supreme Court of Canada. He was the founding president of the Nova Scotia Criminal Lawyers' Association, a Fellow of the American College of Trial Lawyers, and a Fellow of the International Society of Barristers.

Mr. Pink has written and lectured extensively about issues in Canadian criminal justice for more than thirty years. He has been a member of the Faculty of the National Criminal Law Program of the Federation of Law Societies of Canada for the past 28 years. He has taught courses in criminal trial practice and evidence at Dalhousie Law School, and courses in criminal law in the Criminology Program at Saint Mary's University.

The Hon. Michel Proulx, QC, is a senior member of the firm Davies Ward Phillips & Vineberg in Montreal. He was appointed to the Court of Appeal of Quebec in 1989 and sat until his retirement from the bench in 2004. Before his appointment, he had a distinguished litigation practice, mainly in criminal law, representing clients at the trial level as well as before the Quebec Court of Appeal and the Supreme Court of Canada. He also represented interested parties before several federal and provincial commissions of inquiry, including the Cliche Commission, the Malouf Commission, the Keable Commission, and the MacDonald Commission on the Royal Canadian Mounted Police. He also acted as senior adviser to the Dubin Commission of Inquiry into the Use of Drugs and Banned Practices. From 1967 to 1989 Mr. Proulx served as adjunct professor of law at McGill University.

He is co-author, with David Layton, of *Ethics and Canadian Criminal Law* (Irwin Law, 2001), which won the award of the Fondation du Barreau du Québec in 2002 and the Walter Owen Book Prize in 2003.

Raphaël H. Schachter, QC, is a partner at Lavery, de Billy in Montreal and has been a member of the Bar of Quebec since 1969. He practises exclusively in the areas of criminal law, penal law, and statutory law. From 1969 to 1972 Mr. Schachter was a provincial Crown prosecutor, and from 1972 to 1976 he served as a federal Crown prosecutor. From 1976 to 1999 he was a senior partner in the law firm of Lapointe, Schachter, Champagne & Talbot. Mr. Schachter was appointed Queen's Counsel in 1986 and was inducted as a Fellow of the American College of Trial Lawyers in 1994. He is also a member of the Canadian Bar Association, where he served as president of the Criminal Law Section (Quebec Division) for four years. Mr. Schachter has appeared before the courts of every jurisdiction in Canada, both as prosecutor and defence attorney, including, on numerous occasions, the Supreme Court of Canada.

Hersh Wolch, QC, received his law degree from the University of Manitoba in 1965. He practised as a Crown prosecutor for both the province of Manitoba and the federal Department of Justice until 1973, after which he entered private practice. In 1982 he became a Queen's Counsel, and he continues to practise as a criminal defence lawyer throughout Canada. During his lengthy criminal defence career, Mr. Wolch has practised at all levels of court and has experience in all manner of criminal and quasi-criminal litigation, including commercial crime, environmental regulatory cases, and tax prosecutions. His experience includes numerous public inquiries and the successful negotiation of six hostage-taking incidents. Mr. Wolch is best known as the lawyer who successfully fought to free the innocent David Milgaard from prison. The compensation settlement he negotiated on Milgaard's behalf is the largest such settlement in Canadian history.

Mr. Wolch is a member of the Alberta, Manitoba, and Saskatchewan Law Societies. He has lectured on criminal law and procedure at the University of Manitoba, the University of Calgary, and the University of Alberta. He is a member of the International Society of Barristers and the American College of Trial Lawyers.